The American Woman 1987-88

Edited by Sara E. Rix for the
Women's Research & Education
Institute of the Congressional
Caucus for Women's Issues

W · W · NORTON & COMPANY

NEW YORK · LONDON

The American Woman 1987-88

A Report in Depth

First Edition

The text of this book is composed in Goudy Oldstyle, with display type set in Bodoni Bold Condensed. Composition and manufacturing by the Haddon Craftsmen. Book Design by Marjorie J. Flock.

ISBN 0-393-02384-2
ISBN 0-393-30388-8 PBK.

W. W. Norton & Company, Inc., 500 Fifth Avenue, New York, N. Y. 10110
W. W. Norton & Company Ltd., 37 Great Russell Street, London WC1B 3NU

1 2 3 4 5 6 7 8 9 0

Contents

Women in Brief

Appendices

Tables and Figures

Appendix · American Women Today: A Statistical Portrait

Editor's Note

The American Woman 1987–88: A Report in Depth is the first
edition of what is planned to be an annual report on the
status of women in this country. It is designed to keep readers
abreast of changes in the roles of American women and their
families, and to analyze the social, political, and economic
consequences of those changes. "What has happened to the
traditional family?" "How many women are working for pay
and what are they doing?" "Who's watching the children?"
"What is the status of the gender gap? . . . the pay gap?
. . . the parental leave bill?" "How much progress are women
making in politics? . . . in business? . . . in the military?"

These queries are typical of those that are asked of the
Women's Research and Education Institute (WREI), the nonpartisan research arm of the bipartisan Congressional Caucus
for Women's Issues. WREI's special mandate is to channel
sound, scholarly research on women into the national policymaking process, but we have also found ourselves serving as
a clearinghouse for a growing number of journalists, women's
advocates, government workers, union employees, aides to
state and local officials, writers, and students who turn to us
for information on women's issues.

Many call us needing an answer in a hurry: a reporter has
a deadline to meet; a state official is giving a speech that
evening; a student has a paper due the next morning. All that
they need is a quick number or two. But others who contact

us are attempting to marshal facts, evaluations, and expert opinion on a variety of subjects for a variety of reasons, whether it be to help them make a case for legislation, or for changing a company's leave policy, or for the establishment of a new social program. They usually not only want to know "what," but "how," and "why": How are families coping with the changes in women's roles? How has the labor force accommodated the influx of working women? Why hasn't the wage gap narrowed more over time? The answers require evaluations as well as unadorned statistics.

The inquiries WREI receives reflect a growing interest in women's issues throughout American society. More and more politicians at every level of government are seeking the "women's perspective" on the prevailing issues of the day. Employers are increasingly interested in how they can best respond to the unique needs of women workers with family responsibilities. Educators are concerned with how best to encourage more women to enter and remain in such fields as science and engineering. While we at WREI by no means labor under the illusion that we do or could handle all of the public's information needs regarding women, we do compile a great deal of useful information that we feel should be made accessible to a wider audience. To achieve this aim, we decided to publish an annual volume, pulling together the latest data and thinking on a range of subjects of concern to women.

When we brought this idea to colleagues whose judgment we trust and who themselves might refer to a resource of this kind, their reaction was enthusiastic: a comprehensive report on women and the changes in women's lives would be a very useful resource indeed, especially if it were updated regularly. As one whom we consulted put it, the report is "one of those ideas that is so instantly understood that it immediately makes you wonder why someone hasn't already done it." We then submitted a proposal to the Ford Foundation and were rewarded with a grant that put us to work.

We thought long and hard about what an annual report on the status of women should contain. Just as those who call or write to WREI for information have various needs, so, too, would the readers of our book. From the start, our goal has been to appeal to as many types of users as possible by presenting information in several formats and on those subjects that, in our experience, are of particular interest to the public.

We thought it important for the first edition to provide a broad overview of how the lives of women have changed during the course of the twentieth century, with special emphasis on their roles in the family and in the economy. Thus, this volume examines the evolution of women as mothers, wives, workers, and political activists to bring the reader up to date and set the stage for editions to come. The authors of the book's four main chapters discuss in considerable detail the causes and consequences of some of the predominant historical and contemporary trends that have shaped and are shaping the way women conduct their lives today. For the reader who is interested in understanding how and why the status of women has changed, these chapters provide not only a wealth of information but food for thought. Although not all readers will necessarily agree with the perspectives or emphases of the authors, few are likely to disagree on one point that emerges from this book: its title is in a sense misleading, for there is no "typical" American woman!

To assist readers who want information in a hurry, we have provided highlights that summarize the key points in the chapters, "Women in Twentieth Century America," "Women and the Family," "Women and the Economy," and "The Women's Movement in Recent American Politics." And to complement and augment the broad sweep of the long chapters, we have included 14 short chapters, each of which evaluates, close-up, so to speak, the status of women in specific fields or situations, such as the military, business, the theatre, or science.

The section "1986 in Review" lists major legislative, judicial, social, and economic events pertaining to women that occurred during that year. And the statistical appendix, using the most up-to-date data available, paints a picture of women today in charts, tables, and graphs. Readers who prefer not to deal with the detailed numbers in the appendix may find the highlights to the appendix especially helpful.

Our guiding principle for this first edition has always been to serve many purposes for our readers. For those who already know—or think they know—the story of women in America and want the exact numbers to confirm (or, perhaps, refute) their knowledge, we have provided facts and figures, including trend data. For other readers, we have sought to offer the story itself, told by informed observers bringing their personal perspectives and expertise to bear on the shifting landscape of women's lives. We have tried to be comprehensive, but, of course, no single reference volume could answer every question that the serious, or even the casual, reader might ask. Topics in *The American Woman 1987–88* reflect our best judgment as to what might be most useful to the most people. Nevertheless, despite the scope of this volume, we have not been able to address a number of important issues, such as women and health, women and aging, or women and religion. Many of our readers may feel that some of the subjects we have covered—for example, women in broadcasting, or Latina women—deserve more than just a few pages. We agree, and in future editions we intend to expand on many themes treated only briefly here, in addition to generating new material.

Gaps notwithstanding, we are pleased with the wealth of information that we have been able to assemble in this report. We hope that readers will be too.

In the acknowledgments that follow, WREI's Executive Director, Betty Parsons Dooley, makes clear the extent to which so many people contributed so willingly to this book. I wish to add my particular thanks to Anne Stone of WREI, whose exceptional writing ability is reflected on virtually every page. Editing this volume has been a challenge, but has been a far more agreeable one than it would have been without her most willing assistance.

SARA E. RIX

Acknowledgments

ALMOST EVERY PUBLICATION is a collaborative effort, and *The American Woman 1987–88* is no exception. Without the advice, assistance, and encouragement of several foundations and scores of individuals, the Women's Research and Education Institute would not have been able to produce this volume.

At the top of my acknowledgment list must be the generous funders whose support made it possible to undertake the new and ambitious project of producing a yearly report on the status of American women. The Ford Foundation expressed its confidence in us with a grant that underwrites a large portion of the first two editions. We are extremely grateful to the foundation, and to our then-program officer, Amy Vance, for supporting us in this endeavor. Other funders without whose assistance we could not have completed this book are AT&T, Sears, Roebuck and Co., Chevron Corporation, the George Gund Foundation, and RJR Nabisco, Inc. To each we extend our sincere thanks.

One of the first activities in the new project was to establish an advisory board of individuals who represented potential users of *The American Woman 1987–88*—scholars, the media, government officials, policymakers, librarians, and the like. Our advisors provided useful suggestions about content, design, and how best to meet the needs of various readers. Our thanks to Jessie Bernard, Jane Chapman, Beverly Ellerman, Gordon Green, Harriette McAdoo, Brenda Pillors, Sara Pritchard, Anne Radigan, Ida Ruben, Anne Schmidt, Elizabeth Waldman, and Franklin Wallick.

Dial Dickey, Beth Goodell, and Dorothy Rosenbaum spent many weeks laboring over statistical tables for the appendix. Catherine Stone prepared the highlights for chapters one through four; Judith Dollenmayer and Celia Eckhardt pitched in with expert editorial and writing assistance; Michele Lord and Azar Kattan, legislative staffers for the Congressional Caucus for Women's Issues, were always generous with information, time, and expertise. We are grateful to all these women.

Other individuals deserve our thanks because they furnished us with data, recommended authors, reviewed chapters, critiqued our approach, and/or kept us apprised of new developments: Susan Carroll, Arthur P. Endres, Jr., Marianne Ferber, Noralee Frankel, Lisa Garratt, Esther Katz, Susan Keilitz, Carol Muller, Marion Ott, Joseph Piccione, Susan J. Smith, Ronnie Steinberg, Roberta Spalter-Roth, Marley Weiss, Doris Werwie, Claudia Withers, and Leah Wortham.

I want to express my appreciation to the editor, Sara Rix, and assistant editor, Anne Stone, who have devoted most of their energies over the past year to this project, as well as to Susan Scanlan, who also contributed much time and effort to this volume. All three are members of WREI's staff. Editor Sara Rix has my special admiration and gratitude. Without her rigorous scholarship, meticulous attention to detail, awesome organizational abilities, and unflagging energy, there would be no book.

Finally, it should go without saying that our funders and advisers are not responsible for any errors or misstatements

that may be found in the book, nor do the opinions expressed
in the book necessarily reflect the opinions of anyone other
than the authors of the chapters.

BETTY PARSONS DOOLEY
Executive Director
Women's Research and Education Institute

Preface

THE HONORABLE PATRICIA SCHROEDER
and THE HONORABLE OLYMPIA SNOWE
Co-chairs, Congressional Caucus for Women's Issues

IN 1977, WHEN FIFTEEN congresswomen sat down to organize
a caucus that would address the needs of American women,
we did not expect to receive such an impressive tenth birthday present. The *American Woman 1987–88: A Report in
Depth* is indeed a landmark achievement. The Women's Research and Education Institute has presented us with a book
that finally answers the questions about how women are far-
ing in the United States. It will serve both policymakers and
the public as a ready reference on the employment, education, health, and political participation of 51 percent of this
country's citizens. And it will enable our caucus to "make the
case" for women and their families on Capitol Hill.

It was clear a decade ago that the handful of women in
the nation's most powerful legislative body bore a responsibility beyond their own geographic constituencies to women
across America. Then, as now, women comprised less than
five percent of the Senate and House of Representatives. The
Congresswomen's Caucus, a coalition of Republicans and
Democrats from diverse districts, quickly emerged as a natural ally of those who sought to advance the rights and responsibilities of women.

To meet the challenge of their dual roles, the women in

Congress required a research arm to monitor the administration and enforcement of existing laws affecting women, to
provide data on the impact of pending legislation, and to
suggest new areas where congressional attention should be
directed. WREI was established in response to those needs,
and, over the past 10 years, has become our valuable partner
in forwarding the agenda for women on the federal level.

The caucus, under the leadership of Co-chairs Elizabeth
Holtzman and Margaret Heckler, quickly established a record
of achievement: extension of the Equal Rights Amendment
ratification period, establishment of pension rights for divorced wives and widows of public servants, enactment of
flexible and part-time hiring programs in government. Our
work received a special boost when, in 1978, Nancy Landon
Kassebaum of Kansas was elected to the U.S. Senate and
joined the caucus.   .

In 1981, the caucus teamed up with key senators to intro-
duce the Economic Equity Act, a package of tax, retirement,
and child care/support bills designed to secure women's economic rights. The first measures passed under this omnibus
bill increased the spousal Individual Retirement Account
(IRA), established a sliding scale for the dependent care tax
credit, prohibited states from treating military pensions as
communal property in divorce cases, and lifted estate tax
penalties on rural women inheriting farms.

In 1982, the caucus changed its membership and its
name. As the organization evolved, so too did the political
sophistication of the congresswomen. Alliances formed
through the Economic Equity Act demonstrated to caucus
members that a large number of their male colleagues en-
thusiastically shared their commitment to women's issues.
Such alliances increased awareness that women's issues are,

in fact, human issues of equal importance to both men and women. It should also be noted that many congressmen who shared the caucus's goals chaired committees or subcommittees where they could press for passage of caucus bills. Over one hundred men—leaders from both the majority and minority parties—joined the newly designated Congressional Caucus for Women's Issues.

It was no coincidence, then, that almost one-half of the dozen provisions of the Economic Equity Act of 1983 were ultimately signed into law. These included:

- reform of the private pension system to lower the minimum age for pension plan participation and vesting, and require automatic joint and survivor benefits unless both spouses waive them;

- revision of federal civil service pensions to require joint and survivor benefits unless spouses waive them, and continuation of group health coverage for former spouses;

- clarifying the tax-exempt status of nonprofit dependent care organizations;

- establishing community-based child care information and referral services; and

- strengthening child support enforcement through state withholding of past-due support from wages and other forms of income.

Another important legislative victory in the 98th Congress was passage of the Dependent Care Block Grant, targeted to "latchkey" children, the over seven million school-age children of working parents who are left alone in the mornings or who come home in the afternoons to empty houses. This block grant provided monies to states to fund local information and child care referral services, as well as to establish before- and after-school child care programs in existing facilities, such as school cafeterias and neighborhood recreation centers.

It was in 1983, during the 98th Congress, that caucus leadership changed and we began working together as co-chairs. The following year, a caucus member from New York, Geraldine Ferraro, became the first woman in American history to run on a presidential ticket.

The 99th Congress was marked by both success and setback. In many ways, both the caucus and its agenda have entered into the mainstream legislative process; women's equity provisions are routinely written into bills and policies at the drafting stage, rather than as corrective second thoughts later on. The Economic Equity Act has grown to become a 22-point package. We have passed legislation to continue health insurance for former or divorced spouses and for laid-off employees and their dependents. A tax reform bill that will remove low-income women and their families from the tax rolls became law in 1986. Fifteen million dollars for on-site day care for low-income students is contained in the Higher Education Act. The House has taken up a parental leave bill that provides a minimum amount of nonpaid, job-guaranteed leave for the birth or adoption of a child or during the serious illness of a child or dependent. Twenty-six caucus members filed an *amicus* brief in the Vinson case before the Supreme Court, which resulted in a unanimous ruling that workers who are sexually harassed on the job can file for damages if the situation is sufficiently severe or pervasive.

Much remains to be accomplished. The federal government must maintain those programs of vital importance to

American women, particularly poor women. Women, who on the average earn 64 cents for every dollar brought home by men, must obtain economic equity. Further efforts must be made to pass the Civil Rights Restoration Act, which would assure nondiscriminatory policies at all educational institutions receiving federal monies.

At a slower pace than we want, the fight for women's equality progresses. But we are better armed by the data and the insight contained in this invaluable volume.

Introduction

THE HONORABLE JUANITA KREPS

IN THE NINETEENTH CENTURY, most American women remained at home, certainly when given the option. And home was not merely a place. In the charged rhetoric of the day, it was a sanctuary, a potent image of human security, solace, and renewal. Over that sanctuary the wife and mother presided as titulary genius, and thinking about what she did there as work seemed indelicate. To discuss her ministrations in the mundane terms of money and compensation would have been sacrilege. This notion of the centrality of home, which gripped the imaginations of both males and females, helps to explain why women's move into the workplace was fraught with ambivalence, and why equal status for women in the labor force has been so hard to achieve.

Drawing on another pervasive image that may have had even greater appeal for the male psyche, the Congregational bishops of Massachusetts in 1837 called the Grimké sisters to task when they presumed to speak publicly on the subject of slavery. Warning against "the dangers which at present seem to threaten the female character with widespread and permanent injury," the bishops recommended a dependent place for women: "If the vine, whose strength and beauty it is to lean upon the trelliswork, and half conceal its clusters, thinks to assume the independence and the overshadowing nature of the elm, it will not only cease to bear fruit, but fall in shame and dishonor into the dust."[1]

Such views help to explain why American women emerged from the nineteenth century suffering a profound political and economic disadvantage. They were isolated from each other in their separate homes and divided by class, race, and ethnic background. The richly detailed essays in this book trace women's efforts to break out of sanctified domesticities into paid work and public life—an uneven advance from and retreat into the home. Reflecting on the psychic confusion that women carried into the twentieth century, we can understand the tenacious forces arrayed against them, and the fragile condition of their victories.

Although images of ministering angel and clinging vine may have had a comforting appeal, these perceptions did not correspond to reality. Most American women have worked all their lives at jobs that are critical to the economy. Nevertheless, Nancy Barrett describes a conceptual failure that even today limits economists' descriptions of women's work. The household economy employs a substantial portion of our labor resources, but its output is not included in the gross national product. Consequently, as Dr. Barrett notes, "the huge shift of labor resources out of the household economy and into other sectors, such as manufacturing and services, that has occurred since 1960 has been mistakenly analyzed as the arrival of large numbers of 'new' workers. Rather, it should be seen for what it is: a major sectoral realignment that has released nearly half the full-time household workforce into the rest of the economy in the course of a single generation." Over the last quarter century, 28 million women workers have been absorbed into the paid labor force.

Comparing the movement of women out of the home into paying jobs to the earlier movement of people off the farm and into the cities, Dr. Barrett points out that in each

instance technological innovations reduced the time that necessary work required. Farmers got tractors and mechanical
cotton pickers. Homemakers got washing machines and vacuum cleaners. As several contributors to this volume note,
women were also marrying progressively later, having fewer
children, and living longer. Moreover, none of these fundamental directions, though temporarily stalled, seemed likely
to be reversed. Sara Evans emphasizes the fact that "educated
middle-class married women increasingly took the path pioneered by their black and working-class sisters, combining
work inside and outside the family home." The invention of
the pill in the 1960s enabled women to plan their work lives,
making long-term career planning possible for the first time.
As a result, Andrew Cherlin explains, women's lives outside
the home took new paths.

When choice came to extend beyond the initial one of
picking a husband, it turned out that women often wanted
and needed more than what had supposedly satisfied them
throughout history. Among other things, they wanted meaningful work, and they wanted to be paid adequately for it.
They wanted to be self-supporting. In the first half of the
nineteenth century, Margaret Fuller defended women's ambi-
tions: "Let them be sea-captains if they will!" She was thought
fanciful, even outrageous. But Margaret Fuller was on target.
In 1986 there were over 10,000 women in the United States
Marine Corps, almost 700 of whom were officers. Women,
too, wanted to explore, to fly, to analyze, to build. In the
decade of the 1970s, the percentage of all law degrees going
to women jumped from 5.4 to 28.5 percent; in medicine, it
grew from 8.4 to 23 percent. And by the 1980s, more than
two-thirds of all married women with college degrees wanted
to keep working. In 1985, among married mothers, 3.6 mil-

lion more women worked at paying jobs than remained full-time homemakers.

Women also wanted a voice in the public affairs of their cities and states and nation. They wanted to help write the laws and creeds by which they were governed, and they wanted to help interpret them. As Dr. Evans describes it, they began by creating thousands of voluntary organizations in which they could express their new ideas, find new roles, nurture new aspirations, creating in the process "the basic institutions and ideas of social welfare." And in the 72-year struggle for the vote, women learned the political skills of organizing on their own behalf, skills of pamphleteering, public speaking, and lobbying that remain crucial weapons in their struggle for equality.

It is a struggle they have not yet won. In refutation of the American myth that good people who work hard get to the top, women college graduates now earn roughly the same as male high school drop-outs. Their median income for full-time, year-round work is 68 percent that of men's, and for minority women, the figure is much lower. The wage gap, furthermore, is higher for older women. A 55-year-old woman makes approximately the same as one who is 25. Men between the ages of 35 and 55 typically earn twice as much as younger men.

As a result of these pay differentials, women are disproportionately poor and they seem destined to remain so. Their unemployment rates have traditionally been higher than those of men with comparable credentials. The millions who can find only part-time work rarely get health care or retirement benefits. Even those with full-time jobs are concentrated in low-paying, dead-end jobs. Within male-dominated areas of work, they tend to remain in female ghettos. Almost half of

those who marry will divorce, most of them taking on responsibility for raising their children. Child support payments
tend to be low and are often unenforced.

The plight of children growing up in female-headed families is a critical social concern. In a decade and a half, 1970
to 1985, the number of families headed by women grew by
almost 85 percent. One-third of the women who raise their
children alone are poor; among blacks, the figure is over
one-half. A child living with the mother is six times as likely
to be poor as one living with the father or with both parents.
The problem of adolescent pregnancy continues to lock these
children in poverty. According to Andrew Cherlin, "a majority of teens who now bear children do so out of wedlock. . . . By the time they reach 18, four percent of unmarried
white women and 27 percent of unmarried black women have
borne a child." These are the people whose chances of emerging from poverty are most bleak. These statistics speak of
human tragedy and cultural waste.

But women's disadvantages have not led them to agree on
goals for themselves. After they won the vote, for example,
the middle-class reformers, who largely comprised the first
women's movement, split over the Equal Rights Amendment.
Highly visible women like Eleanor Roosevelt and Florence
Kelley believed that the amendment's promise of individual
rights would abandon women to the sweatshops against
which they had fought so doggedly. And although in the
1960s the ERA ceased to be so divisive and most women
leaders rallied to the fight for its passage, issues of race and
class continue to hamper the development of a united movement. As Nancy Barrett points out, a full-employment economy is a necessary condition for women's steady economic
advance. However, even a favorable economic climate fails to

unite women and their organizations behind women's causes.

Marian Lief Palley makes it clear that women have most of the political and organizational tools they need. The next step is to summon the vision, agree on the issues, and use the weapons at their disposal. There are more adult women than men in the United States today, and a higher proportion of females are registered to vote. According to the *New York Times*, 53 percent of those who voted in the 1984 elections were women, and their inclination to use the ballot has been increasing in each of the presidential elections. There is a network of professional women within the federal government who enhance the work of the Congressional Caucus for Women's Issues. Meanwhile, the numbers of elected women at the local and state levels are growing. For assistance, they can call upon some of the small research, litigation, or lobbying groups, such as the Women's Research and Education Institute, the Women's Legal Defense Fund, and the Women's Equity Action League. In addition, there are the broadly based organizations: the National Organization for Women and the League of Women Voters.

These groups and others have discovered the ways of politics and have learned to work in coalition. One such coalition was the 1984 Women's Vote Project, in which almost one hundred women's groups combined in a drive to increase the number of low-income women registered to vote. Another is the Leadership Conference on Civil Rights, which has spearheaded many of the fights over women's issues such as Title IX. In the labor movement, where women's membership increased from 25 to 41 percent of all union members in only a decade, support for their cause is also likely to grow.

Some of the measures through which American women seek to achieve economic advance are reasonably clear: affir-

mative action policies that will open up better jobs, guaran-
tees of pay equity that will eliminate sex discrimination in
the workplace, job training and education for low-income
women, affordable child care, and fringe benefits for part-
time jobs.

But it is important to remember that these and other
questions that are central to the structure and well-being of
families are as important to men as to women. Trends toward
more women in the workforce, fewer children and more re-
tirees, family needs for better public services, and the growth
of single-parent households tax the most thoughtful minds
among us. These issues comprise not a women's but the
people's agenda; it is to this agenda that we must now direct
the attention of men and women, and the institutions
through which we can achieve human progress.

Meanwhile, relegating women policymakers to areas that
have been traditionally considered their particular set of issues is totally incompatible with the levels of education and
professional experience they have achieved. Today's women
leaders in business, government, education, and the nonprofit sector are also concerned with economic growth, the
level of unemployment, the federal deficit, and the quality of
higher education and scientific research—in short, with the
major social dilemmas that have long plagued men's minds.
A better sharing of ideas between men and women will bring
a far sharper perspective and a far greater prospect for solutions to problems both global and family-related.

The
American
Woman
1987-88

Flag bearer for the Women Suffrage Movement.
Courtesy The Bettmann Archive

ONE Women in Twentieth Century America: An Overview

SARA M. EVANS

Highlights

THE MOVEMENT OF women out of the home and into the workforce can be seen, not as a sudden change, but rather as a steady progression that began before the turn of the century and continues today.

• By the late nineteenth century, women had expanded the domestic sphere far beyond the home by creating thousands of voluntary associations, ranging from temperance societies to settlement houses. These associations served women as training grounds for political activism in the interest of social justice.

• As women began to work through these associations to change society in the name of domestic values, they developed skills, self-confidence, and a new sense of their own rights as individuals. In particular, they increasingly claimed their right of citizenship, symbolized most powerfully by the vote.

• In 1900, about one in five women worked outside the home; most of these were young and single. Both women and their employers presumed that their employment would end with marriage. As a consequence, women were segregated into the least-skilled, lowest-paying jobs.

• A small number of women attended college. It was these women, blocked from entry into the male professions, who invented the female professions of nursing, teaching, and social work.

• Urban black women were the only group of married women who presumed a lifetime of work outside the home. Racial discrimination barred blacks of both sexes from the better-paying industrial jobs. Family survival and a high priority on their children's education dictated that black women contribute to the family income.

• By 1910, middle-class white women were forming increasingly effective alliances with black and working-class women around the issue of women's suffrage. The massive mobilization of American women in the decade before the Nineteenth Amendment was ratified included rallies of thousands of "working girls" and the organization of many black women's suffrage clubs.

• After the right to vote was won, veteran suffragists split over the Equal Rights Amendment, introduced by the National Woman's Party in 1923. Many suffragists with a background in the social reform movement believed strongly in female differences, and feared that the ERA would preclude legislation protective of women.

• During the Depression, married women who sought work, even those whose husbands were unemployed, faced a hostile backlash that blamed them for taking "men's" jobs. Although pervasive sex segregation in the labor force meant that women and men rarely competed for the same jobs, many states, cities, and school boards passed laws prohibiting or limiting the employment of married women.

• The concept of social security, as well as other New Deal programs, can be traced to the previous activities of private charities and settlement houses. The irony of the New Deal for women is that it institutionalized "civic housekeeping," redefining the "public arena" away from its roots in local communities and towards a massive and impersonal bureaucracy.

• The union drive of the 1930s drew workers of both sexes, but even a progressive union like the UAW reinforced the segregation of female workers and accepted lower pay scales for women. Both employers and unions presumed that women "belonged" in the home rather than in the labor force, and that working women's income was non-essential.

• The outbreak of World War II ended the Depression and began an economic boom. By 1943, severe labor shortages convinced government and industry to reverse prejudices against married working women, and six million women who had never before worked outside the home entered the labor force during the war years.

• When the men returned home from the war, the gains working women had made in entering new fields of employment were quickly wiped out.

• The expanding post-war economy, however, continued to fuel trends toward the employment of older, married women. Not only had the war removed some of the legal and cultural barriers to the employment of married women, but the number of young, single women seeking employment had decreased because of better educational opportunities and a rising propensity to marry.

• While women provided the most important source of new workers for an expanding economy, the post-war era disassociated women and private life from politics. The feminine mystique defined women's place in a family-centered lifestyle based on new abundance.

• By 1960, there were 20 times more clerical workers than there had been in 1900; 96 percent of these workers were women. One in three women in the labor force was in clerical work.

• Having married younger and had children earlier than preceding generations, women in their 30s and 40s found themselves at home with numerous "labor saving" appliances and without children to care for during the day. Educated middle-class married women were in the vanguard of the army of women who went to work outside the home in the 1960s and 1970s. In contrast, the post-war period of prosperity meant that a working-class husband's wages alone could support a family, and many working-class women were, for the first time, able to—and did—make homemaking a full-time career.

• The 1960s and 1970s saw the rebirth of a feminist movement and the enactment of legislation, including the Equal Pay Act and Title VII of the Civil Rights Act, designed to prohibit discrimination against women in employment.

• By 1980, more than half of all adult women were working outside the home.

Introduction

We owe to women the charm and the beauty of life; for purity of thought and heart, for patient courage, for recklessly unselfish devotion, for the love that rests, strengthens and inspires, we look to women. These are the best things in life; in them men cannot compete with women.

—Dean Briggs, "Remarks," Smith College Quarter Centennial Anniversary *Proceedings*, 1900

As we near the end of the twentieth century it is tempting to look back to its beginning as a time when women and men knew their respective places and roles and lived them out in peace and harmony. Yet our late nineteenth century counterparts felt themselves besieged with change as well. If once they had been sure that a "true woman" was the picture of innocent and submissive domesticity, they may have been startled by the independence and athleticism of the "Gibson girl" or the career aspirations of the college-bound "new woman" or the increasing visibility of working women in factories and offices.

At the end of the last century, most Americans took it for granted that women were "by nature" suited to domesticity, care of the home, and nurture of the young. Implicitly and explicitly, they divided the world into male and female spheres. To men belonged the public world of work and politics, an arena characterized by competition, aggression, and, frequently, corruption. To women belonged the home, locus of the "softer" virtues like beauty and caring and self-sacrifice.[1] Middle-class women in particular accepted "republican motherhood": a moral mission to raise future citizens on whose virtue the future of the republic would depend.

By the turn of the century, however, women were engaged

Information booth in New York, 1914. *Courtesy The Bettmann Archive*

outside the home in a wide variety of activities, ranging from paid work to social reform. The ways in which women became active in public arenas at that time greatly influenced the course of political and economic changes in subsequent years. The links between the beginning and end of the twentieth century form an unbroken chain of historical change in which the past shapes, though it cannot determine, the future. This chapter will first examine the dimensions of change at the turn of the century, trace their political and economic consequences, and then locate the transformations since the Second World War in relation to contemporary perceptions and fears.

The Expansion of the Domestic Sphere and the Emergence of Women's Collective Consciousness

By the late nineteenth century, women had expanded the domestic sphere so far beyond the home that their grandmothers would scarcely have recognized it. Seizing on a shared sense of moral mission as women, they created literally thousands of voluntary associations. Ranging from temperance societies to women's clubs, charitable associations, missionary societies, and settlement houses, these associations occupied a space unrecognized by the simple division of the world into public and private. Although they were defined largely in the language of domesticity, they were public spaces, separate from the family and from institutions of political and economic power like governments and corporations. Such free spaces offered women autonomous places within which they could develop a group identity, experiment with new ideas, and learn the basic skills of public leadership. Within them, women took their moral mission beyond their individual homes and invented new ways of challenging the corruption and misery they found in society (Evans and Boyte, 1986).

In the process, these women created the basic institutions and ideas of social welfare. For example, the middle-class and often college-educated residents of Hull House in Chicago or Henry Street Settlement in New York City developed a wide range of services in poor immigrant neighborhoods and quickly found themselves at odds with corrupt city bosses. The settlement house itself recreated in these teeming neighborhoods a middle-class notion of "home" as a "natural" environment and an expression of personalist values. In Jane Addams's view, settlement work expressed "the great mother breast of our common humanity." With similar intentions, women built a variety of organizations and institutions that served as training grounds for political activism in the interest of social justice. The result was a new political agenda, known as Progressivism, which demanded that the society accept responsibility for public health and safety, factory working conditions, the well-being of children, and the essential needs of the poor. All of these responsibilities were understood as "civic housekeeping" (Addams, 1910).

As women began to work actively and self-consciously to change society in the name of domestic values, they developed skills, self-confidence, and a new sense of their own rights. In particular, they increasingly claimed their right of citizenship, symbolized most significantly by the vote. If men had elected these corrupt politicians, women must vote them out.

The claim of citizenship was in many ways a deeply radical challenge to the ideology of separate spheres for men and women. It asserted the right of the individual woman to stand in direct relation to the state rather than to be represented through the participation of her husband or father. The growing power of the women's suffrage movement rested both on women's collective consciousness, born in female associations, and on increased individualism among women in an urbanizing, industrializing economy (Dubois, 1978; Scott and Scott, 1975).

The Growing Sense of Individuality

Individualism, in the nineteenth century version, was the essence of manliness. From Natty Bumppo to Andrew Carnegie, male heroes made it on their own striving. Women, on the other hand, were seen and saw themselves as defined by ties of kinship: daughter, wife, mother. Their goodness rested in their essential nature, not in their striving or in competition. Yet, in many different ways, women were emerging from familial self-definitions into a sense of individuality.

At the core of this development was the beginning of a new life stage in between those of childhood and marriage. A small but crucial number of upper-middle-class women attended college, where they developed strong relationships with their peers and a transformed awareness of their own potential as women, individually and collectively. These were the women who, blocked from entry into the male professions such as medicine and law, invented female professions of nursing, teaching, and social work, each of which claimed simply to extend women's "natural" domestic impulses. Young college graduates also sparked more audacious grassroots organizing tactics within the suffrage movement. Parades, rallies, and impromptu soapbox speeches shocked Victorian sensibilities, but they seemed natural to young women who took their individualism for granted (Strom, 1975).

The situation was different for working-class, immigrant, and black women. Forced by economic necessity to enter the labor force at an early age, many migrated to the cities in search of work. In 1900, approximately one in five women worked outside the home; most of these were young and single. Low wages, harsh working conditions, and continuing obligations to help support their families sharply limited economic independence for these women. Most of them worked as domestics, isolated in the homes of their employers, granted only half a day per week to themselves. Others toiled in factories, making garments, textiles, paper boxes, or artificial flowers. A few pioneered the new clerical jobs in offices. But both women and their employers presumed that women's work outside the home was temporary, to end with marriage. As a consequence, they found themselves segregated into the least-skilled, lowest-paying jobs. Unions objected to their presence and blocked them from apprenticeship and access to skilled jobs, arguing that if male workers were paid a "family wage," women would not need to work. Despite these obstacles, when wage-earning women organized their own unions, often in alliance with middle-class reformers, they exhibited awesome courage and militancy. In the garment district of New York, for example, the "uprising of the twenty thousand" in 1909 confounded the garment industry and led to a new kind of industrial unionism (Kessler-Harris, 1982: 150–51; Tax, 1980: 205–40).

The only group of married women who presumed a lifetime of work outside the home were urban black women. As black families began to stream north after 1910, they found that racial discrimination barred both women and men from the better-paying industrial jobs. Family survival and a high priority on education for children dictated that black women contribute to the family income. They found their choices restricted to hot and dirty work in industry or commercial laundries, or, most commonly, domestic service. By the 1920s, as white working women found new opportunities in clerical work and other services, black women filled the ranks of domestic workers. Black domestics were older and more likely to be married than their white counterparts. Where young, white, immigrant domestics had lived in their employers' homes, black women adamantly refused, forcing household employers to adapt (Jones, 1985).

As familial identities rooted in a separate female sphere

declined, the coalition of women demanding access to political participation broadened. By 1910, middle-class white reformers had formed increasingly effective alliances with black and working-class women around the issue of women's suffrage. The massive mobilization of American women in the decade before the Nineteenth Amendment to the Constitution was ratified in 1920 included rallies of thousands of "working girls" and the organization of numerous black women's suffrage clubs. Shared exclusion from the individual right of civic participation symbolized their common womanhood. Following their victory, leaders of the National American Woman Suffrage Association joyfully dismantled their organization and reassembled as the newly formed League of Women Voters. Their new task, as they defined it, was to train women to exercise their individual citizenship rights.

Such a reorientation seemed congruent with the popular culture of the 1920s, which emphasized individual pleasures along with individual rights. But popular culture also signaled a dramatic shift in attitudes toward sexuality that simultaneously emphasized and constrained female autonomy. After a century of denial, middle-class culture acknowledged the existence of female sexuality, and, indeed, prescribed sexual pleasure separate from procreative intention. At the same time, it reinforced the traditional goal of marriage in the context of an increasingly competitive "marriage market." And it undermined the powerful bonds between women, reorienting them towards a more emotionally demanding "companionate" marriage and stigmatizing homosexuality and, by inference, relationships between women, as "deviant."

The popular image of the "flapper" portrayed an energetic, hedonistic young woman seeking experience for its own sake and flaunting her sexuality to the horror of her Victorian elders. Movie star Colleen Moore, heroine of the 1923 film, *Flaming Youth*, articulated this rebellious self-assertion to her fans: "Don't worry, girls. Long skirts, corsets, and flowing tresses have gone. . . . The American girl will see to this. She is independent, a thinker [who] will not follow slavishly the ordinances of those who in the past have decreed this or that for her to wear" (quoted in Rosen, 1974: 74). Her ultimate goal, however, was still finding the "right man."

The image of the secretary as a glamorous "working girl" looking for a marriage partner joined the youthful independence and consumer orientation of the flapper to a new ideology about marriage that emphasized companionship, romance, and emotional intimacy. It was this newly created clerical sector that provided an opportunity to weave the "working girl" back into the fabric of socially approved womanhood. The glamour of the secretary's position lay in her proximity to men in the office environment. No longer a male preserve, the office was a public environment in which males and females were accorded separate and unequal roles analogous to their traditional roles in the home. When movies and magazine stories about "office romance" emphasized the importance of marriage as the working girl's ultimate goal, they justified women's work within this limited frame. At the same time, they also obscured the continuing realities of discrimination, the harshness of factory work, and the toil of many rural women in an economically depressed countryside.

In the sexualized consumer economy of the twentieth century, young women learned to market themselves as products. Sales of cosmetics skyrocketed in the 1920s; magazines urged women to develop an attractive "personality"; and the competitive display of female beauty reached new heights in

Office workers in the 1920s. *Courtesy Women's Bureau, Department of Labor, vintage SEIU files*

1921 with the first Miss America beauty pageant in Atlantic City.

Reformers and social workers found that this new individualism, in the context of a growing consumer economy and political conservatism, had weakened their base. Indeed, veteran suffragists found themselves at odds with one another when the National Woman's Party (NWP) introduced the Equal Rights Amendment in 1923. The different meanings of the suffrage victory split the suffragists into opposing camps. Within the NWP, individual freedom and individual rights dictated that women should push ahead to a full constitutional equality: "Equal protection of the law shall not be denied on the basis of sex." For social reformers whose politics were rooted in an understanding of female difference and in a vision of politicized domesticity, the ERA threatened to destroy hard-won legislation protecting women workers. The social reformers continued their efforts, successfully defending protective legislation and winning new programs to provide health education for pregnant women and new mothers through the Sheppard-Towner Act of 1921. But the 1920s were increasingly difficult for social reformers: struggles against child labor, for protection of women workers, and for health, education, and other social services were lost more often than they were won.

Women and the Emerging Welfare State

Out of the reform struggles in the twenties, however, came a new political agenda, one which envisioned an expanded role for the state in assuming responsibility for social welfare. The women (with some male allies) had honed their ideas in institutions of their own creation, particularly the settlement house movement, the National Consumer's League, and the Women's Trade Union League. Even before the great stock market crash in 1929, the National Federation of Settlement Houses initiated a study of the impact of unemployment on family life.

All of these trends collided in ironic and contradictory ways in the Great Depression. The harshness of economic collapse forced a retreat into private life and a focus on the family economy. Women stretched scarce resources to the last penny or crust of bread. They remade old clothes, split worn sheets down the middle and sewed the outside edges together, planted gardens, and canned vegetables. Individualism and adolescent playfulness had no place in the face of hardship and despair.

Married women who sought work—even those whose husbands were unemployed—faced a hostile backlash that blamed them for taking "men's" jobs. In reality, the pervasive sex segregation of the labor force meant that women and men rarely competed for the same jobs. But numerous states, cities, and school boards passed laws prohibiting or limiting the employment of married women. And since cultural norms still ascribed the breadwinner's role to men, those women who lost paid jobs, or were unable to find paid work, found that relief programs for the unemployed consistently discriminated against them.

The irony of the latter could hardly have been greater. Government-sponsored relief drew on the talents and political agendas of women who, for the previous century, had constructed social and institutional responses to the human problems of modern society. By World War I these women had already been advocating a redefined state, a "mother state," that provided protections for the weak and assistance to those in need. In the 1920s they had developed specific proposals for the regulation of labor, health, education, and social welfare. The New Deal, in effect, enacted most of these in the creation of the welfare state. Wage and hour legislation (for example, in the National Recovery Administration and later in the Fair Labor Standards Act) was finally extended to male as well as female workers. Provisions for Aid to Dependent Children, developed in the Children's Bureau of the Labor Department, drew on decades of experience in settlement houses and private charities. Indeed, the entire concept of social security—government-sponsored insurance for the unemployed, the elderly, and fatherless children—as well as expanded public health programs, could be traced to the previous activities of private charities, settlement houses, and the provisions of the Sheppard-Towner Act (Ware, 1981; Chambers, 1962).

A network of women, trained in female reform organizations and strategically placed in the Roosevelt administration, played key roles in the New Deal. Centered around Eleanor

Roosevelt, Secretary of Labor Frances Perkins, and Democratic Party Women's Committee Chair Molly Dewson, this
network represented the last generation of women educated
in the Victorian female subculture that had shaped the progressive movement (Ware, 1981). The female subculture itself, and the mass movement for which it was a base, no
longer existed. Female voluntary associations, with a few exceptions, preserved communal values but did not use them as
resources for political critique. Indeed, the final irony of the
New Deal for women is that it institutionalized "civic housekeeping" while redefining the "public" arena away from its
roots in local communities and towards a massive and impersonal government bureaucracy infused with the values of
efficiency, rational planning, and control by professionals.

Despite this depoliticization, however, the great union
drives of the 1930s and the formation of the Congress of
Industrial Organizations (CIO) drew on the resources of
working-class ethnic communities. When the workers were
primarily male, as in heavy industries like steel, rubber, and
automobile manufacturing, women's auxiliaries profoundly
strengthened their capacity to sustain mobilization and militant action. For female industrial workers themselves, the
CIO strategy of organizing by industry rather than by craft,
and of welcoming unskilled workers, represented a major
breakthrough. In addition, many of the more radical CIO
organizers were committed to the equal inclusion of women
in unions as members and as organizers.

Yet even a progressive and democratic union like the
United Auto Workers (UAW) reinforced the segregation of
female workers, defining certain jobs as male, others as female, and accepting separate and lower pay scales for women.
Both employers and unions accepted the basic tenets of do-

mestic ideology, presuming that women "belonged" in the home rather than in the labor force and that working women's income was secondary and non-essential. The resulting continued segregation of the labor force, and overt discrimination both in job opportunities and in pay, formed the structural basis for later struggles around the issues of equal pay and affirmative action (Milkman, 1976; 1980).

Women in World War II

For the next two decades, the momentum of cultural and economic changes continued under dramatically new conditions. The outbreak of World War II signaled the end of the Depression and the beginning of an economic boom. Half of the southern agricultural labor force migrated to cities. Marriage and birthrates began a sudden spurt, reversing the depressed rates of the 1930s (Anderson, 1981: 76–77). By 1943, severe labor shortages convinced both government and industry to reverse longstanding prejudices against married working women.

Some women responded to the economic opportunities, others to patriotic exhortations to support the war effort. In any case, six million women who had never before worked outside the home entered the labor force during the war years. Millions of others shifted from agricultural, domestic, and service work to skilled industrial jobs previously closed to them. As women entered heavy industries, their rate of unionization increased fourfold. And black women, still discriminated against by industry, began to enter the female jobs, such as clerical work and nursing, which had previously been virtually all white. "Rosie the Riveter" became a national heroine. Strong, positive images of women appeared on magazine covers; advertisements emphasized women's civic and patriotic duty to join the labor force as part of the war effort. The profile of working women represented a marked shift toward older and married women.

At the same time, the media repeatedly assured both women and men that such participation would only be "for the duration" and did not constitute a threat to women's "femininity." A group of 114 electric companies extolled the "modern magic" of electricity in this vein: "She's 5 feet 1 from her 4A slippers to her spun-gold hair. She loves flower-hats, veils, smooth orchestras—and being kissed by a boy who's now in North Africa. *But, man, oh man, how she can handle her huge and heavy press!*" (*Saturday Evening Post,* June 12, 1943: 55).

The Return to Domesticity

Polls taken at the end of the war indicated that most working women did not want their new status to be temporary, but the gains women made in entering new fields of employment were quickly wiped out when the men returned home. Millions of women left the labor force, voluntarily and involuntarily, as men reclaimed jobs in heavy industry. Under intense pressure to return to domesticity, and themselves yearning for security and stability following years of depression and war, younger women quit their jobs to marry and bear children at an astonishing rate. Older women, forced out of higher-paying industrial jobs, found work in the still expanding "feminized" service-sector jobs.

The war had accelerated trends towards the employment of older, married women, and the expanding economy after the war continued to fuel them. A boom in the service sector guaranteed that there would continue to be a very high demand for female workers. And the consumer economy created incentives for women to earn income and increase their families' standard of living. In addition, the war removed some of the legal and cultural barriers to the employment of married women. Several states, for example, removed laws against married women teachers, while several major labor unions and 11 state legislatures adopted the equal-pay-for-equal-work standard (Hartmann, 1982).

World War II also witnessed the end of the women's network that had operated within the New Deal, and the beginning of an era as hostile to reform as the 1920s had been. Mobilization for war pushed women—along with their reform agenda—to the margins of the Roosevelt administration, and the Truman administration, which began in 1945, lacked both links and sympathy with female reformers.[2]

Following the war, women and men alike withdrew into increasingly isolated families. Indeed, the public arena in the post-war era was fraught with danger and complexity. A post-war recession aroused economic fears. Russian explosion of an atomic bomb in 1949 made nuclear war a distinct possibility in the hostile atmosphere of the Cold War. And the House Committee on Un-American Activities warned Americans that communists and subversives lurked in the very hearts of their communities and schools, setting off hysterical witch-hunts in town after town.

Mixed in with deep cultural anxieties about global politics were fears about the changing place of women and changing sexual norms (May, 1984). Social critics at the end of the war charged that women—in public jobs and at home—had deserted their "natural" role. Political scapegoating coupled "frustrated females" with "subversion" in the classroom

(Lora, 1968: 228). A resurgent right wing, represented by organizations such as the John Birch Society and the Ku Klux Klan, practiced defensive and parochial politics, attacking anyone outside the norms of white middle-class culture. It should not be surprising, then, that fear of communists undermining the political and economic order was combined with fear of women undermining the traditional family and therefore the social order. Cold War rhetoric also added a dimension of sexual fear, meshing anti-communism with homophobia in a campaign to purge public employment and the military of "sexual perverts" (D'Emilio, 1983).

The Post-War Economic Boom and the Feminine Mystique

Through the 1950s, however, anxiety gave way to optimism. The enormous strength of the American economy following the war, boosted by the Korean War and sustained defense spending afterward, generated an expanding economy further stimulated by pent-up consumer demand. Burgeoning suburbs absorbed not only middle- and upper-middle-class but also working-class families. Rising incomes, due in part to women's increased employment, placed home ownership within the reach of nearly 70 percent of Americans. Family formation hit new highs, evidenced statistically in a rising propensity to marry, falling marriage ages, and soaring fertility rates.

The dominant optimism turned anxieties on their head, purging complexity and denying change. Faith in technological progress, together with economic growth, led many to predict an end to such social divisions as class and to ideologies based on those divisions. Some even predicted that soon there would be no need for welfare. In this context, what

Betty Friedan termed the "feminine mystique"—defining women almost exclusively in terms of wife and motherhood —functioned smoothly to change women's roles and to deny their disruptive potential.

The feminine mystique defined women's place in the family-centered lifestyle based on new abundance. Pre-war ideas about the centrality of homemaking and motherhood, and popularized Freudian ideas, were incorporated into the consumerist ethos of the post-war middle class. The product was a modern and sexualized version of "republican motherhood," although it actually had little public meaning: "politics" had retreated either to the simple act of voting or to the activities of distant governmental experts. Citizens had become "private citizens." The modern mother's duty was to create a warm haven, a happy family life, a goal *McCall's* defined in 1954 as "togetherness." Woman's role was to maintain the key bulwark of social stability, rather than the training ground for future citizens described by Victorian advocates of domesticity.

The prototypical environment for this family, the suburb, further emphasized the family's separation from public life. Women in suburban families, especially housewives with young children, found themselves in a new kind of female ghetto. At the same time, suburbs effected a new racial and economic segregation of American society. Rural poor people —largely blacks and Appalachian whites—moved into cities abandoned by the more affluent. Behind the façade of a hopeful and self-satisfied popular culture, the numbers of female-headed households among the urban poor had begun to climb, encouraged, ironically, by welfare policies that penalized households with unemployed adult men.

But few acknowledged that those policies had been for-

mulated by a previous generation of female reformers. Indeed, when the Democratic party abolished its women's
division in 1952, it provided a powerful symbol of the disas-
sociation of women and private life from politics (Hartmann,
1982: 155–56). A number of women continued to work
within the political parties, pressing behind the scenes for
increased representation, but their efforts remained invisible
and only marginally effective.

Yet as women faded from the political arena and centered
their lives on the nuclear family, they also continued their
massive entry into another public arena, the labor force.
Throughout the 1950s and 1960s, women provided the most
important source of new workers for an expanding economy,
raising their participation rate by some 10 percentage points
between 1950 and 1970. This trend reflected long-term
changes in both the supply and demand for women workers.

The segregation of the labor force, which had crystallized
in the 1920s and 1930s, reserved heavy and highly skilled
industrial jobs, as well as professional and management positions, for men. The enormous expansion of the service sector
of the economy during and after World War II, however,
occurred frequently in jobs previously designated as "female." Many of these positions extended women's traditional
serving and nurturing responsibilities into offices, schools,
hospitals, and restaurants (Oppenheimer, 1970). That many
were also byproducts of the expanding welfare state constituted an additional, unintended consequence of the policies for which women had fought in the early decades of the
century.

Clerical workers increased their predominance among
working women with the advent of huge corporate and government bureaucracies. By 1960, the number of clerical work-

ers was 20 times what it had been in 1900; 96 percent of them were women. Indeed, nearly one in three women in the labor force could be found in clerical work. The baby boom and rapid urban growth created a sudden demand for teachers at all levels. And the increasing complexity of the health industry multiplied the need for nurses, as well as for paraprofessionals such as nurses' aides and licensed practical nurses.

The pool of young, single, urban "working girls," however, had decreased, because of more numerous educational opportunities and the rising propensity to marry. As in World War II, employers experienced strong incentives to hire married women.

Rather than working before marriage, young women in the 1950s were more likely to move straight from school to marriage, with the expectation that they would work until they had children and possibly again when the children were older. Even more important as a factor affecting the supply of married women workers was that, throughout the twentieth century, the life expectancy of women increased while fertility decreased. In 1900, the average woman could expect to live to the age of 55; in 1910, the birthrate was 30 live births per 1,000 population. By 1950, the life expectancy for women had increased to 71 years and the birthrate—even with the baby boom—had fallen to 24 births per 1,000 population (U.S. Bureau of the Census, 1967: Table 61 and Table 48). Mid-century women also married younger and concentrated their childbearing in the early years of marriage. Together, these changes resulted in new living conditions. Women in their thirties and forties found themselves in houses filled with "labor-saving" appliances and emptied of children, at least during school hours. By comparison, their grandmothers, at the same age, had been preoccupied with the care of small children as well as the production and preservation of food for the family. By the 1950s, furthermore, most women lived in urban areas, the very environment in which the new service-sector jobs existed (Weiner, 1985; Oppenheimer, 1970).

Thus, educated middle-class married women increasingly took the path pioneered by their black and working-class sisters, combining work inside and outside the family home. By the late 1940s, highly educated married women had begun to demonstrate a greater tendency to work outside the home, reversing previous trends, in part because many of the new jobs required significant literacy skills and special training. In the 1950s, the association between husbands' income and female labor force participation began to change. At the beginning of the decade, the less a man earned, the more likely his wife was to be employed. Through the 1950s and 1960s, this pattern gradually reversed (Weiner, 1985). Indeed, married women in middle-income families entered the labor force faster than any other group in the population. For many working-class families, on the other hand, this period of prosperity meant that, for the first time, the husband's wages alone were adequate to support the family; it appears that many working-class wives remained at home, living out the values of the feminine mystique (see Komarovsky, 1962; Rubin, 1976).

The powerful forces of supply and demand meshed with the values of a booming consumer capitalism to justify women's new roles. An "adequate" standard of living came to require home-ownership, automobiles, refrigerators and other appliances, televisions, and college education for children. Thus, many families felt the urgent need for a second income, which, as long as it was defined as secondary and dispensable, could acceptably be earned by a woman (wife). If women worked to "help out" the family, they were not violating social convention. As *Look* put it in 1956: "No longer a psychological immigrant to man's world, she works rather casually, as a third of the U.S. labor force, and less toward a 'big career' than as a way of filling a hope chest or buying a new home freezer. She gracefully concedes the top job rungs to men" (*Look*, October 16, 1956: 35).

By the beginning of the 1960s, signs multiplied of impending change. Popular magazines began to worry about the "trapped" educated housewife. A new organization called Women's Strike for Peace (WSP) proclaimed its opposition to nuclear war in the name of mother love. Most activists in WSP were educated, middle-class housewives. They insisted, however, on the right of housewives to be heard as citizens. And, on November 1, 1961, an estimated 50,000 women left their kitchens and jobs to protest nuclear testing and the arms race.

When the House Un-American Activities Committee called the leaders of WSP to testify about their "subversive" intentions, hundreds of women packed the hearing room, filling it with hubbub and the cries of babies. The committee chair outlawed standing when the audience stood in silent solidarity with the first witness. Then he outlawed applause. The women ran to the front to kiss the witnesses and hand them flowers. Impeccably dressed in hats and gloves, the witnesses remained cool and firm under the committee's sharp questioning. "You don't quite understand the nature of this movement," retired schoolteacher Blanche Posner lectured the committee. "This movement was inspired and motivated by mothers' love for children. . . . When they were putting their breakfast on the table, they saw not only the

Wheaties and milk, but also saw strontium 90 and iodine 131" (Swerdlow, 1982: 502).

In the 1960s, many convergent trends formed the background for new signs of unrest. The great changes of demography and labor force participation undermined domesticity. Marriage ages had begun to creep up again and fertility rates began to fall after 1957. Slowly, almost imperceptibly, the headlong rush into domesticity had begun to reverse. In 1960 the Food and Drug Administration approved a new form of contraception, the birth control pill. For the first time, contraception was thoroughly separated from the act of sexual intercourse. The effectiveness of the pill broadened the possibilities of recreational sex, enjoyed for its own sake in contexts not tied to procreation or even to domesticity.

Working women outside the middle-class mainstream had challenged traditional assumptions in the 1950s. Within the UAW's Women's Department, for example, a tiny staff became increasingly aware that union orthodoxy supported practices, such as protective legislation, that, more often than not, discriminated against women by keeping them out of higher-paying jobs and limiting promotions. But efforts to eliminate separate seniority lists and job classifications based on sex won little favor (Gavin, 1985).

Black women, with long traditions of leadership and activism within black churches and educational institutions, played key roles in the rising protest within the black community against continuing racial discrimination, especially segregation in the South. Rosa Parks, a seamstress and secretary of the Montgomery, Alabama, National Association for the Advancement of Colored People (NAACP), started a mass movement when she refused to move to the rear of a segregated public bus. The boycott that followed her act involved the entire black community of Montgomery for more than a year, and resulted in the creation of the Southern Christian Leadership Conference (SCLC) led by Martin Luther King, Jr. Daisy Bates, president of the Little Rock, Arkansas, NAACP, won a suit to require the integration of the local high school.

When black college students staged a sit-in at Woolworth's lunch counters all over the South in the spring of 1960, it was Ella Baker on the staff of the SCLC who called a meeting of the militant youth and served as a guiding spirit in the founding of the Student Nonviolent Coordinating Committee (SNCC). The civil rights movement that emerged from these activities provided a new model for social change and a language about equality, rights, and community that transformed public discourse. "Freedom now," the movement proclaimed. Citizenship schools taught the basic skills of public participation and reinvigorated the ideals of civic duties and rights. All this ferment changed the idiom of politics, reemphasizing themes of community and civic participation that had long been eclipsed.

The New Feminism

The reemergence of a new, self-consciously feminist movement came from two directions. Professional women, led by women in the labor movement, laid the initial groundwork. At the insistence of Esther Peterson, director of the Women's Bureau in the Department of Labor and a former labor leader, President Kennedy appointed a Commission on the Status of Women headed by Eleanor Roosevelt. The commission set about a reassessment of women's place in the economy, the family, and the legal system. It documented pervasive employment discrimination, unequal pay, lack of social services such as child care, and continuing legal inequality. For the time being, the commission sidestepped the question of the need for an equal rights amendment (which most unions still opposed), but it succeeded in placing women's rights back on the national political agenda (*American Women*, 1963; Harrison, 1980).

The commission also activated a network of professional women, whose position, relative to that of male professionals, had been deteriorating for several decades. Within a year of the national commission's report, similar commissions had been established in most states. Together, they constituted a community of politically sophisticated women well placed to press for policy changes.

Three major federal initiatives provided them with tools. After the commission's report, the president ordered the civil service to hire people for career positions "without regard to sex," and Congress passed the Equal Pay Act outlawing different pay to women and men for the same work. Then, in 1964, Title VII of the Civil Rights Act was enacted to prohibit discrimination in employment on the basis of race, religion, national origin, and *sex*. Soon professional women in the networks of the national and state commissions on the status of women grew concerned about the general non-enforcement of Title VII and women's lack of political clout. In 1966 they organized the National Organization for Women (NOW) to provide a civil rights lobby for women and began to organize grassroots support.

While the professional women moved toward the founding of NOW, younger women active in the civil rights and student movements in the 1960s began to apply their own ideas about rights, community, and equality to themselves.

Activism had given them an opportunity to learn organizing skills and to develop a sharply altered sense of their own potential. Black women in the South presented whites with modes of womanhood that were courageous and self-respecting. Yet the student movement often replicated domestic ideology when it relegated women to kitchens and mimeo machines, and the new "sexual revolution" encouraged by the pill promoted sexual expressiveness in ways that were frequently exploitative of women.

By 1967, a small group of women involved in the student protests decided that they must use their organizing techniques to begin to build a "women's liberation movement." Their focus was less on legal or policy changes than on a frontal challenge to cultural definitions of maleness and femaleness. In consciousness-raising groups they set out to rediscover their own reality by analyzing personal experiences. The problems they identified were external, in a culture and social system that defined women as inferior, and internal, in women's diminished sense of self (Evans, 1979).

As NOW picketed male bars and newspapers with segregated want ads, and women's liberation groups demonstrated at the Miss America Pageant, small beginnings grew quickly into a mass movement. The radical movement's central organizing tool, the small consciousness-raising group, proved a brilliant mechanism for movement building. Within such groups, women discovered that their lives were not unique but part of a larger pattern, and they claimed the power of sisterhood. Since the groups had little or no structure, they could be formed anywhere, from offices to churches to neighborhoods. In effect, consciousness-raising defined the personal issues of daily life—housework, childrearing, sexuality, etiquette, even language—as political issues susceptible to collective action and solution. Nothing was beyond discussion.

The consequence of these spreading encounters was the politicization of informal female networks such as office friendships, church associations, neighborhood kaffeeklatsches, and other voluntary associations. Suddenly women were naming the dilemmas they experienced both at home and at work.

The new feminism began a process of redefinition in response to the breakdown of conventional understanding that women and men had of a social division between public and private life. Women in effect reintroduced the personal into politics, challenging the obsolete language that bifurcated public and private, male and female. But the new life patterns that emerged in the late twentieth century represented a period of experimentation, as women in very different economic and social circumstances worked to make the best of what they accepted to be their life choices. Among themselves, feminists argued vehemently about whether the division between public and private was universal or particular, and whether women were essentially different from or the same as men. The heat of their debate marked the difficulty of devising new categories for this changing reality.

Specific groups of women found their own voices and articulated experiences different from those of the middle-class base of the new women's movement. In consciousness-raising groups, lesbians became visible to themselves and one another. Freed to challenge social definitions of femininity, of sexuality, and of deviance (even when those attitudes persisted in the women's movement itself), they began to discuss the dimensions of a lesbian feminist perspective. They established coffee houses, bookstores, counseling centers, theatres, musical productions, and a variety of feminist enterprises. Lesbian feminism soon became a central intellectual thread in the new movement.

Black women, deeply aware of the need for racial solidarity and sensitive to the racism of white middle-class women, viewed the new movement with caution. They had never internalized a purely private, domestic identity. But within the labor force they had certainly experienced the combined effect of simultaneous racial and sexual discrimination. And within the black movement they had to confront a definition of liberation premised on the reclamation of black manhood, sometimes at the expense of women (see Horton, 1986). By the mid-1970s, strong black feminist voices like those of Alice Walker and Audre Lourde had begun to explore the ramifications of this dual oppression. Black organizers like Bertha Gilkey in St. Louis had begun to proclaim black women's achievements in neighborhoods and communities.

Activists surfaced in other arenas as well. In 1974, clerical workers in Boston and Chicago created a new kind of organization that was modeled on community organizations rather than on traditional labor organizations. Their goal was to tap into and politicize the female networks within offices. In Chicago, for example, Women Employed conducted a nationally televised sit-in at a law office that had fired a secretary for refusing to make coffee. Both Women Employed and 9 to 5 in Boston adroitly used Title VII and affirmative action guidelines to build campaigns against discriminatory employers and to win legal victories. At the same time, women in traditional labor unions created their own organization, the Coalition of Labor Union Women (CLUW). Structurally, CLUW was conservative, remaining within the labor movement and restrained from independent action, particularly in the area of organizing. Yet CLUW broke down the isolation of women within specific unions and forced the labor movement to recognize women as an important constituency for the first time. The appearance of 3,000 women at CLUW's founding meeting in Chicago when only 800 had been expected to attend signaled the intensity of women's interest and need for solidarity (Goodin, 1983).

The emergence of the new feminism in the late 1960s and the 1970s had important political consequences in the form of specific legislation and legal interpretations. The Equal Employment Opportunity Commission (EEOC) began to enforce Title VII prohibitions against sex discrimination more vigorously. More laws, written and promoted by a network of Washington women, provided greater educational opportunities for women and support for female athletics. The Equal Rights Amendment passed Congress in 1972 with the support of such former opponents as unions, the League of Women Voters, and the YWCA. Quickly, the ERA became a symbol of the new feminism's emphasis on individual opportunity and self-expression. Similarly, feminists generally cheered when the Supreme Court ruled in 1973 that abortion in the first trimester of pregnancy was a constitutionally protected private decision between a woman and her physician.

These changing realities, however, not only instigated new forms of social unrest but also deeply affected the daily life experiences and expectations of all women. By the late 1960s, the proportion of women in most professions had begun to rise, reversing a 40-year trend, as did the percentage of women in highly male-dominated fields such as law and medicine. But the stream of young female graduates entering business and becoming professionals after the mid-1970s met more subtle forms of discrimination than their predecessors had experienced. They found themselves in a world that proclaimed equal opportunity but defined career paths in the rhythms of a male life-cycle. In response, many women put off marriage and childbearing.

By 1980, more than half of all adult women were working outside the home. For all its lingering cultural power, the traditional family supported by a father's income was no longer the actual norm. Instead, the dual-career or two-job family was typical for married couples. Furthermore, skyrocketing divorce rates after 1960 and rising unmarried teenage pregnancy led to a substantial increase in the proportion of families headed by single women.

By the mid-1970s, social scientists had discovered what has come to be known as the "feminization of poverty." In ironic juxtaposition to the new female professionals with their supposedly limitless opportunities, poor women and their children got poorer. Unskilled urban males among the poor confronted a constricting and highly unstable labor market. With high rates of male unemployment, women faced severe choices. The welfare system supported (at below subsistence rates) families of women and children, but penalized them if there was an unemployed male present. The labor market, though less racially segregated after the 1960s, continued to be sharply segregated by sex. In general, women had access only to the least-skilled, lowest-paying jobs, few of which paid well enough to support a family.

The persistence of the gap between women's and men's wages, despite the legal tools of affirmative action and equal pay for equal work, generated a central policy debate in the late 1970s and 1980s. The concept of equal pay for work of comparable worth dates from the World War II era, but it reappeared in policy debates and union negotiations in the mid-1970s. At the same time that feminist theorists were searching for the origins of patriarchy as a system, some union organizers and members of the EEOC were recognizing that women's economic disadvantages were complex and systemic. The division of the labor market into male and female jobs had allowed assumptions rooted in the older division of work/home, public/private, and male/female to shape the post-industrial economy. Only in the late 1970s, however, did this discrepancy become the object of social protest.

Conclusion

Many voices speak—or claim to speak—for women in the 1980s. Organized groups advocate policy responses to the crisis in child care, labor force discrimination, and the issue of homosexual rights. Others demand a return to a mythic past of male individualism and female domesticity. Growing stresses of work inside and outside the home frame problems and possibilities.

The backlash against women's increased autonomy gained power through the 1970s. The politicization of personal life has propelled issues like abortion and the ERA into the center of American politics. Indeed, the defeat of the ERA, despite its support by the majority of Americans, indicates the power of organized opposition to the feminist agenda, as well as the depth of cultural anxieties about changes that few understand.

The realities of women's lives, the tensions and stresses of change, the increased self-organization of women, and the policy proposals that they engender, will continue to generate conflict. They seem likely to transform, in ways we can only begin to anticipate, our understanding of the nature of the state, the community, and public and private life.

TWO Women and the Family

ANDREW CHERLIN

Highlights

THE GREAT CHANGES IN the institution of the family over the past few decades have altered the family lives of women considerably. Families have become more diverse. Instead of one dominant family form, there are several: cohabitation, the first marriage, the single-parent family, and remarriage are common, and many women may experience all of these forms during their lifetimes. Moreover, a majority of women now combine family lives with work outside the home.

* At least 90 percent of all women born in this century have eventually married, and at least 85 percent of today's young adult women will probably marry, which means that about one out of six or seven will never marry.

* The divorce rate doubled between the early 1960s and the mid-1970s but since then it has remained level. Nevertheless, at current rates, nearly half of all new marriages will end in divorce.

* In 1980, an estimated 9.2 million U.S. households contained a married couple in which at least one of the spouses was remarried after a divorce. The expanded stepfamily is becoming increasingly common.

• In 1984, according to the Census Bureau, there were 1,988,000 U.S. households with two unrelated adults of the opposite sex. In 1970, the Census Bureau counted only 523,000 such households. Six percent of all unmarried women between the ages of 15 and 44 were cohabiting in 1982.

• After the 1950s—the time of the great post-World War II baby boom when birthrates increased—the birthrate resumed its long-term decline; as a result, women no longer assume that childrearing will occupy all their productive adult years. At the same time, the labor force participation rate of women, notably women with small children, has increased significantly.

• By the age of 18, four percent of unmarried white women and 27 percent of unmarried black women have borne children. Twenty percent of all families with children are headed by women.

• The most common status for American mothers is to be both married and employed outside the home. Combining work and family life has become one of the central family issues of the 1980s.

• 13.8 million married mothers (constituting 46 percent of all mothers who were either married or maintaining families) were employed outside the home in 1985. Still, housewives have not disappeared: as of 1985, there were 10.2 million married women who were full-time homemakers.

• Paid employment is also common among unmarried mothers. For example, in 1985, 69 percent of all single mothers with children between the ages of six and 17, but none younger, were employed outside the home. Single mothers

with younger children are less likely to work for pay, but
still, the proportion who do is impressive—44 percent.

• The family remains the most important source of child care
for working mothers, especially among lower-income families. In 52 percent of two-parent families with children
under age five and an employed mother in 1982, the youngest child was cared for by a family member.

• Only 15 percent of all working mothers in 1982 reported
that their children attended nursery school or day care
centers; the children of another 22 percent were cared for
by a nonrelative outside of the home.

• Foremost among the problems of the growing number of
single mothers is low income. Members of female-headed
families are more likely than those in other types of families
to be poor and to stay poor.

• The majority of "persistently poor" families are female-
headed. However, poverty is not necessarily the result of
changes in family composition. Many, especially blacks, are
poor before changes in household composition. In fact,
those changes (resulting from such events as divorce or the
birth of a child) may be as much a response to poverty as
a cause.

• Among whites, however, a substantial proportion of poor
female-headed households are in poverty because of a
change in family composition—usually a divorce or separation. Although this period of poverty is generally temporary, it can be a very long time for a child.

• Many women and children experience a drop in their standard of living after divorce. Divorced mothers are often
dependent on their own earning power and on normally

modest child support. Census data show that fathers' compliance with child support agreements tends to be low, at least as of 1981.

• Many divorced women ultimately remarry. The chances of remarriage are best for those who are younger, less educated, or white. Women who do remarry after a divorce achieve a standard of living nearly equal to that of divorced men or intact married couples.

• Remarriage is less common among older divorced women. Moreover, during the past few decades, the mortality rate for adult women has declined faster than the rate for men. Consequently, more and more wives are outliving their husbands. Largely as a result, older women are overrepresented among the poor despite a substantial improvement in the standard of living for the elderly overall.

Introduction

By now, the general outline of the great changes in American family life since World War II are well known. Looking back from the vantage point of the 1980s, we can see a roller-coaster pattern of change in marriage, divorce, and childbearing, with the indicators moving in one direction in the 1950s, then surging in the other direction in the 1960s and 1970s before more or less stabilizing in the 1980s. The only consistent source of change throughout the period was the steady march of married women into the labor force. These changes in family life occurred too fast and on too large a scale for our society to adjust quickly to them. They have left many Americans confused and apprehensive about the state of the American family. And they have transformed the family lives of American women.

To review briefly, the 1950s brought the great post-World War II baby boom. Nearly half of all women married

"Combining work and family life has become one of the central family issues of the 1980s." © *Jeffrey D. Smith / Woodfin Camp & Associates*

while they were still in their teenage years. Those who were passing through their peak childbearing years at that time had an average of about three children (Cherlin, 1981). Then, in the early 1960s, these trends reversed. The birthrate resumed its long-term historical decline, so that at today's rates the average young woman will bear fewer than two children. The typical age at marriage rose sharply through the 1960s and 1970s and is still rising in the 1980s: in 1964, the median age at marriage for women was 20.5; in 1974 it was 21.1; and in 1984 it was 23.0 (U.S. Bureau of the Census, 1985). The divorce rate doubled between the early 1960s and the mid-1970s but since then has remained level; at current rates nearly half of all new marriages will end in divorce.

Some observers, perhaps out of nostalgia for the idealized 1950s-style family of two parents, three children, a dog, and a station wagon, mistakenly assume that the patterns of that decade were typical of the way American families always used to be. Actually, the 1950s were in many respects extremely atypical. It is the only period in the past 150 years during which the birthrate rose substantially. The average age at marriage in the 1950s and early 1960s was significantly lower than at any other time in this century. And the divorce rate increased at an unusually slow pace. The reasons for the distinctive patterns of the 1950s are not fully clear. There appears to have been a turn toward the rewards of family, marriage, and childrearing by Americans who were exhausted by the disruptions of the war and the Great Depression. Moreover, the relatively small numbers of young adult men born during the birth dearth of the Depression led to increased employment opportunities and higher earnings for young husbands in the post-war economic boom (Cherlin,

1981). Unless special circumstances such as these recur, a return to the 1950s-style family in the near future is unlikely.

A return to the 1950s is even more unlikely because of the movement of married women into the labor force. Elsewhere in this book, Nancy Barrett reviews this change in detail. It occurred in two steps. During the 1950s, the labor force participation rate of married women with school-age children increased rapidly; then, after 1960, the rate of increase was most rapid for women with children under age six. As Barrett argues, this increase was fueled by the demand for workers in the expanding service sector, where many occupations had become typed as "women's jobs." Although average wages for women are lower than for men, women workers today can expect to make more money than in previous decades. Thus, the cost in forgone earnings of staying home—what economists call the "opportunity cost" of not working outside the home—has increased. Moreover, the lower birthrate means that, unlike previous generations, young women today cannot expect that childrearing will occupy most of their productive adult years. Therefore, it seems highly unlikely that the trend toward married women working outside the home could be reversed substantially.

That there will not be a return to the days when most married women stayed home has important implications for public policy. For it is the case that some policy analysts, concerned about what they see as a deterioration of the traditional American family, urge that public policy encourage the return of married women to the home, or, at least, that no programs be enacted that might further encourage mothers to work. But the historical record suggests that there is little that government can do to influence greatly the proportion of married women in the labor force. Little, that is, except for drastic measures like the mobilization of women's labor during World War II or politically infeasible programs such as paying full-time homemakers the equivalent of their potential market wage. The increase has occurred not because of government action but because of fundamental changes in the structure of our economy. The same could be said of the long-term trend in the birthrate, which will never again be as high as when most of the population lived on farms. For better or worse, then, there is little that our government can do to reverse the fundamental trends that have altered family life in the past few decades. Let us turn to how those trends have altered the family lives of women.

The Family Life Course of Women Today

The family lives of both women and men are more diverse today than they were a generation ago. There is no longer one predominant path that most people travel; rather there is a diversity of family forms and life histories. After entering adulthood, for example, many women will live with a man prior to marriage. This is a recent change; prior to about 1970 cohabitation outside of marriage was uncommon. In 1970 the Bureau of the Census counted 523,000 households with two unrelated adults of the opposite sex; by 1984 the number had grown to 1,988,000 (U.S. Bureau of the Census, 1985). According to the 1982 National Survey of Family Growth (NSFG), a national study of women aged 15 to 44, about six percent of all unmarried women aged 15 to 44 were cohabiting. For most women who cohabit, cohabitation is a stage of life that occurs prior to marriage. For example, the NSFG shows that the proportion of unmarried women who were cohabiting peaked at 16 percent among those 25 to 29, declined to 11 percent among those 30 to 34, then fell further to seven percent among those 35 to 39 and to three percent among those 40 to 44 (Bacharach, 1985). There are no reliable data about the proportion of women who *ever* cohabit at some point prior to marriage, but this lifetime figure is undoubtedly substantial.

Most women, however, will eventually marry. At least 90 percent of all women born in this century have married, with the proportion rising to 96 percent or so for women who entered adulthood during the 1950s. In a 1981 book, I estimated that even with the rise in age at marriage that occurred in the 1970s, recent cohorts of young women would still reach the standard of 90 percent married (Cherlin, 1981). In light of the continuing rise in age at marriage, that forecast may prove too high. It is probably more prudent to predict that at least 85 percent of today's young adult women will marry. This figure can be interpreted in two ways. On the one hand, it suggests that lifelong singleness (possibly in combination with one or more cohabiting relationships) is much more common than in the recent past: one out of seven, or perhaps one out of six, women may never marry. Consequently, remaining single is becoming a more acceptable lifestyle than it was in the past. On the other hand, at least five out of six women will marry. This proportion is higher than current estimates for women in continental Western Europe. Thus, we remain a society that is attached to the institution of marriage more than most other developed societies, though that attachment has weakened somewhat.

Even within marriage, the course of family life has changed. The trends in employment of married women have been discussed above. As for fertility, most couples will have children, though increasingly only one or two. In fact, Charles F. Westoff has estimated that, counting both never-married women and those who marry, upwards of one-fourth of all young women today may never have children (Westoff, 1978). Voluntary childlessness, which was quite uncommon in the 1950s, is becoming increasingly acceptable.

But perhaps the most dramatic change in marriage is the increase in divorce and separation. The current high levels mean that divorce has become a common occurrence in women's lives. The economic implications of divorce for women are profound. Since husbands typically provide the bulk of the family income but women keep custody of the children, a divorce can cause a sharp drop in a woman's standard of living. More will be said about this point below.

Nor is divorce the final phase of family life for most women; a majority of those who divorce will remarry. Among women who divorced a decade or two ago, about three-fourths eventually remarried (Cherlin, 1981). Since then, however, rates of remarriage have fallen, so that the proportion remarried among recently divorced women will be somewhat lower. Remarriage receives much less attention than divorce, undoubtedly because it is not a social problem. But life in remarried families can be complex, and this newly prevalent family form deserves more attention.

Finally, widowhood must be considered. During the past few decades the life expectancy of adult women has risen more rapidly than that of men. Consequently, more and more wives are outliving their husbands, creating a long life stage of elderly widowhood, the existence of which on a large scale is historically novel. Sixty percent of the people aged 65 and over in the United States are women (U.S. Bureau of the Census, 1985). Because of this imbalance, the remarriage prospects of elderly widows (unlike those of elderly widowers) are limited. In 1984, there were 7.8 million currently widowed (and not remarried) women aged 65 and over in the United States, compared to only 1.5 million currently widowed elderly men (U.S. Bureau of the Census, 1985). The situation of elderly widows will be discussed below.

Thus, for many women, family life will consist of a progression through a series of life events, including possibly cohabitation, marriage, childbearing, divorce, remarriage, and widowhood. Not all women will experience all of these stages, of course. But it is increasingly common for a woman's family life course to take on a variety of forms. Prior to the last few decades, it was much more common for a woman to remain celibate until she married and then remain married until she died.

There are other variations in the family life course that deserve mention. One is out-of-wedlock childbearing. Contrary to popular belief, the rate of adolescent pregnancy—the risk that a teenage woman will become pregnant—has declined sharply since 1960. But pregnant adolescents are much less likely to marry than was the case 20 years ago. Therefore, a majority of teens who now bear children do so out of wedlock. Moreover, the rate of pregnancy among older, married women has dropped even faster. Consequently, births to unmarried teenagers account for an increased proportion of all births in the United States. By the time they reach 18, four percent of unmarried white women and 27 percent of unmarried black women have borne a child (Furstenberg and Brooks-Gunn, 1985).

In addition, as the last comparison shows, the differences in the course of childbearing and marriage between black and white women are substantial. Until 1950, black women married at a younger age than did white women; now they marry considerably later, and many more forgo marriage altogether (Cherlin, 1981). What has happened among low-income black women is a separation of childbearing from marriage. Although most will eventually marry, childbearing often precedes marriage by several years. In fact, the place of marriage in the family lives of black women seems to have declined, relative to their ties to extended kin, in the past few decades (Cherlin, 1981). In 1984, just 41 percent of black women aged 25 to 44 were currently married with a husband present in the household, as opposed to 72 percent of white women (U.S. Bureau of the Census, 1985). Black single women are less likely to marry than are white women; black women who are separated are less likely to divorce; and black women who are divorced are less likely to remarry. To be sure, both blacks and whites have been subject to the same trends toward later marriage, a higher ratio of out-of-wedlock births, and more marital dissolution in the past two decades. And there are substantial variations within the black population. Nevertheless, the differences in the family patterns of typical black and white women are striking and will be remarked upon where appropriate later in this chapter.

Women with Children

Let us now examine in more detail the implications of all these changes in family life for women with children. Table 2.1 shows the distribution of families with children under 18 years old according to the employment status of the mother in 1985. Three kinds of families are distinguished: the married-couple family, in which husband and wife are present; the family maintained by a woman, sometimes called a "female-headed family," in which no husband is present; and the male-headed family, in which no wife is present. The table allows us to examine the number of mothers in various family situations, not counting the relatively small number who are neither married nor heading their own households.

As the table shows, the most common status for American mothers is to be married and employed outside the home. There were 13.8 million such mothers in 1985, constituting 46 percent of all mothers who were married or maintaining their own families. Among women whose youngest child was at least six years old, this was by far the most common arrangement: 49 percent versus 28 percent in the next most common status, married but not employed. Among mothers with children under six, employed married women still outnumbered married women who were not employed, but not by much. There also were 6.1 million mothers heading households in 1985. Sixty-nine percent of the single mothers with older children were employed, but a majority of those with children under six were not. Finally, Table 2.1 reminds us that despite the increase in the employment of married women, housewives have not disappeared: there were 10.2 million married mothers who were not working outside the home in 1985.

Work and Family Issues

The sheer number of mothers who are employed—a total of 17.5 million in 1985, according to Table 2.1—shows why combining work life and family life has become one of the central family issues of the 1980s. It is especially important for women because, even in two-parent families, mothers continue to do most of the housework and childrearing. A num-

Table 2.1 • FAMILIES WITH CHILDREN UNDER 18 YEARS OLD BY EMPLOYMENT STATUS OF THE MOTHER, 1985
(numbers in thousands)

	Number of families			Percent distribution		
	Total	With children ages 6–17, none younger	With children under age 6	Total	With children ages 6–17, none younger	With children under age 6
Total families	31,158	17,003	14,155	100.0	100.0	100.0
Married-couple families	24,080	12,587	11,494	79.7	76.8	83.1
Mother employed	13,839	8,005	5,835	45.8	48.8	42.2
Mother not employed	10,241	4,582	5,659	33.9	28.0	40.9
Families maintained by women	6,147	3,800	2,346	20.3	23.2	16.9
Mother employed	3,647	2,620	1,027	12.1	16.0	7.4
Mother not employed	2,500	1,180	1,319	8.2	7.2	9.5
Families maintained by men	931	616	316	*	*	*

*Excluded from the base for percent distribution.

Source: Bureau of National Affairs, Inc., *Work and Family: A Changing Dynamic* (Washington, D.C.: The Bureau of National Affairs, Inc., 1986), p. 315. Figures compiled from U.S. Bureau of Labor Statistics sources.

ber of articles in the media over the past few years have heralded the arrival of the "new father" who shares the childrearing tasks equally with his wife. But upon closer examination, it turns out that many of these fathers are upper-middle-class professionals in cosmopolitan centers such as Manhattan. This media barrage has served to legitimate a greater role for fathers, in itself an important development, but evidence that fathers nationwide are doing significantly more around the house is still inconclusive. Joseph Pleck (1985) compared two national surveys of time use in the 1970s with earlier studies from the 1960s and concluded that husbands of employed wives in the 1970s spent more time with their children than husbands of employed wives in the 1960s. But the pattern of results was complex and somewhat contradictory. Moreover, no good information exists on trends in time use since the late 1970s. There appear to be some incipient changes in the 1980s, but the evidence for them is largely anecdotal: "We are seeing men do more," James A. Levine, director of the Fatherhood Project of the Bank Street College of Education, told the Bureau of National Affairs. "Men *are* becoming more involved with the childrearing, albeit slowly" (Bureau of National Affairs, 1986). Of course, the growing number of single mothers simply have no husband around with whom to share their responsibilities.

Perhaps the most dramatic example of the efforts that dual-earner families are making to combine employment and childbearing is the surprisingly high prevalence of shift work. Harriet B. Presser and Virginia Cain (1983) found that among two-parent families in which both parents work full time, about one-third included at least one spouse who worked other than a regular day schedule. It seems likely that many of these couples have rearranged their work lives so that they still can provide care for their children.

In fact, parents and relatives provide the care for a majority of the children of working couples. In 52 percent of two-parent families with children under five and an employed mother, the youngest child was cared for by a family member, according to a 1982 Bureau of the Census survey (U.S. Bureau of the Census, 1983b). The percentage rose to 63 percent among families with mothers employed part time. The caretaking family members even include a surprising number of fathers: 10 percent of wives who were employed full time and who had a child under five reported in 1982 that their husband was the principal caretaker, as did 20 percent of wives who worked part time. Grandparents were also notable among caretakers, providing primary care for 17 percent of

"The caretaking family members even include a surprising number of fathers."
© *William S. Weems / Woodfin Camp, Inc.*

full- and part-time employed wives. Employed women who are not married obviously cannot rely on husbands for child care (though the survey shows that two percent relied on ex-husbands), but they rely more heavily on grandparents and other relatives than do married women.

These statistics demonstrate that the family plays a significant role in easing the child care problems of working mothers. They show how misleading it is to assume that most children of working mothers are cared for in day care centers. (Only 15 percent of all employed mothers in the 1982 survey reported that their child attended a nursery school or day care center; another 22 percent reported that their child was cared for by a nonrelative outside the home.) The family remains the most important source of care for the young children of working mothers. This is especially true among lower-income families. Among employed women with pre-school-age children in families with incomes below $15,000 in 1982, 59 percent relied primarily on care by relatives. In contrast, 42 percent of those families with incomes of $25,000 and over relied primarily on relatives. In part, this difference may reflect the lesser ability of lower-income parents to purchase group care services. But it also seems to reflect a greater availability of nearby relatives, for it is well known that lower-income individuals tend to live closer to kin.

On the other hand, it is clear that family resources, though often underestimated, are not sufficient for all employed mothers. Thus, increasing attention is being given to corporate and governmental responses that would make the demands of employment and parenting more compatible. These innovations include flexible working hours, part-time employment with prorated benefits, maternity and parenting leave, and better child care services. The U.S. Congress has not entirely ignored these matters. Perhaps the most notable initiative in the 99th Congress was a bill introduced by Rep. Patricia Schroeder that would require employers to provide at least 18 weeks of unpaid leave within a two-year period for employees who choose to stay home to care for newborn, newly adopted, or seriously ill children. Whether or not this bill is passed, the general issues it raises are sure to remain. These include the extent to which government should legislate changes in the workplace that benefit working parents and their children. Some business executives claim that such a benefit would be enjoyed at the expense of other benefits employees would like, or that it would lead to proliferating demands for special benefits. Moreover, they argue that a more collaborative effort by corporations and government, rather than a legislative mandate, is the way to produce change in this area. But supporters of the legislative approach respond that without government prodding, little change is likely to occur.

At the moment, corporations seem to be moving toward accommodating working parents, though the number who have done so remains modest. Dana Friedman of the Conference Board has estimated that, as of 1985, 2,500 companies were providing some form of child care assistance. This is only a small percentage of all large and medium-sized companies, but it represents a fourfold increase since 1982. Most of these companies seem to favor providing flexible benefit packages that can be used to pay for child care. Some employees obviously would be assisted by on-site centers, but many working parents appear to prefer other arrangements, including care provided in the home or nearby. Thus, the provision of benefits and information may allow more parents to satisfy their preferences than would a heavy emphasis on on-site child care centers.

Single Mothers

The growing number of single mothers who are raising children—about 20 percent of all mothers, according to Table 2.1—face other problems as well. Foremost among these is low income. As Barrett notes in chapter three, the proportion of poor persons living in female-headed households has increased dramatically in recent years, and over half of all children living in poverty are in households headed by women. This phenomenon has come to be known as the "feminization of poverty."

Not only are the members of female-headed households more likely to be poor in any given year, but they are also more likely to remain poor. The Panel Study of Income Dynamics (PSID), carried out by the Institute for Social Research (ISR) at the University of Michigan, has been following a nationally representative sample of 5,000 families since 1968. The ISR investigators report that, between 1969 and 1978, 28 percent of the families that were "temporarily poor" (defined as poor just one or two years out of the 10) were female-headed; but that 61 percent of the "persistently poor" families (defined as poor eight or more years out of the 10) were also female-headed. Black families were heavily over-represented, as well: 62 percent of the persistently poor families were black, compared to 19 percent of the temporarily poor. In fact, 31 percent of all the persistently poor were found to be living in families headed by non-elderly black women (Duncan, 1984).

Given the growth in female-headed families, especially among blacks, many observers have assumed that changes in family structure are largely responsible for the increase in the poverty population. It is assumed that the increase in divorce and separation in the 1960s and 1970s, coupled with low levels of child support, have impoverished many previously middle-class women and children, while out-of-wedlock child-bearing has had similar effects among the near-poor. Yet recent empirical studies suggest that the effects of changes in family composition on poverty rates have been exaggerated. Analyzing the PSID, Mary Jo Bane found that only about half of the female-headed and single-person white households living in poverty had become poor when household composition changed; some were poor before the household change, others were not poor until well afterward. And, among blacks, just a fifth of female-headed and single-person households living in poverty had become poor when household composition changed; in contrast, 45 percent were already poor before the household change. Thus, among whites, what Bane calls "event-driven poverty"—a fall into poverty due to a family event such as divorce—accounted for perhaps half of the occurrences of poverty among families in the PSID. Among black families, event-driven poverty was much less common. Bane argues instead that much of the poverty of black female-headed families was a "reshuffling," in which people who were already poor changed their family structure. Bane draws the following conclusion: "Although there has indeed been a dramatic and shocking increase in female-headed households among blacks and an equally dramatic feminization of black poverty, one cannot conclude that much of the poverty could have been avoided had families stayed together" (Bane, 1986: 231).

In others words, changes in family structure, especially among blacks, may be as much a response to poverty as a cause. One cannot simply blame the persistence of poverty on the rise in divorce and teenage childbearing, because many of the mothers in poverty were poor before they divorced or gave birth. One would have to look at other factors to understand fully the causes of poverty, for example, the labor market situation of black men. Changes in family structure do play a role in producing poverty, but the role has been overemphasized. According to census data, 15 percent of whites and 35.5 percent of blacks were below the official poverty line in 1983. Bane estimated that even if there had been no changes in the proportion of female-headed families or of other household types over the previous two decades, 13 percent of whites and 28.5 percent of blacks would still have been poor in 1983. Further, she finds that changes in family structure had little influence on the substantial rise in poverty in the early 1980s.

Nevertheless, Bane's analysis does confirm that among whites a substantial proportion of poor female-headed families are in poverty because of a change in family composition, usually a divorce or separation. For most white women and their children, a spell of poverty after a divorce will be temporary, but even a few years in and out of poverty can be a very long time for a child. The economic hardships that women and their children face after divorce have received much attention recently, especially with the publication of Lenore J. Weitzman's (1985) in-depth study of the issue. Weitzman argues that the changes in divorce laws from fault-based grounds to no-fault grounds have hurt divorced women economically. The new laws assume that husbands and wives are equals, but in reality most wives have far less earning potential than their husbands. Older wives, especially, may not have worked for wages in decades. Even younger, better-educated wives may have worked only part time or withdrawn from the labor force when their children were young, thus forgoing the opportunity to develop a career.

Consequently, settlements that award the wife half of the family's property (often forcing the sale of the family home in the process) leave the wife and children dependent on her earning power and her ex-husband's child support payments. And census data show that fathers' compliance with child support agreements is low. In 1981, for example, only 49 percent of mothers who were supposed to receive child support payments reported receiving the full amount; 28 percent reported receiving nothing. Moreover, the amount of child support agreed upon or awarded by the court is modest: a mean amount of $2,460, or about $200 a month, per family in 1981 (U.S. Bureau of the Census, 1983a). Nor, as Weitzman notes, are these awards typically indexed for inflation.

The result is that many women and their children see their standard of living fall after a divorce. (Despite changes in custody standards, mothers continue to retain custody of their children in nearly nine out of 10 divorces.) Weitzman's most startling and most widely quoted claim is that "on average, divorced women and the minor children in their households experience a 73 percent decline in their standard of living in the first year after divorce. Their former husbands, in contrast, experience a 42 percent rise in their standard of living" (Weitzman, 1985: xii). Thus "divorce is a financial catastrophe for most women" (ibid.: 339). These figures, however, overstate the case. Weitzman's sample of divorced men and women in the Los Angeles area, from which she derives her estimates, is useful but not without limitations.[1] Far better for assessing the economic effects of divorce is the PSID, which, as we have seen, was designed to provide national estimates of the changing economic circumstances of American families. Greg J. Duncan and Saul D. Hoffman, who

analyzed the PSID data, and Weitzman used similar techniques to adjust pre- and post-divorce income for the change
in household size and composition that occurs after a divorce.
But Duncan and Hoffman (1985b) reported that, one year
after a divorce or separation, adjusted family income for all
women had dropped by nine to 25 percent of its pre-divorce
level (depending on the exact method of calculation) and had
risen by three to 13 percent for men.

In addition, the PSID data suggest that the averages for
women conceal large variations. The fall in living standards
was much sharper for women whose families initially had
been in the top half of the income distribution: 29 percent
of women from these relatively affluent pre-divorce families
had experienced a drop in adjusted income of more than half
by one year after the divorce (Duncan and Hoffman, 1985b).
In contrast, 19 percent of women from less affluent pre-
divorce families had comparable income drops, and 38 percent actually had experienced a rise in adjusted income by
one year after the divorce. These more detailed figures suggest
that the women who suffered most were middle-class and
upper-middle-class wives whose husbands' earnings were
large and whose own labor market experience was limited. It
is these older, middle-class homemakers who have the most
to lose from a divorce and for whom the consequences seem
most unfair. Yet divorce is more common among younger
families (the median age at divorce for women is about 31)
and among lower-income families, where the wife has relatively less to lose. My point is that on this issue, as on so many
others, one cannot speak of the effects on women in general
without ignoring important variations. Clearly, our society
treats unfairly the wife of a business executive who leaves her
for his secretary after 30 years of devoted housework, enter-

taining, and child care. Yet the situation is different for a 27-year-old mother who is employed full time as a nurse and decides to leave her husband. In the latter case, it is unlikely that the divorce will be an economic catastrophe for the mother, though she may experience some hardship, and she is likely to view the divorce as psychologically beneficial as well.

Still, there is no justification for the inequities that do exist. Studies such as Weitzman's suggest that middle-class fathers do have the money to pay agreed-upon child support without undue economic sacrifice. Yet less than half of the fathers pay in full. Many fathers, it seems, drift away from their children after a divorce, often starting new families. In a national survey of teenage children, Furstenberg and his colleagues (1983) reported that half of those with divorced or separated parents had not seen their fathers within the past year. That fathers must be held responsible for the support of their children after a divorce is one of the few elements of family policy on which liberal and conservative policymakers have agreed in recent years. The result was the passage of the Child Support Enforcement Amendments of 1984, which greatly strengthened enforcement procedures against non-compliant, middle-class men. This law appears to be an important step, but it is too soon to evaluate its success. Yet it is important to realize that child support enforcement, valuable though it is, is not of much use when the father is unemployed or unknown. Bane (1986: 231) cautions: "Child and spousal support may help alleviate the poverty of many white households, but it can make only the smallest dent in the problem of black poverty."

Remarriage

A complete consideration of the effects of divorce on women must take remarriage into account. Even though re-marriage rates are lower for divorced women than for divorced men, the extent of remarriage among divorced women is substantial. In the PSID, 20 percent of the white women had remarried within one year of the time when they were first observed to have separated from or divorced their hus-bands. Forty-six percent had remarried within three years and 54 percent within five years (Duncan and Hoffman, 1985a). Some observers dismiss remarriage too quickly. Weitzman, for example, notes that the probability of remarriage declines with age and argues that "the assumption of remarriage is clearly inappropriate for all divorced women over thirty" (1985: 204). She subsequently devotes little attention to the effects of remarriage on the economic situation of women and children. But a majority of women who divorce while in their thirties do eventually remarry (Koo and Suchindran, 1980). And, as stated above, over half of all divorces occur to women aged 31 or under, whose probability of remarriage is even higher.[2]

As with divorce, it is misleading to generalize about the remarriage possibilities of all women. What seems to occur is that divorced women whose skills and economic resources are limited, or who are younger, are likely to remarry; in contrast, women with more resources, those who are older, and those who are black are less likely to do so. Women with resources, such as a college or postgraduate degree, have less economic need to remarry. Those who are younger may be more attrac-tive to men as potential spouses, since it is still acceptable in our culture for a man to marry a younger woman but less acceptable for a woman to marry a younger man. Thus, older divorced women face competition in the marriage market from the large number of younger women, both never-married and previously divorced. In addition, black women can expect fewer economic gains from remarriage, on average, compared to white women because of the poorer labor market position of black men.

The result is that divorced women who are younger, less educated, or white tend to remarry, and in so doing recoup most of the economic ground they lost after their divorces. Because of the economic benefits of remarriage, the average divorced woman in the PSID (including those who had remarried) was better off economically three years after the divorce than she had been before the divorce (Duncan and Hoffman, 1985a), though still not as well off as the average divorced man, who had improved his standard of living even more. Five years after the divorce, women in the PSID who had remarried had a standard of living nearly equal to divorced men or to intact married couples. Remarriage is clearly a route out of economic difficulties for many divorced women.

Yet the other side of this story is that women who cannot remarry or who choose not to remarry tend to remain at an economic disadvantage. Five years after the divorce, the adjusted family incomes for women in the PSID who had not remarried were 94 percent of their pre-divorce levels, on average. Meanwhile, the adjusted family incomes of remarried couples and intact couples had increased by 25 to 30 percent, due to rising real incomes as well as extra earners. And the PSID researchers concluded that most of the women who remained unmarried would not have been helped that much by a remarriage anyway; because of their poorer marriage market position (their older age or their race), the predicted earnings of the typical men they might have married were quite modest. Just as clearly, remarriage is not a route out of economic difficulties for all divorced women. (Moreover, many of those who do remarry are likely to spend a few economically difficult years as a single parent.)

Economic considerations aside, being in a remarriage is an increasingly common status for women. In the United States in 1980, there were an estimated 9.2 million households that included a married couple, one or both of whom was remarried after a divorce. In about 40 percent of these households, one or both spouses had children less than 18 from previous marriages (though some of these children were living elsewhere with custodial parents; see Cherlin and McCarthy, 1985). When children from previous marriages are present, a "stepfamily" is formed. The most common arrangement is for the wife to bring her children, if any, to the household while the husband's children remain with his ex-wife. Thus, relatively few women are full-time stepmothers (an estimated 338,000 in 1980); many more are married to full-time stepfathers (2.2 million in 1980). The addition of a stepfather to the family is not always problem-free. The mother and her children may have developed ways of interacting during years of single-parenthood that are disrupted by the remarriage. For example, a teenage child may have taken on a parent-like role vis-à-vis younger children in order to fill the void left by the departed father; it may not be easy to relinquish such a role. Or a child undergoing puberty and dealing with his or her own emerging sexuality may have difficulty accepting his or her mother as someone actively involved in a new, sexual relationship. Stepsiblings brought together by the remarriage may not be sure what kind of relationship to establish with each other.

In general, there is a lack of widely accepted guidelines for how stepparents and stepchildren ought to behave in a remarriage (Cherlin, 1978). A woman who marries a divorced man with children does not replace the children's mother; rather she becomes an additional figure. The existence on a large scale of these relationships is recent; not until the 1970s did the number of marriages ending in divorce surpass the number ending in the death of one spouse. Consequently, the kinds of taken-for-granted norms that govern everyday behavior in first marriages are often absent in remarriages. But as this family form becomes more common, norms are beginning to surface. For example, when I first began to study remarriages about 10 years ago, there was confusion among stepparents and family counselors about whether a teenager from one spouse's previous marriage ought to be able to date a teenager from the other spouse's previous marriage. Now nearly all stepparents and counselors to whom I mention this hypothetical situation take the same position: no dating among stepchildren.

These emerging norms seem to be moving in the direction of expanding the concept of the family to include step-relationships and other quasi-kin ties. Indeed, family ties after remarriage often extend across two or three households. The result is that our commonsense equation of "family" with "household" often breaks down.[3] The basic question of what constitutes a family and what its boundaries are becomes less clear.

For young and middle-age women in remarriages, these cross-household links most often take two forms: (1) associating with an ex-husband or (2) associating with a new husband's ex-wife and her children. Neither form necessarily occurs; as noted above, many fathers virtually sever their ties with children from disrupted marriages. Relations with ex-husbands obviously can be difficult and acrimonious, though they are not always so. Less noticed but also stressful is being a part-time parent to the husband's children. The part-time stepmother may see these children for short visits, as on weekends, or for longer but irregular visits, as during school vacations. But because the children still live with their mother, the part-time stepmother's role is ambiguous. She cannot replace the children's mother; yet when the children are at her home she is cast into a parent-like role. Given the lack of clear behavioral guidelines, families must often work out accommodations to these situations for themselves.

Before leaving the topic of remarriage, let me note that it plays less of a role in the lives of black women because they are less likely to remarry. In the PSID study, only 42 percent of the black women had remarried within five years after a divorce or separation, compared to 58 percent of the white women (Duncan and Hoffman, 1985a). As noted above, this differential is most likely caused by the poorer labor market position of black men. Over the past few decades, black women have made far greater strides in their occupational attainments relative to white women than have black men relative to white men. Thus, black women who are separated or divorced have relatively less to gain from remarriage, on average, than do white women. And many black women from low-income backgrounds may conclude reluctantly that public assistance offers a level of support that is more secure than, and reasonably close to, what could be provided by a prospective spouse.

Older Women

The most important recent development in the lives of older women is the substantial improvement in their standard of living that has occurred over the past 20 years. As is well-known by now, the great increases in government programs for the elderly have boosted their incomes relative to the population under 65. In 1959, 35 percent of persons 65 and over were poor, compared to 22 percent of the population under 65. But by 1982, the elderly poverty rate was actually lower than that of the non-aged—14.6 vs. 15.0 percent (U.S. Bureau of the Census, 1984). Moreover, these figures exclude the often substantial noncash benefits that flow to the elderly, most notably Medicare benefits but also food stamps, housing subsidies, and so forth. By one estimate, the proportion of elderly who are below the poverty standard after consideration of these noncash benefits falls to four percent (Preston, 1984).

The increased economic well-being of the elderly is probably the greatest achievement of the much maligned war on poverty, and it is an achievement that has benefited older women as well as older men. Peter Uhlenberg and Mary Anne Salmon (1986) demonstrated that the incomes of women aged 65 to 69 and 75 to 79, married and unmarried, rose substantially between 1960 and 1980. Moreover, the increases tended to be relatively larger among the poorest women, so that inequality of income among older women declined during the same period. And these comparisons once again exclude noncash benefits, which go disproportionately to women with lower incomes.

Still, elderly women continue to be overrepresented among the poor. This is due mainly to the aforesaid prevalence of widowhood and low levels of remarriage. Among all women 65 to 74 in 1984, 39 percent were currently widowed, compared to just nine percent among men 65 to 74 (U.S. Bureau of the Census, 1985). Elderly widows are more likely to be poor in any given year than are elderly married women, and they are more likely to remain poor for several years. In the PSID study, five percent of all households were headed by elderly women, but 15 percent of all the "persistently poor" households between 1969 and 1978 were headed by elderly women (Duncan, 1984). So despite the general economic progress, the problem of poverty still persists for a minority of the elderly, a minority that is disproportionately composed of widows.

Because of the prevalence of widowhood, the family lives of elderly women tend to revolve around intergenerational ties to children and—with lower mortality—increasingly to aged parents. Elderly women are not, in general, cut off from kin. To be sure, many are living alone, but studies show that most elderly women (and men) see at least some of their children and grandchildren regularly. In a national survey of grandparents, about half reported seeing a grandchild the day of the interview or the previous day (Cherlin and Furstenberg, 1986). But except in times of family crises, grandparents do not play a major role in the day-to-day decisions of children and grandchildren. They leave parenting to the parents and become, instead, valued, symbolic figures and sources of support in reserve. But when a crisis such as a divorce occurs, grandparents often step in and provide important assistance. Since mothers retain custody of children after most marital dissolutions, maternal grandparents tend to become more deeply involved in helping out after divorce. One of the consequences of more frequent divorce is that grandchildren in disrupted families often develop deeper ties with their maternal grandparents than grandchildren from intact families have with either set of grandparents.

Thus, divorce may be creating a "matrilineal tilt" in inter-generational relations, as observers such as Gunhild Hagestad (1986) have noted. In fact, Hagestad argues provocatively that the gap between the family worlds of older women and older men is widening. Due to the increased longevity of women and to higher levels of marital disruption, she argues, older women's family lives more often center on vertical kinship ties across the generations. Older men, she states in contrast, more often have strong horizontal ties to their current wives. Therefore, elderly men often receive support from spouses but elderly women must rely more often on their daughters or their own older parents. Some observers question how well middle-age women will be able to meet the needs of their older mothers for support in the future, given that middle-age women are much more likely to be employed than was the case a few decades ago. The nature of multi-generational linkages in an age of longevity, frequent marital dissolution, and changing work roles for women is an important topic for further study.

Conclusion

That the family lives of American women have changed greatly in recent decades hardly needs to be said. A diversity of family forms and paths through the family life course has replaced the relative homogeneity of the 1950s. Most women now combine family lives with work outside the home. I have argued that these changes in women's family lives are likely to persist.

Women, like men, place a greater emphasis today on achieving personal satisfaction and individual growth in their relationships. In part, they do so because the generally high standard of living frees most Americans from day-to-day worries about subsistence and gives them the luxury of concentrating on their sense of personal satisfaction. Although personal satisfaction is by no means the only reason why women are seeking employment, for an increasing number of women, individual satisfaction is maximized by combining family roles with employment outside the home. This is a combination that has long been viewed as optimal for men; it therefore could be argued that its extension to large numbers of women constitutes a major advance in personal well-being. Similarly, the freedom to end a marriage to an abusive husband undoubtedly increases the welfare of women.

Yet there are costs to these changes, costs that have become more visible as the numbers of working parents and marital disruptions have increased. Our economic institutions have not yet adjusted to the fact that most workers no longer have a spouse at home to take care of family matters. Until such adjustments are made, two-earner couples and employed single parents will face difficulties in combining family life and work life. Our social institutions have not adjusted to the large numbers of female-headed families that have been formed by marital dissolution and, secondarily, by out-of-wedlock pregnancies. Recent reforms that treat divorced women as the economic equals of divorced men have penalized older women with limited work experience. The lack of strong child support enforcement (until recently at least) has hurt the standard of living of middle-class mothers and children. Moreover, we are just beginning to explore the implications of these changes for the longer lives of elderly women. Issues such as these will dominate discussions of the family lives of American women in the near future.

THREE Women and the Economy

NANCY BARRETT

Highlights

THE INCREASE in women's labor force participation over the last 25 years has brought with it questions of equal employment opportunity, pay equity, and family services that were less frequently raised when the paid labor force comprised largely males and single women, and child care and other household duties were managed by full-time homemakers.

- The number of women working or looking for work has increased by roughly 28 million over the past 25 years.

- The huge shift of labor resources out of the household economy and into other sectors such as manufacturing and services is not due to an influx of new workers, but to women who are remaining in the workforce rather than dropping out upon marriage or a first pregnancy.

- The most dramatic increase in labor force participation has been among middle-class, well-educated women who formerly would have dropped out of the labor force during their childrearing years.

- In 1960, fewer than 20 percent of married women with pre-school-age children were working outside the home, compared with more than 50 percent today.

- Seventy percent of married women with college degrees were either employed or looking for work in 1981, compared with 50 percent in 1971.

- The percentage of women pursuing advanced professional degrees has increased substantially. From 1970 to 1979, the percentage of graduates earning degrees in law who were women jumped from 5.4 to 28.5 percent, and in medicine from 8.4 to 23.0 percent.

- Despite advances made in women's educational attainment and employment opportunities, women remain overwhelmingly concentrated in low-paying female occupations.

- In 1985, 70 percent of all full-time employed women were working in occupations in which over three-quarters of the employees were females.

- Over one-third of all employed women work in clerical jobs.

- Women tend to be employed in low-paying jobs with no on-the-job training and little security, and thus they are often among the first fired.

- In almost all areas of employment, women are overrepresented at the bottom and underrepresented at the top.

- The average female worker is gaining in experience and should be progressing more rapidly up the job ladder than is actually the case.

- Women college graduates who work full time, year round, have earnings roughly on a par with male high school dropouts.

- The concentration of women in low-paying occupations, their ghettoization within male-dominated professions, and their lack of upward mobility translates into a lower average wage for women than for men.

- The median earnings for women working full time, year round, in 1985 were 68 percent of men's earnings, up from 61 percent in 1978.

- The slight improvement in the wage gap is not due to women moving into higher-paying jobs but to a recession that has had a disproportionately negative effect on the high-wage, male-dominated sectors of the economy.

- The wage gap between men and women increases with age. Younger workers of both sexes enter the labor force in the lowest pay categories, but men are more likely to advance in earnings while women remain behind. A 45- to 55-year-old woman makes approximately the same wage as a woman of 25.

- During the 1970s, adult women experienced higher unemployment rates than adult men: 6.0 percent for women compared to 4.5 percent for men.

- In the 1980s, the average unemployment rates for both women and men rose and were virtually identical at 7.2 and 7.1 percent, respectively. Between 1980 and 1985, 6.9 million new jobs were created in the female-dominated sectors of sales and services, while 500,000 jobs were lost in the male-dominated sectors of manufacturing, mining, construction, and transportation.

- The decline of full-time homemaking as the predominant occupation for married women has been accompanied by a rapid increase in the number of women seeking part-time jobs. Roughly one-third of the shift out of homemaking has been into part-time employment.

- About three-quarters of women working part time are in the low-paying sales, clerical, and service occupations.

- Women workers' low part-time pay is accompanied by the virtual absence of fringe benefits or opportunity for advancement.

- Female jobs have traditionally been and remain undervalued because of their association with unpaid work in the home and because women are not seen as important economic providers.

- Although women, on average, earn less than men, their contributions to the economic resources of families are substantial.

- For all families, and especially for black families, a second paycheck makes a significant difference in living standards and substantially reduces the incidence of poverty.

- Women with paid jobs still bear most of the responsibility for housework. The shift to paid employment has not meant an offsetting decline in the number of hours most women spend in the household economy. Thus, women now contribute more total hours to the economy (both paid and unpaid) than they did before the shift.

Introduction

It is practically impossible to open a newspaper or magazine today without finding an article on some aspect of women's changing economic status. Indeed, the proliferation of these accounts and their sometimes contradictory messages are often more bewildering than informative. Does the growing number of female professionals mean progress for women, or does the persistence of a male-female pay gap signify a lack of progress? Are women becoming financially more independent, or more likely to be in poverty?

Public policies such as Title VII's mandate of equal employment opportunity for women, affirmative action programs, social security for divorced homemakers, and child support enforcement programs, to name only a few, have occasioned considerable debate regarding the practicality or even the desirability of women's changing roles. Government programs like Aid to Families with Dependent Children are strained for resources and subject to growing criticism as they try to deal with problems for which they were never designed. The idea of comparable worth as a way to achieve pay equity for women has staunch defenders and equally vocal critics. What are the best public policy choices, and why is it so difficult to establish a consensus on their implementation?

This chapter establishes a framework for evaluating these issues and presents the most recent information on women and the economy. It begins with the recognition that the many economic changes taking place for women are linked to one of the most important social transformations of post-war America, namely the decline in full-time homemaking as the predominant "occupation" of married women, especially those with children, and the concomitant increase in the numbers of these women working outside the home in paid employment. In 1960, fewer than 20 percent of married women with pre-school-age children worked outside the home, compared with over 50 percent today. The number of women working or looking for work outside the home has increased by roughly 28 million in 25 years, involving an absorption of more than a million additional women workers per year into the job market.

Perhaps not solely by chance, the increased labor force participation of women followed on the heels of the civil rights movement for racial justice and coincided with other egalitarian political influences that resulted in growing attention to feminist objectives.

From the perspective of the household economy, women's new work roles have wrought other changes. With a majority of married women working outside the home, the traditional family with a full time homemaker is no longer the norm. While two-earner families have substantially higher average incomes than single-earner families, there is less time available for work in the home. Practically everyone has felt the effects on family life, effects that have been negative as well as positive. Consequently, support for women as workers is often viewed as disruptive to families, making policy implementation controversial and the policy debate emotionally charged.

Of course, economic factors are not at work in a vacuum. Traditional perceptions of women's social roles can limit women's economic opportunities. At the same time, economic factors have contributed to reduced fertility and higher divorce rates. The high poverty rate among families maintained by women, for example, is clearly the outcome of a complex socioeconomic nexus.

While this chapter focuses on economic influences, it is important to bear in mind the social, political, and institutional environment that conditions women's economic choices and opportunities. These issues are addressed in other chapters.

The Transformation of the Household Economy

Until fairly recently, homemaking (unpaid work in the home) was the main occupation of married women with children. In 1960, when 85 percent of married women with children were full-time homemakers, there were about 40 million adult women so employed. Compared with a manufacturing sector comprising 17 million workers, the household economy was (and continues to be) a sizable employer of labor resources and a large part of our economy. Considering the unpaid housework also performed by workers with paid jobs, the household economy is quite large relative to the economic activity that goes on in offices, shops, and factories.

Because the output of the household sector is not included in the official gross national product (GNP), it is usually not considered part of "the" economy. Similarly, homemakers are not considered part of the labor force. Consequently, the huge shift of labor resources out of the household economy and into other sectors, such as manufacturing and services, that has occurred since 1960 has been mistakenly analyzed as the arrival of large numbers of "new" workers. Rather, it should be seen for what it is: a major sectoral realignment that has released nearly half the full-time household workforce into the rest of the economy in the course of a single generation.

In many respects, this movement of labor out of the household sector is similar to what occurred much earlier in the farm sector of the economy. Improvements in productivity both within the home and on the farm reduced the amount of time required to do necessary tasks. Moreover, in the home economy, the longer life expectancy of women and lower birthrates combined with higher levels of education for women to reduce the advantages of full-time homemaking relative to employment outside the home. Rising wages made economic opportunities outside the home more attractive, just as was the case for workers leaving the farm some decades ago. As the lure of the city drew second and third generation farm workers from the land, so too improved labor market opportunities for women have drawn them into the paid labor market.

The major impact of the household transformation, as would be expected, has been on married women with children. The extraordinary increase in the proportion of married mothers with pre-school children who are working outside the home is documented in Table 3.1. This shift out of full-time homemaking is still going on. In the past five years alone, the overall labor force participation rate for women has increased by three percentage points, and for married

Table 3.1 • LABOR FORCE PARTICIPATION RATES OF
ALL WOMEN AND MARRIED WOMEN BY AGE
OF CHILDREN

	All women	Married, spouse present		
		Total	Children 6 17	Children under 6
1950	28.3	23.8	28.3	11.9
1960	37.7	30.5	39.0	18.6
1970	43.3	40.8	49.2	30.3
1980	51.5	50.1	61.7	45.1
1985	54.5	60.8	67.8	53.4

Source: U.S. Department of Labor, Employment and Training Report of the President (Washington, D.C.: U.S. Government Printing Office, 1979); U.S. Bureau of Labor Statistics, "Labor Force Activity of Mothers of Young Children Continues at Record Pace," News, Release No. USDL 85-381, September 19, 1985.

mothers of pre-school children it is up by more than eight percentage points.

Of course, the "shift" is not due to an army of homemakers suddenly entering paid employment. Rather, it largely comprises women who are remaining in the workforce rather than dropping out upon marriage or first pregnancy. Because many are delaying childbirth, these married mothers on average are older and have considerably more work experience than did the average married women with children a generation ago.

Table 3.2 shows women's labor force entry and exit rates for the period 1968–77. Entry rates for full-time and part-time workers increased only slightly, while exit rates declined substantially for both groups.

Table 3.2 • LABOR FORCE ENTRY AND EXIT RATES OF
           WOMEN, 1968–1977

	1968	1970	1972	1974	1976	1977
Rate of:						
Entry into full-time labor force[1]	2.3	2.5	2.6	2.7	2.9	2.9
Exit from full-time labor force	4.2	3.6	3.6	3.5	3.2	3.0
Entry into part-time labor force[2]	2.7	2.9	2.9	3.0	3.0	3.0
Exit from part-time labor force	17.9	14.8	13.8	12.7	12.1	11.5

[1]Full-time labor force includes women working full time, women working part time but who desire full-time work, and unemployed women seeking full-time work.

[2]Part-time labor force includes women working part time voluntarily and unemployed women looking for part-time work.

Note: The rate of entry into or exit from the labor force is equal to the number of women who entered (or left) the labor force in an average month in the year under study, divided by the number of women in the labor force in the previous month.

Source: Carol Len and Robert W. Bednarzik, "A Profile of Women on Part-time Schedules," *Monthly Labor Review*, 101, October 1978, p. 10.

It is also important to recognize that the shift from full-time homemaking to paid employment has not meant an offsetting decline in the number of hours most women spend working in the home. Although women with paid jobs spend fewer hours on average in the home economy than do full-time homemakers, women still bear most of the responsibility for housework. Unlike the farm workers who moved to the city, homemakers who take paid jobs do not leave their old occupation behind. This means that women now contribute more total hours to the economy (both paid and unpaid). Few families can afford to purchase all their household services from professionals and, as is the case with reliable child care, such services are often not available. This incompleteness of the household-economy transformation is a critical factor for women in paid employment. And the strains associated with the double burden on women of a paid job and housework, or with other family members being newly responsible for household tasks, create added stress for families.

Understanding women's changing roles as stemming in part from changes in the household economy has a number of advantages. First, it improves our awareness of the forces behind women's participation in paid employment and the related effects on fertility and marital stability. Clearly, the transformation of the household sector is rooted in some of the same irreversible events that occurred in agriculture some decades ago. In each case, the change in people's work lives meant dramatic changes in personal lifestyles.

Because the household transformation is so recent, stereotypes of women as unpaid household workers and nurturers whose husbands provide their economic support still condition societal attitudes about women in paid employment. There remains a deep-seated belief that work should be divided along gender lines, resulting in the occupational segregation of women into jobs that reflect stereotypes from the household economy.

This stereotyping of women's work interacts with two other factors based on women's former homemaker roles. One is the notion that women's work is not worthy of monetary reward comparable to that for men's work, and the other is that women are not financially responsible for their families. These beliefs result in a persistent devaluation of women's work relative to men's when account is taken of the comparable worth of their jobs in terms of skill and responsibility. These beliefs also produce policy responses like welfare payments instead of jobs for women who maintain families. Failure to provide needed social services—child and dependent care and the like—also stems from misconceptions about the household transformation.

The factors that have radically altered the sex composition of the workforce are fundamentally different from those behind other demographic changes. Equal employment opportunity for women was most surely aided by widespread concern over racial injustice, but treating all women's employment problems as similar to those faced by victims of racial discrimination is a mistake. While women may be "disadvantaged" by cultural stereotypes, many are well educated and possess administrative and organizational skills that can be useful in paid employment. However, recognizing the link with the household economy clarifies the policy debate. To the extent that a consensus over men's and women's familial roles is lacking, there will be antagonism over equal employment opportunity issues.

In pursuing policies to improve women's economic position, we cannot look to labor market solutions alone. For instance, it is well documented that women who work in paid employment continue to do most of the housework. Many people who support the concept of equal pay for women stop short of advocating an end to the sex-based division of labor within the household economy. The very suggestion that the Bureau of Labor Statistics collect data on hours spent in housework is met with great resistance and allegations of governmental invasion of privacy, despite the fact that these data could be collected using the Current Population Survey that is already in place.

The collection of information by a government agency on hours spent in housework would be an important first step in establishing this activity as "work," while at the same time revealing the extent of the disparity between men's and women's contributions. It is not very likely that equality for women will be achieved in paid employment unless tasks in the household economy become the equal responsibility of men and women. And putting the facts on the table could be a vehicle for change, as was the case when a government survey revealed the low incidence of child support payments by fathers.

Women's Unemployment

The transformation of the household sector created a cadre of job-seeking women and a new source of unemployment.

Since full-time homemakers are not counted as labor force participants until they seek paid work, had the household transformation not occurred, many women would not have been included in the unemployment count, and the national rate would have been lower. During the 1970s, as stagflation made it difficult to reduce unemployment to a previously acceptable level, issues regarding women's unemployment became central to the debate over the national unemployment target. In considering whether the unemployment target should be revised, some people argued that only the male rate should be used as a policy target. Others suggested a "weighted rate" in which women's unemployment would receive a lesser weight than men's. Another issue was the allegation that women's unemployment creates less of a hardship than male unemployment. But implicit in the entire discussion was the view that women's presence in the paid labor force was somehow less legitimate than men's.

The debate over women's unemployment became part of an upheaval in social policy and consciousness. Policymakers took advantage of the emotional aspects of the issue to take attention away from the restrictive economic policies that were the major cause of high unemployment in those years. As with the transformation of the agricultural sector, a satisfactory adaptation of the economy to the transformation of the household sector would require a full-employment economy.

At that time, however, women experienced higher unemployment rates than men, and the growth of the female workforce was seen as contributing to even higher unemployment. During the 1970s, the unemployment rate for adult women (aged 20 and over) averaged 6.0 percent compared with the 4.5 rate for adult males. Still, the higher rate for women was only partly related to their labor force entry or reentry. In general, low-paid workers of either sex tend to have relatively high unemployment rates. This is because they tend to lack on-the-job training and seniority, and consequently are the last hired and first fired. Although women are less likely than men to be employed in sectors of the economy that experience cyclical unemployment, this factor did not outweigh the relative lack of seniority and work experience that then kept women's unemployment rates above male rates.

During the 1980s, the overall unemployment picture has changed dramatically. Between 1980 and 1985, the average unemployment rates for adult women and men were virtually identical at 7.2 and 7.1, respectively. Although unemployment rates for both groups increased substantially as the economy experienced a deep recession, the rate for men increased disproportionately, due both to a decline in jobs traditionally held by men, and to an expansion of job opportunities for women.

Between 1980 and 1985, 6.9 million new jobs were created in the female-dominated sectors of sales and services, while 500,000 jobs were lost in the male-dominated sectors of manufacturing, mining, construction, and transportation. Over this same period, the female labor force grew by 5.6 million and the male labor force by three million. Clearly, the growth of the female labor force was far more easily accommodated by job openings in sales and services than was the growth of the male labor force accommodated by jobs in the goods-producing sectors. But although there was a relative expansion of jobs traditionally held by women, these tended to be lower-paying than the jobs lost in the goods-producing areas.

Within industry and occupation groups, the unemployment rates of females remain above those of males, as shown in Table 3.3. Some of the same factors that were at work in the 1970s are still present. Women have less seniority and on-the-job training than men within the same industry. Moreover, although this pattern is changing, as noted above, adult women in the labor force are still much more likely than men to be entering for the first time, or reentering after a period of unpaid homemaking. Forty-five percent of unemployed adult women were in these categories in 1985, compared with 21 percent of unemployed adult men. For men, losing a job was a much more common reason for unemployment than for women: 69 percent of unemployed men had lost their jobs, compared with 41 percent of unemployed women. Unem-

Table 3.3 • UNEMPLOYMENT RATES BY OCCUPATION, INDUSTRY, AND SEX, 1985[1]

	Women	Men
Occupational		
Managerial and professional	2.8	2.2
Technical, sales, and administrative support	5.4	3.8
Technicians	3.7	2.9
Sales	7.1	3.5
Administrative support including clerical	4.9	4.7
Services	8.8	8.7
Precision production, craft, and repair	10.1	6.9
Operators, fabricators, and laborers	13.0	10.7
Farming, forestry, and fishing	10.4	7.9
Industry		
Mining	7.4	9.9
Construction	10.0	13.4
Manufacturing	9.9	6.6
Durable	9.3	7.0
Nondurable	10.5	5.9
Transportation and public utilities	4.1	5.6
Wholesale and retail trade	8.7	6.7
Finance, insurance, and real estate	3.6	3.3
Services	6.2	6.3

[1]Persons 16 and over.

Source: U.S. Department of Labor, Bureau of Labor Statistics, *Employment and Earnings* (Washington, D.C.: U.S. Government Printing Office, January 1986), pp. 164-65.

ployed women were somewhat more likely to have left their last job voluntarily than were men, perhaps reflecting a more abundant supply of jobs in the female-dominated sectors.

A recent study found no sex differences in quit rates when personal and job characteristics were held constant (Blau and Kahn, 1981). However, voluntary quit rates have been low in recent years for both men and women, as overall unemployment has remained at historically high levels for both sexes.

Women are more likely than men to fall into the category of "discouraged workers." These persons, not counted among the unemployed, are those who report they have stopped looking for work because they think no jobs are available. In 1985, 1.4 percent of the potential female labor force was discouraged from looking for work, compared with 0.8 percent of the men. Many economists would add discouraged workers to the official unemployment figures to estimate the real extent of involuntary joblessness.

Structural Unemployment and Displaced Workers

Economists distinguish between "cyclical" unemployment that results from inadequate aggregate demand, and "structural" unemployment that arises from special factors causing pockets of unemployment among certain groups or in certain areas, even when jobs are plentiful in general. But there are two separate sources of structural unemployment, requiring quite different policy responses.

The first is the historically more familiar lack of skills and work experience, usually related to such factors as age, poverty status, and low educational attainment. Traditional measures to relieve this type of structural unemployment have been education, skill-training programs, and public service employment targeted on low-wage population groups. A safety net of modest unemployment insurance and welfare benefits is also provided. Many women who lack education, skills, and work experience fall into this category, but so do many male workers.

Another kind of structural unemployment involves workers in certain manufacturing industries that have suffered from changing energy prices, international trade, pollution controls, and other factors. Workers laid off in these industries possess skills and work experience and represent a spectrum of demographic groups. Most have been well paid, with relatively long tenure on the last job, and view themselves as middle-class Americans.

When jobs are lost in particular industries, macroeconomic stimulus can create new jobs elsewhere in the economy, but skills are not always transferable, and the new jobs may not pay as well as the lost jobs. In 1984, the Department of Labor conducted a special survey which counted 5.1 million "displaced" workers, defined as persons who had worked for at least three years before being dismissed because of a plant closing or layoff. A substantial proportion, 35 percent, of these displaced workers were women. They were less likely than men to have been reemployed by January 1984 and were about 2½ times more likely to have left the labor force (Flaim and Sehgal, 1985).

Displaced Homemakers

The distinction between the unskilled and the "displaced" structurally unemployed worker is of particular interest in analyzing women's unemployment. Women are usually thought to be one of the demographic categories that constitute the group known as "disadvantaged." In fact, while some women are truly disadvantaged, many others are more correctly seen as displaced workers, "unemployed" because of the transformation of the household sector.

We have seen that the growth in the female labor force participation rate has resulted largely from the failure of younger women to leave the labor force to take up full-time homemaking as their mothers and grandmothers did. However, each year a substantial number of "displaced homemakers" with a long job tenure (at home) are looking for paid employment. Low-wage jobs may be inappropriate for many of these women, especially the well educated and those with usable skills. Where displacement resulted from marital disruption, there is typically inadequate support from former husbands. As of 1981, only about 15 percent of divorced and separated women had been awarded alimony; fewer than half received the full amount of child support they had been awarded (Blau and Ferber, 1986: 125).

Policy responses should build on these women's prior education and previous work experience as homemakers, recognizing the substantial skill development entailed in household administration. Their financial needs as household heads or important contributors to family economic resources must also be recognized.

Although there is a considerable body of data on workers who have been displaced from paid jobs, little is known about the skills and work experience of displaced homemakers. As mentioned earlier, policies to support women as their work roles change have been and will continue to be hampered by the lack of data on the household economy comparable to our data for the paid labor market. The initiation of a data collection project for the household sector is long overdue, and should be high on the policy agenda for those interested in the economic status of women.

However, the fact that time spent in homemaking goes unrecognized as a qualification for work in paid employment suggests that the choice of a career as a full-time homemaker is potentially risky, given today's high divorce rates and the failure of many former husbands to provide adequate support. Many families are in poverty because the women who maintain them lack the prior paid work experience they need to land a high-paying job.

Trends in Women's Employment Patterns

Although the transformation of the household sector has created a truly revolutionary change in women's work, women's occupations in paid employment have remained remarkably traditional. Despite the attention afforded to a female astronaut or Supreme Court justice, statistics show that women remain overwhelmingly concentrated in female-dominated occupations. And where they have moved into formerly male domains, they remain on the bottom rungs of the job ladder, or are tracked into predominantly female "ghettos"—relatively low-paying subcategories of jobs held by women within higher-paying occupations dominated by men.

In 1985, 70 percent of all women employed full time were working in occupations in which over three-quarters of the employees were female.[1] Part-time workers are even more heavily concentrated in predominantly female occupations. Admittedly, there has been some change in the occupational profile of women workers since 1970, as shown in Table 3.4. Women have increased their representation in the managerial

Table 3.4 • OCCUPATIONAL PROFILES OF WOMEN AND MEN, 1970 AND 1982

Occupation	Percent of women in occupation		Percent of men in occupation		Percent of all employees in occupation who are women	
	1970	1982	1970	1982	1970	1982
Professional and technical	14.5	19.8	14.0	17.5	38.6	43.2
Managers and administrators	4.5	8.2	14.2	13.2	15.9	29.2
Sales workers	7.0	4.3	5.6	5.7	43.1	33.4
Clerical workers	34.5	38.4	7.1	7.1	74.6	78.4
Craft workers	1.1	2.3	20.1	22.3	3.3	2.5
Operatives	14.5	11.7	19.6	11.8	30.9	39.7
Nonfarm laborers	0.5	1.2	7.3	6.5	3.6	10.8
Private household	5.1	1.0	0.1	—	97.4	96.7
Other services	16.5	12.4	6.6	8.3	60.2	49.8
Farm workers	1.8	—	5.6	1.6	16.8	10.3
Total	100.0	100.0	100.0	100.0	37.7*	40.1*

*In millions.

Note: Beginning in 1983, the occupational classifications in the Current Population Survey were changed. Consequently, it has become difficult to compare changes in representation in the broad occupational categories before 1983 with more recent changes. Where appropriate, the new classifications have been used in these chapters. Totals might not sum exactly due to rounding.

Source: U.S. Bureau of Labor Statistics, Employment and Earnings (Washington, D.C.: U.S. Government Printing Office, January 1983).

and professional categories and decreased it in the sales and service categories. And while both women and men have tended to move from "blue-collar" to "white-collar" occupations as the manufacturing sectors have declined, occupational changes for women have been more dramatic than for men. Nevertheless, over a third of all employed women work in clerical jobs, and the proportion of the female workforce in clerical work has increased since 1970. The dynamic for change in women's labor force activities seems to be much

weaker than the forces that propelled so many women into
paid employment to begin with.

It is not surprising that a major impact of the household
transformation has been in the professions, since the most
substantial increase in labor force participation has been
among middle-class, well-educated women who formerly
would have dropped out of the labor force during their childbearing years. By 1985, the proportion of women aged 25 to
34 in the labor force who had attended college actually sur-
passed that of men. This gain was accomplished by an explosive increase in the labor force participation rate of college-
educated women in this age group over the decade 1975 to
1985—from 69 to 83 percent for college graduates and from
58 to 76 percent for those who had completed one to three
years of college—combined with an increase in the percent of
college graduates and advanced-degree recipients who are
women. Between 1970 and 1979, the female proportion of
degree recipients increased at all levels, rising from 43 to 48
percent of bachelors' degrees, from 40 to 49 percent of masters' degrees, from 13 to 26 percent of doctoral degrees, and
from 5 to 24 percent of first professional degrees (Randour,
et al., 1982).

Seventy percent of married women with college degrees
were either employed or looking for work in 1981, compared
with 50 percent 10 years earlier. Moreover, the rise in career
expectations among this group, aided by Title IX legislation
that, among other things, prohibits discrimination against
women in higher education, has substantially increased the
number of women pursuing advanced professional degrees in
fields like law and medicine. From 1970 to 1979, the percentage of graduates earning degrees in law who were women
jumped from 5.4 to 28.5, and in medicine from 8.4 to 23.0
(Randour, et al., 1982).

The growth in the female labor force has been accommodated, at least in part, by job openings in the service sector. *Courtesy Martha Tabor*

In considering these gains, however, it is important to bear in mind that the broad occupational categories listed in Table 3.4 mask important segregation patterns within more detailed occupations. A study of nearly 61,000 workers found that only 10 percent were in job titles that had both men and women assigned to them (Bielby and Baron, 1986). There is a substantial pay gap between men and women within the broad occupational categories that reflects a concentration of women in relatively low-paying specialties within them. For instance, in medicine, women predominate in specialties like pediatrics and nutrition, both of which pay considerably less than a male-dominated specialty like surgery. And the few women attorneys entering prestigious law firms are often assigned to library research rather than to the courtroom, or to the less prestigious and less lucrative fields of trusts, estates, and domestic relations (Fox and Hesse-Biber, 1984: 131).

In academic jobs as well, the status of women is below that of men. Women academics are located disproportionately in two-year and four-year colleges and state universities with heavy teaching loads not conducive to research. Nationwide, women on college faculties account for only 10 percent of full professors but 50 percent of instructors and lecturers (ibid.). Moreover, male faculty members are concentrated in the physical and social sciences and professional schools, while women predominate in the lower-paying arts and humanities.

The computer field is projected by the Bureau of Labor Statistics to be one of high employment growth in the coming decade. Because this field is so new, women theoretically should be at no disadvantage compared to men in occupational choices and opportunities for advancement. However, occupational segregation of women is already apparent in the computer field. In 1985, only about one-third of the 530,000 computer programmers were women, compared with two-thirds of the 779,000 computer operators and word processors. Median weekly earnings for computer programmers in 1985 were $542, compared with $284 for computer operators.

Within the "sales occupations" category there is strong gender segmentation. For instance, while women account for 82.7 percent of apparel salesworkers, who have average weekly earnings of $171, they are only 7.7 percent of motor vehicle and boat salesworkers, who earn a median of $400 per week.

Gender-typing of jobs within formerly male-dominated fields is not the only reason for the relatively high pay gap within them. Another factor is the way in which men and women move up the job ladders in these fields. From government civil service to university faculties, private corporations, banks, and insurance companies, women are overrepresented at the bottom and underrepresented at the top. Fewer than five percent of federal civil servants at level GS 16 and above are women, compared with 77 percent in grades 1 through 4 (Smith, 1979: 40). Job ladders for many predominantly female jobs such as secretarial are much shorter than for male jobs; that is, opportunities for advancement disappear after a few promotions. This pattern of women's greater representation in the lower echelons of the job hierarchy repeats itself in practically all large business organizations.

Data from a 1981 special survey by the Bureau of Labor Statistics corroborate these observations. The National Survey of Professional, Administrative, Technical, and Clerical Pay provides details that separate entry-level, experienced, and senior-level positions within occupations. A recent study of these data concludes that "growth in women's employment in the experienced work levels has not been as noticeable as at the entry level" (Sieling, 1984: 30). Among professional accountants, for instance, women held 46 percent of the entry-level jobs (paying an average of $1,377 per month), but only five percent of the senior jobs (averaging $2,928). Among auditors, women held 36 percent of the entry-level jobs and eight percent of the professional jobs. The figures are similar for other male-dominated job categories.

One could speculate that the reason women are underrepresented in the higher echelons of the job ladder is that they lack seniority or relevant work experience. Although it is true that many women interrupt their working life at some point when they are raising children, the trend is for women to remain at work longer than they used to. Then too, male workers frequently change jobs and even occupations. This is becoming more common as male workers are increasingly displaced from jobs. According to the Bureau of Labor Statistics, in 1983 the median tenure on the job was 3.3 years for women, compared with 5.1 years for men. There was little or no difference in the length of job tenure between men and women up to the age of 30.

The household transformation has increased women's attachment to the workforce. Because women today are less likely than in the past to drop out of the labor force when they marry and bear children, the average female worker is gaining in experience and should be progressing more rapidly up job ladders than is actually the case. Moreover, the scarcity of opportunities for upward mobility in female-dominated occupations, and in female ghettos within predominantly male occupations, suggests that the problem is not solely intermittency of participation among women workers, but rather a job environment that fails to provide women the same promotional opportunities that male workers enjoy.

The Earnings Gap and Pay Equity Strategies for Women

Since the passage of the Equal Pay Act of 1963, there has been legislative support for eliminating wage disparities based on sex. At that time, median earnings for women working full time, year round were about 60 percent of men's earnings. That ratio held remarkably constant throughout the 1960s and 1970s, despite the rapid change in women's work roles associated with the household-sector transformation and the passage of an impressive body of legislation mandating equal employment opportunity. Although there has been a barrage of anecdotal reporting about upwardly mobile women, the statistical evidence shows that despite radical changes in women's work and family roles, there has not been a substantial narrowing of the pay gap between men and women. The previous description of women's employment patterns provides a foundation for understanding why the pay gap persists. The pay gap is inextricably bound up with the sex-based division of labor that characterizes our economy. The concentration of women in low-paying occupations, their ghettoization within male-dominated professions, and their lack of upward mobility all translate into a lower average wage for women than for men. This means that the pay gap cannot be closed simply by enacting a law. Rather, pay equity will require a radical realignment of the occupational profiles of men and women, or alternatively, a major restructuring of the pay scales in men's and women's jobs. Egalitarian views of social justice may favor pay equity for women, yet there is a conflict with the deeply entrenched social expectations regarding differences in men's and women's work roles. It is important to face this dilemma squarely in seeking policy remedies.

The Role of Occupational Segregation

The persistence of the wage gap despite the Equal Pay Act demonstrated that pay equity for women could not be achieved simply by mandating equal pay for equal work. In a labor market segregated by sex, equal pay for equal work, however important to establish in principle, is not the main issue.

Female-dominated occupations and industries are the lowest paying. A recent study by the Bureau of Labor Statistics shows a strong inverse relationship between the percent of an industry's employees that is female and the level of average hourly earnings (Norwood, 1982: 2). A ranking of 52 industries in July 1982 shows that the apparel and textile products industry had the highest percentage of women workers (81.9 percent), and ranked 50th in average hourly earnings. The bituminous coal and lignite mining industry, on the other hand, ranked 52nd in percentage of women employees (5.1 percent) and first in average hourly earnings.

Roughly one-third of all women work in clerical occupations, where median weekly earnings in 1985 were $286 for full-time workers of both sexes. This compares unfavorably with a median weekly wage for all full-time male workers of $406, but is roughly equivalent to the median of $277 for full-time female workers.

Table 3.5 shows earnings for groups of predominantly female and predominantly male occupations. Forty percent of all adult women employees hold jobs in the female-dominated categories listed. (Men are not similarly concentrated in a few job categories.) While these jobs vary considerably in terms of the education, skill requirements, and responsibility involved, women's jobs are generally lower-paying than men's jobs. For instance, a licensed practical nurse averages $294 per week, compared with $363 for a truck driver and $406 for a furnace operator. A child care worker averages $169, and a bank teller $219, compared with $276 for an unskilled construction laborer.

Recognition that the pay gap is largely the result of occupational differences between men and women led to a focus on providing equal employment opportunity (EEO) in higher-paying, male-dominated job categories as the best way to achieve pay equity for women. Title VII of the Civil Rights Act of 1964 was the legislative basis of the EEO mandate, and this was followed by a series of court decisions and executive

Table 3.5 • EARNINGS[1] IN SELECTED OCCUPATIONS, 1985

	Percent female	Median weekly wage (in dollars)
Predominantly female occupations		
Secretary/typist	97.7	276
Receptionist	97.6	225
Licensed practical nurse	96.9	294
Private household	96.2	132
Child care worker	96.1	169
Registered nurse	95.1	434
Teacher's aide	93.6	196
Bookkeeper	91.5	272
Bank teller	93.0	219
Data entry keyer	90.7	277
Textile sewing machine operator	90.8	178
Health service worker	89.9	210
Librarian	87.0	391
Elementary school teacher	84.0	412
Cashier	83.1	178
Predominantly male occupations		
Extractive occupations	1.1	501
Fire fighting/prevention	1.4	436
Truck driver	2.1	363
Construction trades	2.0	393
Airplane pilot/navigator	2.6	738
Construction laborer	3.1	276
Material-moving equipment operator	3.2	360
Furnace operator	3.6	406
Welder	4.8	371
Engineer	6.7	661
Lathe operator	9.6	339
Police officer and detective	10.1	424
Architect	11.3	488

[1]Usual weekly earnings of full-time workers.
Source: U.S. Bureau of Labor Statistics, unpublished tabulations.

orders that shifted the policy focus from merely prohibiting employment discrimination to actually promoting improved representation of women in higher-paying occupations and industries. The motive behind these efforts was not necessarily to integrate occupations as an end in itself (although many proponents of equality for women support occupational integration as a way to eliminate stereotypes), but rather to reduce the pay gap.

But women have made only modest inroads into the high-paying sectors of the economy. And, as noted earlier, where women have been successful in penetrating nontraditional occupations, they are ghettoized into lower-paying, female enclaves within them, or concentrated on the lower rungs of the seniority ladder. The result is that the pay gap between men and women is often greater in male-dominated occupations than in female-dominated ones.

Because women are generally located at the bottom of the job hierarchy and men at the top, there is a considerable difference in how the level of their earnings is distributed within the same category of work. In 1982, 16.2 percent of women managers and administrators earned less than $200 per week, compared with only 3.2 percent of men. On the other hand, only 14.9 percent of those women earned more than $500 per week compared with 51.3 percent of the men. Among craft workers, 28.4 percent of the women and only 7.0 percent of the men earned less than $200 per week, while 7.7 percent of the women and 23.9 percent of the men earned more than $500. Similar patterns were also found in the specific occupations within these general categories. (Mellor, 1984: 24).

The concentration of women at the bottom of the distribution of earnings results in a wage gap that increases with age, as shown in Table 3.6. Young workers of both sexes enter the labor market in the lowest pay categories, but the men are more likely to advance in earnings while the women remain behind. This is either because women are in occupations without opportunities for upward mobility, or because they are denied access to the opportunities that are available to men.

Another way of looking at the problem is to examine the age-earnings profile. Male earnings advance rapidly between ages 25 and 35, with men between 35 and 55 typically earning more than double that of younger men. Women's earnings, as a rule, rise modestly between ages 16 and 25 and then remain virtually flat. A 45- to 55-year-old woman makes approximately the same wage as a woman of 25, reflecting the fact that the vast majority of women are in dead-end jobs. Men, on the other hand, seem to experience considerable upward mobility.

Occupational segregation, ghettoization, and lack of up-

Table 3.6 • THE RATIO OF FEMALE TO MALE EARNINGS BY AGE GROUP AMONG FULL-TIME, YEAR-ROUND WORKERS, 1975 AND 1984

Age group	1975	1984
All ages	59.5	68.2
16–24	75.9	87.5
25–34	64.7	74.3
35–44	51.9	63.2
45–54	52.5	60.4
55–64	55.0	60.8
65+	55.9	65.9

Source: U.S. Bureau of the Census, Current Population Reports, Series P-60, No. 105, *Money Income in 1975 of Families and Persons in the United States*, and Series P-60, No. 149, *Money Income and Poverty Status of Families and Persons in the United States: 1984* (Washington, D.C.: U.S. Government Printing Office, 1977 and 1985).

ward mobility deserve great emphasis, but other factors contribute to the pay gap as well. For instance, women work fewer hours per week than men, and despite gains among younger women, have slightly less education than men on the average. However, differences in education and hours worked account for a relatively small part of the pay gap. Together, in 1982, they contributed 3.7 percentage points to a pay gap of 35 percentage points (Mellor, 1984: 26).

Lack of work experience and intermittent labor force activity of women are sometimes thought to contribute significantly to their lower earnings. However, a recent study by the Bureau of the Census reports that work interruptions explain only a small part of the earnings disparity between women and men. The bureau found that even if women's education, experience, and interruptions were the same as men's, the earnings gap would be reduced by only about five percentage points (U.S. Department of Labor, Women's Bureau, 1985).

Pay Equity Strategies

Implementation of the laws and executive orders that followed the passage of Title VII focused on moving women into higher-paying, male-dominated occupations, either by eliminating barriers to women's entry or by encouraging women to seek these careers. It was increasingly recognized that the distinction between institutional and attitudinal barriers is to some extent a false dichotomy, since attitudes as well as social and economic institutions are the products of a history of sexual stratification.

During the 1970s, attention turned to the question of upward mobility for women, and the practice of "tracking" women and men, ostensibly in the same occupation, through different internal labor markets of firms or promotions systems of trades and professions (Bergmann, 1976). For instance, a firm may hire male and female economists with bachelors' degrees at the same pay rate, but after a time provide management opportunities for male economists while assigning the women to be research assistants. After a few years, the men are promoted and earning considerably more than the women, who are found to be "not qualified" for the higher positions because they lack management experience.

Equal employment opportunity only at the entry level will not eliminate the wage gap if men are later provided superior job opportunities within the firm. Unfortunately, it is more difficult to monitor internal pay and promotion practices than the entry-level offers that are publicly advertised. Although firms may be forced to demonstrate that they have not discriminated in hiring, they are not under similar public scrutiny when it comes to promotions, unless they are monitored by their own employees.

Comparable Worth

The persistence of occupational segregation has led to the advocacy of a more direct approach to pay equity for women, namely equal pay for work of comparable value. This means compensation on the basis of the skill and responsibility entailed in the job, and not on the sex of the person performing it. Female jobs have traditionally been and remain undervalued because of their association with unpaid work in the home and because women are not seen as important economic providers. It was shown earlier, for instance, that an average child care worker earns far less than an unskilled construction laborer and a licensed practical nurse averages less than a truck driver. Jobs done predominantly by women tend to be low-paid, regardless of the skill and responsibility they require.

Because societal expectations condition the career patterns of many women, it is unrealistic to expect a rapid elimination of their occupational segregation. More than 60 percent of women (or men) would have had to change jobs in 1981 in order for the occupational distribution of the sexes to be the same (Blau and Ferber, 1986: 166–68). Most women apparently find no alternative to accepting the low pay offered in traditionally female occupations. In turn, because female labor is relatively cheap, employers have little incentive to structure women's jobs efficiently and to provide on-the-job training and opportunities for professional development. An effective comparable worth pay strategy that raises women's earnings could force a reevaluation of job quality in traditional female occupations.

While redress of the inequities caused by the undervaluation of work traditionally done by women is vital, continued progress in reducing occupational segregation of women is also important to weaken stereotypes regarding women's work. Improving women's access to male-dominated occupations and establishing comparable worth compensation in female-dominated occupations are important ways to reduce the pay gap.

Education

Women and men at the same level of educational attainment still experience substantial differences in earnings, as shown in Table 3.7. Women college graduates who work full time, year round have earnings roughly on a par with male high school dropouts. This suggests that simply providing women with more education will not, by itself, eliminate the pay gap, although it may be an important element of employment strategy for low-income women.

Table 3.7 • YEARLY EARNINGS BY SEX AND EDUCATIONAL
ATTAINMENT OF FULL-TIME, YEAR-ROUND
WORKERS, 1984 (in dollars)

Educational attainment	Female earnings	Male earnings
Fewer than 8 years	9,828	14,624
1–3 years high school	11,843	19,120
High school graduate	14,569	23,269
1–3 years college	17,007	25,831
College graduate	20,257	31,487
1 or more years postgraduate	25,076	36,836

Source: U.S. Bureau of the Census, Current Population Reports, Series P-60, No. 149, Money Income and Poverty Status of Families and Persons in the United States: 1984 (Washington, D.C.: U.S. Government Printing Office, 1985), Table 7.

Recent Trends in the Pay Gap

After several decades of virtual stagnation, the pay gap has narrowed slightly. In 1978, the earnings ratio was 61 percent; by 1985, it was 68 percent. Most of this "improvement," however, was not the result of women moving into better-paying jobs. Rather, as noted earlier, there was a deep recession that had a disproportionate effect on the high-wage, male-dominated sectors of the economy. The same factors that caused men's unemployment rates to rise caused their real earnings to fall. Thus, the appearance of greater equality between men and women is actually the result of a deterioration in labor market conditions facing male workers rather than an absolute gain for women.

While women's earnings have barely kept pace with inflation, men's have fallen behind. In 1985, women's median weekly earnings of $283 would have purchased $172 in 1978 dollars, or about the same as their actual 1978 earnings of $166. Men's 1985 median weekly earnings of $410 would have purchased $249 in 1978 dollars, substantially less than their actual 1978 earnings of $271.

As the economy adapts to lower oil prices and an exchange value of the dollar more favorable to exports, it is likely that the goods-producing sectors will once again expand. It will be important to monitor progress on the pay equity front as the growth of these high-paying employment opportunities occurs. Without further reduction of occupational segregation, or progress in achieving comparable worth pay increases for women in traditional jobs, the pay gap could once again widen as job opportunities for male workers improve.

Part-time Employment

The decline of full-time homemaking as the predominant occupation for married women has been accompanied by a rapid increase in the number of women seeking part-time jobs. Roughly one-third of the shift out of homemaking has been into part-time employment. Since the early 1960s, the part-time workforce has grown nearly three times as fast as the full-time workforce.

Many married women, as well as women who maintain families, see part-time employment as a way to benefit from the social and financial advantages of paid employment while still having time to meet home and family responsibilities. About one-third of employed married women and about one-sixth of employed divorced and separated women with pre-school children work part time.

However, for many women, the same attitudinal changes that caused them to leave full-time homemaking are causing them to deplore the low-paying, menial, dead-end work that part-time employment typically has offered. No longer an intermittent workforce, part-time workers want pay equity, fringe benefits, job security, and opportunities for upward mobility. For women who maintain families, a part-time job that pays well may mean the difference between at least partial self-sufficiency and complete welfare dependency, not to mention a much needed source of stability and self-esteem. And a part-time job can serve as an important bridge to full-time work when children enter school and family responsibilities become less demanding.

Despite their aspirations for improved part-time opportunities, however, the fact remains that about three-quarters of women working part time are in the low-paying sales, clerical, and service occupations, with hourly earnings about 25 percent below those of full-time female workers, who are more likely to be in higher-paying occupations. Adult women who worked part time averaged $111 a week in 1985. Coupled with low part-time pay rates is the virtual absence of fringe benefits, apart from federally mandated social security and unemployment insurance. And the dead-end nature of most part-time jobs provides very little opportunity for the training and upward mobility that could translate into higher pay and improved job security.

Few nondisabled men between the ages of 25 and 55 work

part time. However, more egalitarian sex roles would be facili-
tated by improved part-time job opportunities for men, ones
that would not necessitate a severe loss in income, status, and
opportunities for upward mobility. As long as part-time jobs
remain low-status, sex-segregated, and more acceptable for
women than for men, traditional inequalities in the time
women and men devote to child care and housework will
continue. Except in unusual circumstances, it is not now
possible for both husband and wife to work part time and
earn as much as if only the husband worked full time.

Already, the standard 9 A.M. to 5 P.M., Monday through
Friday work week is becoming less sacrosanct, as employers
are experimenting with flexitime and alternative work
schedules for their full-time employees. Job-sharing is also in
an experimental stage, and seems to be a fruitful approach for
some professional couples. All these advantages in flexible
scheduling should improve opportunities for part-time employees, whose "part-timeness" would not be so conspicuous
under these arrangements.

If women are to move successfully into traditionally male
jobs in paid employment and men into traditionally female
work in the home, it is clear that more flexible work arrangements are needed for families with children. It is in no one's
interest that flexibility be associated with low pay and status
and with "women's work." Indeed, it is paradoxical that the
household transformation that has thrust women into new
work roles, and is widely viewed as a force for egalitarian
social change, should have relegated so many to low-paying,
dead-end jobs.

Because women are far more likely to be seeking part-time
employment than are men, there is a danger that all women
will be stereotyped as only "needing" part-time work. Women

who want full-time work are currently twice as likely as men to be working part time because they cannot find a full-time job. Because the transformation of the household sector remains incomplete in the sense that women have not left housework behind, the stereotype of the partially committed woman worker remains.

Higher-paying, part-time job opportunities have the potential, at least, for moving families out of the welfare system, and providing continuity of work experience for married women who may later seek full-time work. Equal employment opportunity programs must begin to focus, as a top priority, on the provision of part-time jobs for both women and men outside the traditionally female occupations and in the higher-paying skills and professional categories.

An even bolder approach would be a shortening of the work week for all, creating the possibility for both men and women to contribute equally to home and family responsibilities. Realistically, however, part-time work will continue to be disproportionately used by women, even with improved opportunities, and this will reinforce women's responsibility for unpaid work in the home.

Women's Contribution to Family Income

Although women earn less than men, on average, their contributions to the economic resources of families are substantial. In husband-wife families, a wife's earnings make a significant difference in living standards. In fact, the financial status of today's husband-wife families is closely linked to women's earnings. For black married couples, for instance, median income in 1984 was $14,502 when the wife was a full-time homemaker, compared with $28,775 when she was in the labor force.[2] For whites, the median income was $24,246 when the wife was a full-time homemaker compared with $35,176 when she was in the labor force. The poverty rate in 1984 among black couples with two earners was only 5.4 percent compared to 27.1 percent for black couples with a single worker. Among white couples with two workers, the poverty rate was 3.8, compared with 9.7 for white couples with a single worker. Thus, for all families, and especially for black families, a second paycheck makes a great difference in living standards, and substantially reduces the incidence of poverty.

But when women are the sole providers, their families are far more likely to be in poverty than are other families. The transformation of the household economy has involved more than simply the increasing participation of married women in paid employment. It has also been accompanied by a higher divorce rate and an increase in out-of-wedlock childbearing, thrusting many women into the role of sole provider. In 1984, nearly 20 percent of all families with children were maintained by women, up from 10 percent in 1970. Nearly 60 percent of all black children under 14 now live in families maintained by women.

Women and Poverty

The so-called "feminization of poverty" stems from the fact that almost half of all families with children maintained by women, and over half of those maintained by black women, live in poverty. By comparison, only one in 11 husband-wife families with children lives in poverty. With nearly half of all new marriages ending in divorce, the likelihood of a family becoming female-headed and moving into poverty for some period of time is quite substantial.

The number of families maintained by women grew by more than 80 percent between 1970 and 1984, when 10.1 million families had a woman as their principal breadwinner.

During the 1960s, the United States made tremendous progress in reducing both the absolute and relative incidence of poverty. The poverty rate dropped from 22.2 to 12.1 percent. Since then, the poverty rate has increased, as the profile of the poverty population has shifted dramatically. As of 1984, the poverty rate stood at 14.4 percent, down slightly from its 1983 level of 15.2 percent, but well above the rate experienced in the late 1960s.

The increase in the number of families headed by women and their high risk of being poor are the main factors behind the failure of the poverty rate to decline. During the 1970s, the number of poor persons living in male-headed households declined, but those in female-headed households increased in even greater numbers. Since 1980, the deep recession caused the poverty rate to increase in households with a male provider, as well as among those maintained by women. Still, in 1984, over half of all children living in poverty were in households headed by women. A child is four times more likely to be poor if he or she lives with only the mother (or other female provider) than with either the father or both parents present in the household.

Because families maintained by women average more children than other families, the "feminization of poverty" has greatly increased the risks of poverty for this nation's children. Although the overall poverty rate in 1984 was a shockingly high 14.4 percent, the poverty rate among children under 18 was 21 percent. Among black children the poverty rate was 46.2 percent and among children of Spanish origin it was 38.7 percent. And since the probability of being born into a female-headed family is far greater for blacks than for whites, the feminization of poverty has exacerbated the poverty gap between black and white children. This fact is at odds with the widely held perception that racial inequality has diminished.

Policies aimed at reducing poverty should be based on the recognition that among its main causes are women's low earnings and the failure of absent fathers to provide support. In 1984, 77 percent of nonmarried (single, divorced, widowed, and separated) mothers with school-age children (and none younger) were in the labor force, as were 53 percent of those with pre-schoolers. Among employed women aged 25 to 54 who maintained families, 85 percent worked full time, with median weekly earnings of $266. This amounts to $13,800 for the full-time, year-round earner *at the median* (in other words, half of all earn less than that), compared to the official 1984 poverty threshold for a family of three of $8,277 and $10,609 for a family of four. Subtracting the payroll tax contribution (6.7 percent for employees in 1984), and a modest $10 per day for all employment-related expenses including child care, transportation, meals away from home, and clothing, reduced the median disposable income of a female provider who worked full time, year round, to $10,275. And with a 10.4 percent unemployment rate for women who maintain families, many women were not able to find work year round, so that they earned less than the year-round median.

Fewer than half of all households maintained by women receive child support, and cash welfare payments are generally not available to women who work, although the working poor are frequently eligible for food stamps and other non-cash benefits. In 1984, median household money income from all sources for families maintained by women was $12,764, compared to $27,307 for households with a male provider.

Although welfare benefits are woefully inadequate, they become an attractive alternative for many women, especially those at the lower end of the earnings distribution. In 1985, 3.7 million families, comprising 10.8 million individuals, were part of the Aid to Families with Dependent Children (AFDC) program, and the overwhelming majority of these families (80 to 90 percent) were maintained by women. The median value of cash and noncash benefits to AFDC recipients was in the range of $7,000, when food stamps, school lunches, and medical benefits were included.

The welfare system has the added attraction of reliability, while the jobs most low-income women hold are unstable at best. Moreover, the amount of red tape required to establish AFDC eligibility provides a strong incentive to remain in the system, once enrolled. If an enterprising woman takes a job and goes off welfare, she knows it will take time and effort to get back into the system if she loses her job. Today, literally millions of women and children are caught in this welfare trap, effectively prevented from taking control of their own lives and entering the mainstream of society.

At the very minimum, welfare benefits should be linked to inflation. Moreover, the eligibility rules of welfare programs like AFDC, food stamps, and Medicaid need to be changed so they do not penalize participants who take low-wage jobs. But welfare will never be a solution to the poverty problem; it can only mitigate poverty's effects. Instead, there should be a major commitment to improving job opportunities for women, including the provision of training for those who lack skills, public service employment for those who need work experience, and implementation of pay equity strategies like comparable worth and equal employment opportunity.

Child Care

Child care is a serious problem for all working mothers, but it is especially serious for women who maintain families since they frequently lack the financial resources to purchase adequate care. More than 10 million pre-school children now have mothers who work, and yet we lack a national child care policy. Although there is occasional hand-wringing over the "latchkey child" phenomenon, the inference is that the problem stems from maternal irresponsibility rather than a systemic failure.

Lack of a national child care policy is symptomatic of the country's ambivalence about the household transformation and the fear that support services for working mothers could have adverse effects on family life. However, failure of government to lead in its development and implementation only adds to the economic problems of families. Although economic factors dictate that most women will not return to full-time homemaking, the demands of child and other dependent care produce heavy strains on women who work outside the home. And although national statistics are not available, there is little evidence that fathers, even when they are present in the household, are shouldering much of the burden.

Lack of affordable and reliable child care is a major factor perpetuating women's low economic status. It is a strong impetus to welfare dependency, since the cost of child care can prohibit low-income women from working. Moreover, it creates unsettling role conflicts for many women, exacerbating the considerable strains that women already experience in their work lives.

"Lack of affordable and reliable child care is a major factor perpetuating women's low economic status." *Courtesy Barbara Hadley*

Employment and Training Programs for Poor Women

Employment and training programs were an important part of the government's anti-poverty initiatives during the 1960s and 1970s. While early programs focused on low-income males, during the 1970s the economic needs of young women became increasingly recognized.

Employment and training programs for low-income individuals have sometimes been maligned, often because of exaggerated expectations regarding their outcomes. It is unrealistic, for instance, to expect a young mother who has dropped out of high school to become adept at a skilled trade in a few months. Paradoxically, when programs are targeted on the most disadvantaged, their outcomes seem the most dismal, yet careful statistical analysis shows conclusively that the poorest participants generally benefit the most.

Despite the fact that past programs have enrolled males disproportionately, women tend to gain more than men. A longitudinal follow-up study of over 6,000 participants in programs under the Comprehensive Employment and Training Act (CETA) during the 1970s found average (mean) gains of 19 percent in post-participation earnings for women (25 percent for minority women) and only four to five percent for men. Earnings gains were found to be greatest for "persons with limited earnings backgrounds," and for middle-aged or older women who were reentering the labor force (Westat, 1981).

Other studies report similar findings. Using 1977 data, the Urban Institute found that public service employment programs increased earnings for white women by $882 to $990 in the first post-program year and by $1,035 to $1,144 in the second. For black women, the gains were $1,126 to $1,196 in the first year and $608 to $678 in the second. There were similar gains for women in an on-the-job training program. On the other hand, the same study found no significant gains for men who participated in the public service employment program, and a very small gain for white men only from the on-the-job training program (Simms, 1986).

Since 1981, there have been major cutbacks in governmental employment and training programs for women who maintain families. But the statistics paint a consistent picture of the success of past programs in raising earnings of poor women and encouraging them to maintain a more permanent connection to the workforce. While the gains are admittedly modest relative to the magnitude of the poverty problem, they offer evidence that a jobs-oriented approach to the problem is feasible as a long-run strategy, and surely preferable to the current welfare system.

Overview and Conclusions

It is a mistake to dismiss the events taking place in women's working lives today with the adage: "Women have always worked." The significance of the household transformation is that it has dramatically altered the typical woman's work patterns, and rendered obsolete many deep-seated societal attitudes and expectations regarding not only women's work, but women's social and political activities as well. These changes are not limited to the workforce but also involve the family and other sex-role relationships.

Recent Experiences of Women Workers

There has been encouraging progress for some women, particularly young, college-educated women who are entering high-paying professions like law, medicine, and business in record numbers. On the other hand, there appears to be considerable sex segregation within those fields, and women are grossly underrepresented in the highest ranks. It remains to be seen whether, as more women move into these elite occupations, their representation might become more uniform across specialties and in the higher ranks.

Other changes seem less positive. The proportion of women who work in relatively low-paying clerical jobs continues to increase, although some clerical workers may have

"moved up" from even lower-paying service jobs. The reduction in the male-female wage gap since 1980 is largely the
result of the decline in high-wage, male-dominated manufacturing employment, rather than any real progress for women.
Whether the wage gap widens as falling energy prices and a
declining dollar reverse the decline in the goods-producing
sectors of the economy will depend on the extent to which
women find equal employment opportunity with men in the
higher-paying jobs.

Finally, the situation of the poorest women seems particularly intractable. The number of families maintained by
women continues to grow, and their poverty rate stubbornly
refuses to fall significantly. Given the fact that black families
are far more likely to be maintained by women than white
families, poverty among this group is increasing the poverty
gap between black and white children at an alarming rate.
Efforts to reduce racial inequality in our workplaces, high
schools, and colleges will be in vain unless the economic
needs of poor women, who are nurturing the next generation,
are addressed.

An Economic Policy Agenda for Women

All of us, women and men, and the institutions we shape
and by which we are shaped, are affected by the changes
brought on by the transformation of the household sector. A
whole set of long-held, mutually reinforcing attitudes and
institutions will have to be rethought to accommodate wom-
en's new roles.

No single policy or program can address the needs of all
women workers. For professionals in male-dominated occu-

pations, affirmative action may be needed. For women in traditional jobs, comparable worth offers a potential source of higher pay. And for those trapped in the welfare system, job training and public employment programs could serve as a bridge or gateway into secure jobs paying a living wage.

But these women also have many needs in common. Some of these needs arise from the common stereotypes women experience, the devaluation of women's work, the institutional barriers women face, and women's socialization to sex-specific roles. Others are more pragmatic, such as the need for affordable and reliable child care, and the double burden of household and financial responsibilities.

Women's policy agenda should also include two items that are not strictly "women's issues." The first is full employment. Clearly, a slack economy is ill-suited to large numbers of workers changing jobs. The successful shift out of agriculture was accomplished at a time of booming demand. The household shift has been accompanied by growth in the service sector and in other jobs traditionally held by women.

But the availability of a job cannot, by itself, assure a successful transition for women. Women need full employment in *good* jobs that enable them to support themselves and their families. This means improved access to high-paying jobs now held mostly by men. High unemployment creates competition for these good jobs, and the economic problems associated with accommodating all job-seekers take on social implications. Only in a full-employment context will high-paying jobs for women not be viewed as male losses.

A second issue is the question of deficit reduction and the effectiveness of government social programs. Failure to enact a tax increase to pay for needed social spending is having an adverse effect on programs for women. Employment and training programs, food stamps, and other benefits for women who maintain families are all getting the budget ax. And any discussion of funding a national child care program is politically unrealistic when budget dollars for social programs are scarce.

Clearly, no one wants to pay higher taxes. But the budget debate should include a discussion of social needs and responsibilities, as well as the long-term budget implications of failing to act now. Dollars spent on employment and training programs for poor women are essential to enable them to achieve even modest success as workers. Private employers will simply not hire women who lack basic educational and social skills. And it is unrealistic to expect that child care for the millions of families who need it will be forthcoming without at least some government involvement.

Programs that enhance women's employability have the potential for reducing future budget outlays. And social investments in the well-being of children may also reap long-term benefits.

There are other areas where government support is needed to further women's employment needs in the private sector. People should not be misled by anecdotal success stories into believing that equal employment opportunity goals have been achieved when statistical evidence demonstrates that such is not the case. Enforcement of Title VII should be strengthened, and more widespread use of affirmative action programs and comparable worth pay plans should be encouraged. Better part-time employment opportunities and flexible work-scheduling are needed. And, finally, government statistical agencies should begin collecting data on the household economy to assess the extent to which men's work roles in the home are changing in ways that complement women's new roles in paid employment, and to improve our awareness and assessment of the human capital embodied in our female labor force.

FOUR **The Women's Movement in Recent American Politics**

MARIAN LIEF PALLEY

Highlights

THE WOMEN'S MOVEMENT may be seen as both a set of interest groups involved in lobbying on behalf of equal rights for women and an amorphous, unorganized social movement of women and men who support equal opportunities for women and sympathize with a number of specific goals. This chapter focuses on the groups in the women's movement.

• Though often accused of focusing too narrowly on the Equal Rights Amendment and a woman's right to abortion, women's groups, in fact, lobby and work for political change on myriad issues, including pension benefits, insurance equity, day care, and Title IX.

• Groups in the movement have been acting to foster improvements in conditions for women in the past two decades, during which time there have been notable legislative, administrative, and judicial successes, changes in female voting patterns, and an increase in the number of women elected to public office.

• Most groups in the feminist community are essentially leadership, rather than mass-membership, organizations. In other words, they do not, in general, actively seek to enroll, or to provide a range of services to, individual members. Rather, they tend to be composed of staff who concentrate on either lobbying or electoral activities in attempts to influence public policy.

• The traditional women's membership organizations, while not "feminist" (that is, not having as their primary focus equal rights for women), are an important factor in the women's movement and can often be mobilized to provide the broad-based community support that the feminist groups, generally lacking extensive grassroots structures, cannot do as readily.

• On most issues, there is conscious coalition building among the groups in the women's movement. One group may assume leadership, but many groups will participate in working toward a particular goal. Coalitions that ally groups lacking a significant membership base with large-membership organizations help the movement demonstrate to decisionmakers that an issue has wide public support.

• Women's groups have also learned to work with groups outside the women's movement when appropriate.

• As more groups and more people become involved in issue-specific coalitions, however, the need to present a united front to the media and decisionmakers may require compromise on particular issues, with the result that feminist positions may be diluted.

• Before women's groups could put any set of reasonable demands before political decisionmakers, women themselves had to become aware that they shared a set of problems for which political solutions existed. During the late 1960s and early 1970s, the National Organization for Women (NOW), among other new organizations, played a key role in encouraging this awareness.

• Interest groups in the women's movement have profoundly influenced the policy process. They have deeply affected the development of new attitudes, and have been instrumental in redefining problems and issues among the public at large, as well as among decisionmakers. They have persisted in working to develop sound policy and are vigilant in monitoring the implementation of laws.

• The groups in the women's movement have been most successful in influencing the decisionmaking process when they have directed their political energies to issues perceived by the general public, as well as by decisionmakers, in terms of "role equity" rather than "role change." In large measure, the political remedies sought by the women's movement have been addressed to economic inequality and perceived injustice.

• The groups in the women's movement have been accused of reflecting a middle- and upper-middle-class bias in selecting problems to address with political solutions. As the problems of working-class and poor women have become more acute, however, their economic and social concerns have been drawing increasing attention from the feminist groups.

• Most observers concede that there are differences in the intensity with which the two sexes hold their positions on social issues, such as reproductive freedom, or national security issues, such as defense spending. It may be possible to mobilize women to vote for or against candidates at least partly on the basis of the candidates' positions on these particular issues. But it is important to remember that differences between the sexes in party identification and voting also can be associated with economic issues.

- Voting studies of the 1980 and 1984 elections demonstrated that women voted differently from men. These gender differences in political preferences appear to continue today. They can be attributed to positions on the economy and defense, as well as to the perceived anti-women views associated with President Reagan and his supporters in Congress, state legislatures, and statehouses.

- Women outnumber men among the voters; for that reason alone the views women hold on political issues cannot be ignored by candidates for public office. If women in the electorate have different expectations about politics and political issues than men, candidates must at least listen. If they dismiss out of hand what they hear, new voting patterns may emerge.

Introduction

The term "women's movement," which is used to identify the wide range of groups and individuals who support the goals of equal rights for women, is best understood as two separate but related components. On the one hand, the women's movement is a set of interest groups involved in lobbying on behalf of equal rights for women. On the other, it is a rather unwieldy social movement that draws on a broad, diverse population of both men and women who want equal opportunities for women and support special goals, such as free choice regarding abortion, an equal rights amendment, comparable worth, public support for day care, and the various titles of the Economic Equity Act. There are also radical, separatist, socialist, and anarchist feminists who have different goals. Since representatives of the latter political perspectives represent a small minority of the overall movement and thus have been unable to influence the mainstream political process very much, this chapter will limit its discussion to the first two components.

Groups in the women's movement have been acting to foster improvements in conditions for women for the past two decades. During this time, there have been notable legislative, administrative, and judicial successes, changes in female voting patterns, and growth in the number of elected women officials. The groups, as well as the social movement, have begun to exert influence in national politics; as a national phenomenon, the women's movement is a force with which decisionmakers must now contend.

Lobbying and electoral activities are two strategies used by movement activists to influence public policy. Interest groups have directed their energies toward lobbying for policy changes. Some of these groups also have focused their attention on the electoral arena as women in state and local jurisdictions become more politically active and interested in seeking public office. Moreover, because women are now more likely to vote than men, they cannot be ignored as voters.

This chapter will also discuss the two approaches to political involvement: lobbying and electoral. The first section examines the groups in the movement and how they have operated to influence the enactment and implementation of legislation. The second section examines women as voters, as candidates for public office, and as a new force that all candidates must consider. Throughout this chapter, the terms "women's movement" and "feminist movement" will be used interchangeably.

Groups in the Movement and How They Operate

The women's movement as a set of interest groups comprises several types of organizations. The feminist political community embraces mass-based feminist organizations, single issue groups, litigation groups, research groups, and electoral groups. Traditional women's organizations, often not associated in the public mind with the women's movement, lend significant support to the movement and represent yet another kind of group. Like many classification schemu, this one does not always designate mutually exclusive categories, but it does provide some basis for understanding the different roles performed by various groups.

The primary feminist mass-membership group is the National Organization for Women (NOW), which in 1985 had a membership of 158,000 women and men. Based in Washington, D.C., NOW also has local affiliates that work to influence state and local policymaking. The National Women's Political Caucus (NWPC) is another mass-membership group with 77,000 members. The single-issue groups are concerned with specific issues, such as education, abortion and pension rights. The National Abortion Rights Action League (NARAL) is the largest of the single-issue groups. Like NOW, it includes state and local affiliates that operate to influence subnational decisionmakers. NARAL is also Washington-based and actively works to influence national decisionmaking and public opinion. In addition, the women's movement embraces litigation and research groups. The Center for

Women Policy Studies, a research group, and the Women's Legal Defense Fund (WLDF), a litigation organization, are two such organizations.

The electoral sector of the women's movement directs most of its attention to the election of candidates for public office who support the goals of the women's movement. It includes many groups such as the National Women's Political Caucus (which, as noted above, is also a mass-membership organization), and political action committees (PACs) of some of the mass-membership and issue-specific women's groups, e.g., NOW and NARAL. NWPC has focused considerable attention and activity on electing women to public office and as delegates to national nominating conventions. It also lobbies and is active in Washington-based coalitions and campaigned hard to ratify the ERA. But over the years, the electoral process has been NWPC's primary concern.

Although traditional women's organizations do not have as their primary focus equal rights for women, during the past 20 years of the women's movement, many of them have become indispensable partners to feminist groups. The League of Women Voters (LWV), the American Association of University Women (AAUW), and the National Federation of Business and Professional Women's Clubs (BPW), to name only a few, are mass-based groups with grassroots structures. When appropriate, they can be mobilized to provide broad-based community support that the feminist groups cannot do as readily because, by and large, they do not have mass memberships and an extensive grassroots network.

Most groups in the feminist community are essentially leadership, not mass-membership, organizations. Leadership groups do not actively pursue or maintain opportunities for individual membership in the organization. Rather, they are composed primarily of the staff—for example, the National Women's Law Center. Other groups, like the Women's Legal Defense Fund with 1,500 members (Gelb and Palley, 1987), have small membership bases and thus tend to operate as leadership groups. Obvious exceptions to the leadership group model include NOW and, to a lesser degree, NARAL and NWPC. The traditional women's groups have large memberships. In 1980, for instance, United Methodist Women had nearly 1.25 million members and the General Federation of Women's Clubs included 600,000 members (Gelb and Palley, 1982). These groups can be called upon to marshal broad-based support when needed.

When, on the other hand, it is politically astute to develop an issue quietly so as to minimize the mobilization of highly vocal opposition, leadership groups in the movement, with their limited dependence upon mass membership, can work to the advantage of the feminist community. Therefore, in the period just before Congress passed Title IX of the Education Amendments of 1972, the law that bars discrimination against women in education, the women's groups worked out of the public eye. Passage of Title IX was achieved in part as a result of pressure from feminist groups, but its enactment is usually attributed to Representative Edith Green and Senator Birch Bayh. When the 1972 amendments were being debated in Congress, attention and debate focused on portions of the legislation other than Title IX. By assuming the role of "silent partner" rather than engaging mass support for the amendment, feminist groups caught the potential opposition unaware. The opponents of the legislation did not mobilize in time to block enactment; an effective opposition arose only afterward, when the full implications of the law began to be realized.

On other occasions, the traditional women's groups have

been called upon to apply the pressure from constituents that is often necessary to mobilize congressional support. This strategy proved useful during the campaign to influence members of Congress to pass the Equal Credit Opportunity Act of 1975. Traditional women's groups lent grassroots organizational support to the campaign to persuade senators and representatives that broad-based enthusiasm existed in favor of the legislation. Groups such as the National Council of Jewish Women organized telegram campaigns in their local affiliates to draw mail volume from their membership.

The groups in the women's movement have been reasonably successful in achieving their goals. Leaders of the feminist organizations have recognized that there are certain "rules of the game" they must follow in order to achieve any success in the American political system. As relative newcomers to the political process, most of these leaders have been careful to operate within the implicit restrictions of these mainstream rules (Gelb and Palley, 1982).

The women's groups have been most successful in influencing the decisionmaking process when they have directed their political energies to issues defined and then perceived by the general public and decisionmakers as "role equity" rather than "role change." Role equity calls for the extension to women of rights that are now enjoyed only by men. Issues relating to this are presented as relatively narrow in their implications; they permit policymakers to seek uncontroversial, low-cost advantage with feminist groups and voters. Thus, legislation has been enacted that provides equal credit opportunity and pension reform. By contrast, role change issues appear to alter the dependent roles of women as wives, mothers, and homemakers. This, in turn, raises for some people the possibility of greater sexual freedom, independence, and the transformation of existing values. A visible, sometimes very powerful opposition is aroused by efforts to address policy concerns that imply role change for women. It is increasingly difficult, however, to separate economic from political problems, and thus to distinguish the political from the economic barriers that hinder women; the spheres are clearly related. In large measure, the political remedies sought by the women's movement have addressed economic inequality and perceived injustice. When political solutions have been sought for issues defined as unjust in noneconomic terms, the women's movement has often been less than successful. Thus, free choice regarding abortion and the Equal Rights Amendment have been perceived in terms of role change, not role equity; as a result, they have aroused strong opposition.

The issues on which the women's rights movement has chosen to focus have varied, but the Equal Rights Amendment and concerns for freedom of choice about abortion have remained fundamental. Success on these two issues has been mixed. The ERA failed to receive support in enough state legislatures to become part of the Constitution. Congressional passage of amendments prohibiting the use of Medicaid funds for most abortion procedures has eroded abortion rights, as have anti-abortion riders attached to foreign aid legislation and Defense Department appropriations. The women's movement has, however, preserved the basic principle of freedom of choice through constant vigilance in the judicial system. Though the Supreme Court has upheld the constitutionality of the Hyde amendment, it has not retreated from its 1973 decision in *Roe v. Wade*, which held that the "right to privacy" includes the decision to have an abortion, and that the state's "compelling interest" to regulate abortions increases after the first trimester of pregnancy. The Court rejected the view that an unborn fetus has a constitutional "right to life."

Strategies for addressing specific issues have changed, since social and political conditions influence the selection of issues. In general, however, the "issue turf" has been divided among women's groups, with different groups taking the lead on particular ones. On issues relating to abortion, NARAL regularly has assumed leadership; on equal credit opportunity legislation, the Center for Women Policy Studies has played a prominent role; and on pension rights and unisex insurance legislation, the Women's Equity Action League (WEAL) has been a primary actor.

Dividing the issue turf is not an exclusionary method. Quite the contrary: on most issues, there is conscious coalition building. One group may assume leadership, but many groups will participate in working to achieve a common goal. Some highly successful formal coalitions have been developed to strengthen issue positions and lobby to improve conditions for women. Among the more successful of these efforts are the National Coalition for Women and Girls in Education, the Campaign to End Discrimination Against Pregnant Workers, and the Coalition on Women and Taxes.

Feminist leaders have recognized that coalition building permits groups with nonexistent or small membership bases to ally with large membership organizations to demonstrate to decisionmakers that an issue has substantial public support. Different groups also bring their own expertise to a collective effort. Research groups, litigation groups, and electoral groups all have different strengths they can bring to bear on a campaign to change the *status quo*.

Women's groups have also learned to develop coalition

strategies that reach beyond their own ranks to include a broader range of interests. A recent example is their activity in response to the Supreme Court's 1984 decision in *Grove City College* v. *Bell,* narrowly interpreting Title IX of the Education Amendments.

At issue in this case was the scope of Title IX, the law barring sex discrimination in educational programs and activities receiving federal funds. Was an entire institution, or only the particular program that received federal funds, bound not to discriminate on the basis of sex? Although the law had long been interpreted as reaching throughout the institution, the Court, in a 6–3 decision, held that the federal government does not have institution-wide authority to enforce an anti-sex-discrimination law whenever an educational institution receives federal aid for specific programs. The justices held that only the programs (in this case, the student financial aid office) must comply with Title IX. The impact of this decision extended beyond sex discrimination and Title IX to Title VII of the Civil Rights Act (prohibiting employment discrimination on the basis of race, religion, and national origin as well as sex), Section 504 of the Rehabilitation Act (the disabled), and the Age Discrimination Act (the elderly), since all of these laws contain similar language.

To organize support for the Civil Rights Restoration Act, legislation that would have the effect of overruling the *Grove City* decision, women's groups collaborated with many other civil rights, feminist, senior citizen, and handicapped organizations. The Leadership Conference on Civil Rights (LCCR) has acted as an "umbrella" for this coalition, which, after some early success, has been facing problems staying together because the Catholic Conference, a coalition member, has a differing view on abortion rights.

As more groups and more people become involved in issue-specific coalitions, however, they may be forced to compromise their particular positions to present a united front to the media and to decisionmakers. Coalition building has often united, on one issue, groups that disagree or remain neutral on other issues. Thus right-to-life groups joined with feminist groups, civil rights groups, and labor unions in the Campaign to End Discrimination Against Pregnant Workers. The campaign was involved actively in the process that led to enactment of the 1978 Pregnancy Discrimination Act.

This strategy of compromise can sometimes dilute feminist concerns. If one assumes that interest-group politics inherently demands narrowly focused positions on specific policies (Berry, 1984), then coalition strategies run counter to the basic premise of interest-group participation in politics. In fact, coalitions sometimes behave like political parties in that they require participant groups to tone down adamant positions in order to maintain a broad ideology.

There are many advantages to coalition building, however: first, the pooling of resources to support issues; second, greater access to decisionmakers; third, the added advantage of pre-existing networks and special expertise; and, fourth, expanded opportunities to build new networks.

Extensive networking has occurred among feminist activists. Besides developing networks among themselves and among leaders of supportive organizations, they also have developed and maintained relationships with members of Congress, as well as congressional and executive agency staff. They are kept well informed of relevant events by their public-sector supporters in Congress and the bureaucracy, and so they often receive advance notice of amendments that may be offered to a particular piece of legislation that would dilute the effectiveness of the proposed law, or administrative proposals that might weaken anti-discrimination regulations. As a result of these relationships, movement groups are often able to organize themselves to anticipate adversity. The women who lead them are politically astute players on the Washington political scene; they are well prepared and never appear without having done their "homework" on an issue (Gelb and Palley, 1982).

All feminist groups—be they method-specific or single-issue groups—aim to improve conditions for women: method-specific groups are research and litigation organizations, while issue-specific groups address single issues such as education or pension equity. The multi-purpose groups such as NOW and WEAL use a variety of methods in pursuing their multiple-issue concerns. It is in the interest of them all to work together, particularly because the opposition they face is often formidable. Thus, the organizational response of coalitions seems necessary, and the extensive networks that they have built are essential.

Opposition to the goals of the women's movement comes from several quarters. On role-change issues, such as ERA and abortion rights, opposition tends to come from "pro-family" conservatives and "right to lifers" who are often conservative on a broad range of other social and political issues. On abortion, these groups are bolstered by the organizational strength of both the Catholic Church and fundamentalist Protestant sects, including the "electronic church." On issues defined and perceived in terms of role equity—such as pension rights, unisex insurance, and comparable worth—the linchpin of opposition is typically the industry or social group that perceives it will suffer most from a change in the *status quo*. Thus, the insurance industry's lobbying arm led the opposition to unisex insurance due to the cost associated with changeover, and the National Collegiate Athletic Association (NCAA) vigorously fought implementation and full compliance with Title IX of the Education Amendments of 1972, since it, in effect, required that additional funds be committed to women's athletics, perhaps at the expense of men's sports programs.

The Women's Movement and the Policy Process

Interest groups in the women's movement have profoundly influenced the policy process. They have deeply affected the development of new attitudes. They have been instrumental in redefining problems and issues among the population at large as well as among decisionmakers; they have persisted in working to establish sound policy; and they have diligently monitored policy implementation.

In the past two decades, attitudes about women's roles in American society have changed substantially. Betty Friedan's groundbreaking 1963 book, *The Feminine Mystique,* described the contradictions faced by educated middle-class American women. The value of individual success was minimized by women themselves, who believed they were limited to the traditional female roles of wife and mother. Friedan wrote about the plight of these educated women whom society consigned to housekeeping and child care. Others, such as Kate Millett and Germaine Greer, also critiqued the conditions women confronted in fast-paced, achievement-oriented twentieth century America.

During the same period, the state commissions on the status of women were organized, bringing together women concerned with sex-specific issues and accumulating evidence that legally sanctioned inequality for women was widespread in American society. In 1966, at the Third Annual National Conference of State Commissions on Women, conference organizers prevented a group of women from submitting a formal motion urging legislation to forbid sex discrimination. This act disappointed conference participants, causing a number of women to walk out. Among them was Ms. Friedan, who, with other commission members, was soon instrumental in organizing NOW as a women's rights organization.

Several other feminist organizations emerged in the late 1960s and early 1970s. In 1968, WEAL was created as an alternative to NOW; in 1971, the NWPC was organized. During this initial period, WEAL did not support freedom of choice about abortion; NOW has always endorsed this right for women.

Particularly significant in the early stages, NOW made political statements about concerns that were defined as women's issues. People were made more aware of women who were dissatisfied with their circumstances. Also, women began to discuss with other women ambivalence about their roles and, in some cases, had their own consciousness put into sharper relief. They realized that personal problems and role anxieties they had thought unique were common among a great many other women. In fact, before women's groups could put any set of reasonable demands before political decisionmakers, women themselves had to become aware of the problems they shared for which potential solutions existed. Once a significant cadre of women understood this, men could also be made conscious of these problems. Both men and women are needed to support changes in the laws and create sufficient political leverage to implement regulations. Recent poll data now indicate an awareness and concern on the part of both sexes for improving conditions for women (Thom, 1984).

In the movement's formative years, the media often ignored or mocked feminism and its organized interest groups. Today the media are not as blatant in their disregard of the movement and its issues. Whether the media's present attitude is the cause or the effect of changed popular attitudes, the majority of American men and women endorse the principles of equal educational opportunity and an equal rights amendment to the Constitution. Finally, the majority of both men and women approve of women working outside the home—a significant shift in opinion since before the women's movement.

One criticism leveled at the interest groups is that they do not represent or reflect the needs of working-class and poor women—young and old—and of women who choose to stay at home to care for their families. Put in somewhat different terms, the group component of the women's movement has been accused of having a middle-class and upper-middle-class bias in selecting problems to define as issues. Though they have always supported a government role in providing day care programs, the groups in the women's movement have not been in the forefront of efforts to develop such programs or to organize special facilities and programs for mothers of young children (Hewlett, 1986; Kamerman, 1985).

Until recently, feminist groups also have been charged with focusing scant attention on the problems of poorly paid, largely unorganized working women, as well as poor women and their children who depend on public assistance for survival. Though it may be unfair criticism, the movement has been judged harshly for spending too much time and energy on the Equal Rights Amendment and abortion rights, losing sight of a vast array of economic and social concerns that especially affect poor women (Hewlett, 1986). Since the problems these women face have become more acute—at least partly due to federal program cutbacks and a sluggish economy—the feminist groups have begun to pay closer attention to them.

Comments like those above provide some grist for the arguments of women's movement critics. Nevertheless, several points should be made to put the criticisms in perspective. First, though the ERA and the ongoing campaign to protect freedom of choice have required considerable time and effort, other issues have also been addressed by women's groups. The structure of the organized women's movement enhances the possibilities for multi-issue campaigns. Because the wide variety of groups brings together so many issues and approaches, the danger of narrowing to only a few topics is almost nonexistent. The mass-membership organizations, such as NOW, act as bridges between the numerous issue-specific groups in the movement and the unorganized, somewhat amorphous mass movement that actively supports issues of concern to women.

Many feminist groups concentrate on specific issues or possess special expertise they can bring to bear on a policy campaign. There is, in other words, a specialization of function that predominates in the movement. That helps to explain why many people see the women's movement as anchored primarily on the ERA and abortion rights. NOW is the mass-membership organization that usually attracts the most media attention, and its primary issues are also perceived to be the ratification of the ERA and freedom of choice, even though NOW has been involved in numerous issue campaigns.

The nonmembership groups (essentially leadership groups, such as the Project on Equal Education Rights [PEER] and the Center for Women Policy Studies) work outside the limelight to define problems and influence public policy. Thus, while battles continue around role-change issues like ratification of the ERA and the protection of abortion rights, other interest groups have been securing several pieces of significant role-equity legislation. The Equal Credit Opportunity Act, the Pregnancy Discrimination Act, and, most recently, the Retirement Equity Act, all exert important effects on women's lives.

In addition, women's groups have been involved in a campaign for national unisex insurance legislation, the Civil Rights Restoration Act, and comparable worth legislation. Though the issue of comparable worth is being addressed more aggressively by state and local legislatures and courts than in the federal arena, groups in the national women's movement, along with a number of labor unions, have been responsible for defining comparable worth as an issue and keeping it in the public eye and on the policy agenda.

The litigation groups, such as the American Civil Liberties Union's Reproductive Freedom Project (ACLU-RFP) and the pro-choice groups, especially NARAL, have actively litigated to protect women's abortion rights. NARAL, as well as most other members of the feminist interest-group community, has also been working in Congress to retain abortion rights and reproductive counseling facilities. Moreover, several groups outside the women's movement, Planned Parenthood and the Alan Guttmacher Institute in particular, have worked actively with feminists to champion women's right to reproductive freedom, including abortion rights. Not only have these groups mounted concerted campaigns directed at political decisionmakers, they have worked to maintain the public's concern about protecting these rights in the face of strenuous opposition from several quarters. Religious groups like the Catholic Church, the Church of the Latter Day Saints, and some fundamentalist Protestant sects have mobilized to oppose freedom of choice, as have socially conservative women and men. Symbols and taboos, such as "baby murder," have been manipulated with some success in this ongoing campaign against role change.

It is useful to consider closely an issue campaign other than the ERA or abortion rights in order to understand more clearly the way in which the group component of the women's movement operates. In the 1980s, movement groups have spent much of their energy on the Economic Equity Act (EEA). The EEA is a multi-title act that includes provisions for pension equity, unisex insurance, stricter enforcement of child support laws, and more extensive day care coverage for children of working parents.

One of the EEA titles enacted by Congress in 1984 was the Retirement Equity Act. A number of women's groups were involved in the campaign for this legislation, which is intended to make pension law more responsive to the particular circumstances of women. WEAL, as well as the Women's Rights Project of the Pension Rights Center and the AAUW, were involved from the outset. Among other groups joining forces to mobilize congressional support for this legislation were the Older Women's League (OWL), the National Federation of Business and Professional Women Clubs, and the National Organization for Women (NOW).

A significant role in the campaign for passage of the Retirement Equity Act was played by the bipartisan Congressional Caucus for Women's Issues. Led by caucus Co-chairs

Patricia Schroeder (Democrat-Colorado) and Olympia Snowe (Republican-Maine), key caucus members and staff not only helped inform other members of Congress about the need for this legislation but also worked closely with women's groups to develop strategy.

In general, the Congressional Caucus for Women's Issues has become an important focal point for the legislative campaigns of women's groups. The caucus has provided leadership in introducing legislation and developing and disseminating information, and has acted as a clearinghouse, especially in the fight for various titles of the EEA, the keystone of the caucus's legislative agenda.

Rep. Patricia Schroeder, (D-CO), right, talks with Rep. Olympia Snowe, (R-ME) outside the Capitol Building in Washington. The two women chair the Congressional Caucus for Women's Issues. *AP / Wide World Photos*

Efforts to pass the pension equity legislation, as well as the problems that it sought to remedy, drew very little media attention. Most people were unaware of the activities of groups involved in the campaign to enhance women's pension benefits. Visible concern and greater attention were directed toward ERA and abortion rights. Nevertheless, or perhaps partially as a result of this media apathy and public ignorance, women's groups came together to develop a strategy and a unified position.

After the Equal Rights Amendment—which the president opposed and which the national Republican party did not endorse—failed to be ratified by the states, it was the Republican majority in the Senate that provided leadership instrumental in moving the Retirement Equity Act through Congress. The law passed was not perfect, but it was a good start (Gelb and Palley, 1987).[1]

There was little vocal opposition to the principle of pension reform legislation, and public opinion polls indicated considerable support for more equitable pension rights for women. The Nondiscrimination in Insurance Act (H.R. 100) title of the EEA, on the other hand, has encountered heavy opposition in the insurance industry and in Congress. This proposed "unisex insurance" law would prohibit discrimination in the establishment of both premiums and benefits (including annuities) on the basis of sex, race, color, or national origin.[2] The women's groups that assumed early leadership positions in the campaign for unisex insurance were WEAL, BPW, and AAUW. Several other groups in the movement have since become involved.

On the other side of the issue are the umbrella organizations for the life insurance industry: the American Council of Life Insurance (ACLI) with 575 corporate members, and the Committee for Fair Insurance, a coalition of 34 corporations that was established to fight H.R. 100. As the industry's unified campaign against H.R. 100 developed, the Task Force on Insurance Discrimination of the LCCR began to work for the bill. The task force's membership is drawn from the women's movement, unions, religious organizations, and consumer groups. In addition, several unions and professional organizations have supported the campaign. The American Federation of State, County and Municipal Employees (AFSCME) and the Electrical Workers Union, as well as the American Nurses Association, have been most notable in lobbying for unisex insurance legislation (Gelb and Palley, 1987). So far, the coalition's efforts have met with disappointment.

Not only have the women's groups fought for legislation, they have also remained vigilant in monitoring the implementation of laws. Careful monitoring of the implementation process—particularly the development of regulatory guidelines to carry out the law—allowed the movement to realize the greatest benefits from Title IX (before the Grove City decision). In this case, feminists had several primary goals, involving both the legislative and regulatory processes. While the bill was in Congress, feminists sought to prevent Title IX from exempting revenue-producing sports, such as football; they fought to prevent riders to the Department of Health, Education and Welfare (HEW) appropriation that would restrict the implementation of Title IX; and they sought to ensure that final regulations would not be subject to congressional review (for fear that such a review might weaken the regulations).

After Title IX was enacted, the women's groups worked to design acceptable guidelines for carrying out the law.

Under the aegis of the National Coalition for Women and Girls in Education, the groups used litigation tactics and publicity, as well as close monitoring of the regulation-writing process, for the entire period between passage of the law and the issuance of final regulations. The coalition maintained a united front and the image of broad-based support, the latter made possible by melding the resources of mass-membership groups with those of specialized research and litigation groups. Moreover, support from elected officials, as well as agency and congressional staff, strengthened the hand of women's groups in the decisionmaking process. The guidelines issued by HEW in December 1979 were acceptable to groups in the feminist community, even though they did not meet their highest hopes (Gelb and Palley, 1982).

Implementation of Title IX was also closely watched by local women's groups. Local school districts, colleges, and universities complied in varying degrees as a result of the pressures these groups brought to bear. As discussed elsewhere in this book, participation by women in school athletic programs grew considerably in the decade after enactment of Title IX. Certainly the success of American women in the 1984 Olympics can be related to implementation of Title IX.

Women in the Electoral Process

Participation

Most observers concede that there are differences in the intensity with which the two sexes hold their positions on social issues, such as reproductive freedom, or national security issues, such as defense spending.

Economic problems are probably the most highly charged

issues for most voters, however, and there is no dispute that today a disproportionate number of women are economically deprived. Three out of every five adults officially designated as having incomes below the poverty line are women, and women head nearly half of all poor families in the United States. The report of the National Advisory Council on Economic Opportunity noted that "if wives and female heads of household were paid the wages that similarly qualified men earn, about half of the families now living in poverty would not be poor" (*Washington Social Legislation Bulletin*, August 23, 1982: 27). If economic conditions continue to be a primary influence on voting, as most analysts believe, men and women may well cast their votes differently on election day.

How have women's concerns been translated into electoral performance? The *New York Times*/CBS News poll estimated that, in the 1984 elections, 53 percent of the voters were women. Moreover, there was a slight majority of women voters in every age group (the *New York Times*, November 8, 1984: A-19).

Historically, the fact that potential female voters outnumbered potential male voters did not seriously concern either major party. Before 1980, women were less likely than men to vote (Poole and Zeigler, 1985),[3] and their political attitudes were believed to parallel those of men. However, the results of the 1980 and 1984 presidential and congressional elections indicate that neither of these conditions seems to prevail any longer.

In 1980, although there were more women than men at the polls, the difference in actual numbers was not statistically significant. On a percentage basis, the voter turnout was about the same for women as for men. By 1984 the percent of eligible women voters who cast their ballots exceeded the comparable figure for men. Moreover, since there are more women than men of voting age in the population, the absolute number of women among voters will be greater than the absolute number of men, even if the percentage turnout is approximately the same for both sexes.

Voting studies of the 1980 and 1984 elections demonstrated that women voted differently from men. In *Voters' Choice*, Gerald Pomper (1975) expressed the then-popular view that there are "no political differences between men and women that can be attributed to the factor of sex itself." 1980 was the year in which the voters challenged the conventional wisdom. According to polls conducted on election day by the Gallup Organization, the *New York Times*/CBS and the University of Michigan Center for Political Studies, 49 percent of women preferred Ronald Reagan and 44 percent of women preferred President Carter; men gave Mr. Reagan a much greater margin: 53 to 38 percent ("Who Cast Their Votes . . . ," 1984: 2132). The *Los Angeles Times* and the ABC News/*Washington Post* polls indicated that in 1984 the gap remained (ibid.). Women gave President Reagan 56 percent of their votes and Walter Mondale 44 percent, while men went for the president by 63 to 37 percent.

It appears that these differences in political preferences between men and women continue today. They can be attributed to positions on the economy, defense, and national security, as well as to the perceived anti-women views associated with President Reagan and his supporters in Congress, state legislatures, and statehouses (Klein, 1985).

Women's voting has also influenced the outcomes of recent congressional races. For example, when liberal Democratic Representative Barney Frank defeated his more conservative Republican opponent Margaret Heckler for a congressional seat in a redrawn Massachusetts district, his victory was considered in part due to the women's vote. This race underscored a telling lesson for candidates: women will not win women's votes simply on the basis of sex loyalty; issues are important factors. In the 1984 Iowa senatorial race, the defeat of incumbent Senator Roger Jepsen was seen, in some measure, as caused by the votes of women. Similarly, in Illinois, Democrat Paul Simon defeated incumbent Republican Charles Percy, and in Michigan, Democrat Carl Levin defeated his Republican challenger. The *New York Times* /CBS exit poll showed Simon receiving 55 percent of the female vote and 46 percent of the male vote, while Percy drew 48 percent of the male vote and just 40 percent of the female vote. In Michigan, the gap was clear, too. Fifty-two percent of women voters and 47 percent of men went for Levin; Jack Lousma received only 46 percent of the female vote and 49 percent of the male (Center for the American Woman and Politics, 1984; 1986).

Significantly, male support for women's equity issues is proportionately the same as women's support. Also, men endorse an equal rights amendment and free choice regarding abortion in about the same proportion as women. As noted earlier, however, it is generally believed that women hold positions on women's issues more intensely than men do. Thus, it may be possible to mobilize women to vote for or against candidates at least partly on the basis of the candidates' positions on these issues. Nevertheless, it is important to remember that differences between the sexes in party identification and voting can be associated with economic issues as well. The Frank election is a case in point.

In 1984, when asked whether or not they felt the Reagan economic program had helped or hurt the U.S. economy, 53 percent of women as compared to 44 percent of men answered that Reagan had done only a fair or poor job. When asked how President Reagan was handling inflation and the rising cost of living, men responded positively 57 percent of the time, while only 43 percent of women thought he was doing a good job (Thom, 1984).

Looking ahead, it is difficult to know what specific issue or cluster of issues will become most salient in dividing the sexes at the polls. Clear preferences are now being expressed, that is certain; also, there are likely to be more women than men voters in the years to come. To some extent, the organized women's movement has been focusing on these differences since ERA ratification failed. Fundraising efforts by the PACs associated with women's interest groups, along with specific electoral targeting of women's group opponents, seem to have drawn additional attention to the issues of importance to these groups. Consequently, candidates are finding it more and more difficult to ignore the number of female voters.

Women as Elected Officials

Are American voters as likely to vote for a woman as for a man? Pollsters for the *Los Angeles Times* suspected that some people who would refuse to vote for a woman for public office might be reluctant to admit that to a canvasser. They tried a more indirect approach to determine the influence of a candidate's sex on voter decisions. Two hypothetical candidates for governor were invented in late August 1984. One candidate was described as a business executive who was married, had two children, and was a native New Yorker. The other candidate was presented as a lawyer who was married,

had three children, and was a native midwesterner. For half
of the sample, the New York native was described as "she."
"She" lost to her opponent, the native midwesterner, 54
percent to 27 percent. For the other half of the sample, "she"
was the native midwestern lawyer. "She" lost again, this time
by a margin of 43 percent to 38 percent ("Beneath the Enthusiasm for Women Candidates," 1984: 1743).

In November 1984, women candidates were not as successful in their election bids as one might have expected,
given the proportion of voters who were female. Leading the
list of losers was Rep. Geraldine Ferraro, who lost her bid for
the vice-presidency when Walter Mondale was defeated. In
addition, all nine women senatorial challengers to incum-
bents and 43 women House hopefuls were defeated. After the
1984 congressional elections, women held 23 of the 435 seats
in the House of Representatives and two seats in the Senate
(Center for the American Woman and Politics, 1986). In the
states, women made some electoral gains in 1984. According
to the National Women's Education Fund, 14.3 percent of
the membership of state legislatures was female, up from 13.3
percent in 1982; women candidates won 56.3 percent of their
general election campaigns in 1984. In Vermont, Democrat
Madeline Kunin won the gubernatorial election, and in 1986,
women held 26.1 percent of the seats in the Vermont state
legislature, up from 18.8 percent in 1983 (Center for the
American Woman and Politics, 1983; 1986). The increase in
the number of women holding public office is becoming significant, especially in county and municipal governments. In
the decade prior to 1984, the number of women holding
county office grew from three percent of elected officials to
eight percent. By November 1985, four of the 100 largest
cities in the United States had women mayors. Though these

figures do not reflect the proportion of American adults who are female, or the female proportion of the electorate, they certainly reflect a larger role for women in electoral politics.

Will the growing presence of elected women officials affect policy decisions? The evidence is not yet in. If one looks at the women who have served in Congress and in state and local positions, the answer is ambiguous. Most elected women officials have been more conscious than their male colleagues of the concerns of women on questions of role change and role equity and have backed policies to improve conditions for women. But some elected women have not been as sympathetic. In 1981, the Center for the American Woman and Politics surveyed both elected and appointed state and local officeholders, trying to determine if female and male officeholders held the same views on several issues of specific relevance to women. The survey found that women officeholders were indeed more supportive of an equal rights amendment to the Constitution than their male counterparts, and they were also more likely to oppose a constitutional amendment that would forbid abortions in most or all circumstances. These positions were not, however, held by all female officeholders.

Since economic redistribution may be necessary to achieve greater equity for women, political decisions that transcend women-specific issues must be considered. On issues such as minimum social security insurance benefits and AFDC levels, as well as on broader redistributive issues like the income tax rate structure, liberal women officeholders may possibly be more supportive of policies that will enhance opportunities for women, while conservative women may be less likely to offer their encouragement and their votes. Women voters seem to be aware of this situation, and they sometimes support politically liberal men rather than their conservative female opponents.

Though it would be a mistake to assume a perfect relationship between liberalism and the Democratic party or conservatism and the Republican party, there is a general tendency among voters to draw these correlations. In January 1986, the New York Times/CBS poll found that 50 percent of female respondents favored the Democratic party while 40 percent favored the Republican. The comparable figures for men were 45 percent and 45 percent respectively (the New York Times, May 11, 1986: A-22). Since women are more likely than men to support candidates whom they perceive to be liberal, this distribution is not surprising.

Conclusion

Women as a force in American politics remain a new factor. They have mobilized into a sometimes formidable nexus of interest groups, and when role-equity issues are at stake, they have been quite successful in achieving their goals. This is so because the principal leaders have become consummate "game players" in American politics. It is likely that these groups will continue to help define issues and strive to meet their goals in the political process. Many of their achievements have been incremental, which will probably continue to be the case. Women and men have changed their attitudes considerably regarding the appropriate role of women in society. And despite the criticisms leveled at feminist interest groups, these attitudes are not likely to return to what they were before the women's movement began to have an impact on public awareness.

Patterns of female voting and officeholding have also

changed in the past two decades. Women outnumber men among the voters; for that reason alone, the views women hold on political issues cannot be ignored by men or women who run for public office. If women voice different expectations about politics and political issues than men, candidates must listen. If they listen and then dismiss out of hand what they hear, new voting patterns may emerge. Though a majority of women voted for President Reagan in 1984, despite his outspoken opposition to many women's rights issues and his clear opposition to a number of programs that benefit poor people—disproportionately women and their children—it is important to remember Ronald Reagan's unusual personal appeal to voters. Because most candidates do not remotely approach his extraordinary hold on a forgiving electorate, they may treat women voters lightly at considerable risk to their political fortunes.

1986 in Review

January 15 / At a news conference on Martin Luther King, Jr.'s birthday, U.S. Attorney General Edwin Meese reaffirms his commitment to ending the use of goals and timetables to promote the hiring of more women and minorities by federal contractors.

January 28 / Astronaut Judith Resnik and Christa McAuliffe, a school teacher from New Hampshire, are among the seven crewmembers killed in the explosion of the space shuttle Challenger.

February 3 / U.S. District Judge John Nordberg of the 7th Circuit, ruling that Sears, Roebuck and Co. was not guilty of sex discrimination in hiring, promotion, and pay, throws out one of the largest cases (*Equal Employment Opportunity Commission* v. *Sears, Roebuck and Co.*) ever brought by the Commission (EEOC). The suit against Sears was based on statistics showing that women were underrepresented in certain types of jobs at Sears, rather than on specific instances of discrimination.

February 4 / In his State of the Union address, President Reagan orders a major evaluation—to be completed by December 1—of federal welfare and family policies by the White House Domestic Council, headed by Attorney General Edwin Meese.

February 11 / At his press conference, the president reaffirms his administration's opposition to using numerical quotas, goals, or timetables to benefit groups victimized by discrimination. (The president's remarks notwithstanding, consensus is lacking in the president's cabinet on this issue: Labor Secretary Brock has made clear his view that affirmative action programs are still necessary to overcome patterns of job discrimination.)

February 24 / The Supreme Court, in a summary affirmation, lets stand the decision by the 7th U.S. Circuit Court of Appeals in *Hudnut* v. *American Booksellers' Association*. The decision struck down as unconstitutional an Indianapolis, Indiana, ordinance that defined pornography as discrimination against women.

March 4 / U.S. Rep. William Clay, joined by principal House of Representatives advocates Patricia Schroeder, Mary Rose Oakar, Austin Murphy, Stewart McKinney, George Miller, and Senate sponsor Christopher Dodd, announces the introduction of H.R. 4300, the Parental and Medical Leave Act of 1986. H.R. 4300 would provide 18 weeks of unpaid, job-protected leave to parents for the birth, adoption, or serious illness of their child, as well as 26 weeks of unpaid, job-protected leave for employees who are unable to work due to a serious health condition.

March 9 / More than 100,000 women and men participate in the National March for Women's Lives in Washington, D.C., demonstrating their support for women's rights to birth control and legal abortion. Thirty thousand march in Los Angeles—in the rain—for the same cause.

March 10 / U.S. Department of Health and Human Services (HHS) announces that $7.1 million in funds for the Family Violence Prevention and Services Act are now available to the states for distribution to nonprofit, community-based organizations that provide direct services to family violence victims. The funds had been delayed for two years because HHS failed to write the regulations necessary to guide implementation of the program.

March 20 / Congress sends H.R. 3128, the FY86 Budget Reconciliation (deficit reduction) bill, to the White House for the president's signature. Included in this legislation is the first component of the Economic Equity Act of 1985 to clear the Congress. It would require employers to maintain group health insurance coverage for up to three years for individuals who face termination of their benefits due to such events as divorce and widowhood. Beneficiaries would pay 102 percent of the total premium (both the employee and the employer contribution, plus a two percent administrative cost), but would nevertheless benefit because group health insurance is typically far less expensive than individual health insurance. Other positive aspects of H.R. 3128 for women include requiring states to provide Medicaid coverage for the prenatal and postpartum care of low-income women in two-parent families where the chief wage earner is employed, and allowing states to provide poor pregnant women with a broader range of services than they provide for other beneficiaries under Medicaid.

March 21 / Debi Thomas wins the world figure skating championship in Geneva, Switzerland. Thomas, a pre-med student at Stanford University, is the first black to win the gold medal in a world skating competition.

April 1 / Under a pay equity settlement between the American Federation of State, County and Municipal Employees (AFSCME) and Washington State announced on December 31, 1985, the state will give pay equity salary increases to about 35,000 employees starting this month. Among the employees receiving substantial salary increases are clerk-typists, nurses, social caseworkers, and librarians.

April 17 / The Pulitzer Prizes for 1985 are announced. Among the winners: Edna Buchanan, *Miami Herald,* for general news reporting; Mary Pat Flaherty (with Andrew Schneider), *Pittsburgh Press,* for specialized news reporting; Katherine Ellison (with Lewis M. Simons and Pete Carey), *San Jose Mercury-News,* for international reporting; Carol Guzy (with Michel du Cille), *Miami Herald,* for spot news photography. Elizabeth Frank wins the letters-biography award for her *Louise Bogan: A Life.*

Ann Bancroft reaches the North Pole by dogsled, May 1, 1986.
© *Jim Brandenburg*

May 1 / Ann Bancroft, with five male colleagues, reaches the North Pole by dogsled. Bancroft, an American, is the first woman to have reached the Pole without mechanical transportation, and she and her team are the first known to have gained the Pole by dogsled without resupply en route.

May 6 / The U.S. Bureau of the Census reports that in nearly 20 percent of two-paycheck households in 1983, the wife earned more than her husband. Overall, however, husbands had average earnings more than double the earnings of their working wives, if part-time and part-year workers are included.

May 8 / Lucile Atcherson, the first American female Foreign Service Officer, dies at the age of 91.

May 12 / The U.S. House of Representatives passes H.R. 4745, the Sexual Abuse Act of 1986, revising statutes covering sexual offenses on federal property. The bill would replace the three existing federal rape statutes with four gender-neutral gradations of sexual assault; it would also repeal the marital rape exemption that, under existing law, prohibits the federal prosecution of a spouse if the couple is living together.

May 14 / Nebraska makes history when its primary voters of both major parties nominate women candidates for governor. Both Helen Boosalis, the Democratic candidate, and Kay Orr, the Republican candidate, have years of experience in politics and public service.

May 19 / The Supreme Court, ruling in *Wygant* v. *Jackson Board of Education*, makes clear that affirmative action plans giving blacks or women preferential treatment in hiring and promotion are not inherently unconstitutional. The Court rejects the U.S. Solicitor General's argument that affirmative action is constitutional only if used to benefit actual victims of past discrimination.

May 19 / Connecticut Superior Court Judge Joseph Chernauskas rules that the Boy Scouts of America did not violate sex discrimination laws in denying Catherine Pollard's application to be an official Scoutmaster.

May 28 / Terrie A. McLaughlin is named Outstanding Cadet in the U.S. Air Force Academy's class of 1986. The first woman to achieve that distinction since women were first admitted to the academy in 1976, McLaughlin is also the outstanding cadet in engineering and electrical engineering.

Terrie A. McLaughlin is named Outstanding Cadet in the U.S. Air Force Academy's class of 1986. She is the first woman to achieve that distinction. *Courtesy U.S. Air Force Academy*

May 30 / Basketball player Nancy Lieberman joins The Fame, a Springfield, Massachusetts team, thus becoming the first woman to play in a men's professional basketball league (the U.S. Basketball League).

June 11 / The Post Office and Civil Service Committee of the U.S. House of Representatives favorably reports out H.R. 4300, the Parental and Medical Leave Act, without amendment. (The bill has also been referred to the Education and Labor Committee.)

June 11 / The Supreme Court, ruling in *Thornburgh* v.

American College of Obstetricians and Gynecologists, upholds by a narrow margin (5-4) its 1973 decision in *Roe* v. *Wade* establishing a woman's constitutional right to have an abortion, and strictly limiting state power to regulate with regard to abortion. (The Reagan administration filed a brief in *Thornburgh* asking the Court not only to affirm a state's right to regulate extensively with respect to abortion but to overrule *Roe* v. *Wade.*)

June 19 / The Supreme Court rules unanimously (in *Meritor Savings Bank, FSB* v. *Mechelle Vinson*) that sexual harassment in the workplace, even if it does not result in job or promotion loss, violates Title VII of the Civil Rights Act (barring discrimination in the workplace on account of sex, race, religion, and national origin). According to the Court, "Without question, when a supervisor sexually harasses a subordinate, that supervisor discriminates on the basis of sex."

June 19 / The Senate confirms Dorcas Hardy as Commissioner of Social Security. Hardy, previously Assistant Secretary of Health and Human Services for Human Development Services, takes over the Social Security Administration from Acting Commissioner Martha McSteen.

June 19 / The *New York Times* decides that "Ms." is fit to print. The *Times* has concluded that the honorific has "passed sufficiently into the language to be accepted as common usage."

June 24 / The House Education and Labor Committee favorably reports out H.R. 4300, retitled "The Family and Medical Leave Act of 1986." The committee adopted an amendment offered by Rep. William Clay (see March 4, above) that includes the care of elderly parents among the purposes for which job-protected, unpaid leave could be taken. The amended bill also exempts from coverage employers with fewer than 15 employees.

June 27 / The Supreme Court rules (in *Ohio Civil Rights Commission* v. *Dayton Christian Day Schools*) that religious organizations are not exempt from a state's investigation into charges of sex discrimination. In a unanimous opinion, the Court holds that "the elimination of prohibited sex discrimination is a sufficiently important state interest" to warrant investigation.

July 1 / In a unanimous decision, the Supreme Court rules (in *Bazemore* v. *Friday*) that discrimination continuing after enactment of Title VII of the Civil Rights Act (prohibiting discrimination in employment on the basis of race, sex, religion, and national origin) violates the law. Although the plaintiff in this case charged racial discrimination, the implications of the decision are important with regard to sex discrimination, especially with respect to pay equity.

July 2 / The Supreme Court, in two separate decisions *(Local 28 of the Sheet Metal Workers' International Association* v. *Equal Employment Opportunity Commission* and *Local Number 93, International Association of Firefighters* v. *City of Cleveland)*, again signals its approval of affirmative action programs that are narrowly tailored to remedy a specific and proven problem of employment discrimination. The Court again rejects the administration's view that only specific, identified victims of discrimination may seek relief under Title VII.

August 14 / Rear Admiral Grace M. Hopper, at 79 the nation's oldest active military officer, retires from the U.S. Navy. Hopper was co-inventor of the computer language COBOL.

August 17 / The White House Conference on Small Business convenes. Reflecting the rapid growth in the number of businesses owned by women, 30 percent of the conference delegates are women.

August 26 / The U.S. Bureau of the Census releases 1985 poverty statistics. Poverty rates for almost all persons and family types were somewhat lower in 1985 than in the previous year, but female-headed families were still over five times as likely as married-couple families to be poor in 1985.

September 7 / Martina Navratilova wins her third U.S. Open and celebrates her victory by announcing that she is donating $150,000 to the Women's Sports Foundation's "Aspire Higher," a program giving travel and training grants directly to female athletes who might otherwise not be able to afford to continue competing. Navratilova's gift is believed to be the largest personal charitable contribution ever made by a female athlete.

September 9 / Voters of both major parties in Maryland nominate women as their candidates for the U.S. Senate. Linda Chavez, formerly staff director of the U.S. Commission on Civil Rights under President Reagan, is the Republican candidate. Barbara Mikulski, a five-term U.S. Representative, is the Democratic candidate. Also as a result of today's primary, one Maryland congressional race is between two women: incumbent Republican Helen Bentley vs. Kathleen Kennedy Townsend.

September 17 / H.R. 4300, the Family and Medical Leave Act, receives a rule from the House Rules Committee, and is thus cleared for consideration by the full House of Representatives. Because of the press of other business, however, it seems doubtful that the House will act on H.R. 4300 before the 99th Congress adjourns.

September 22 / Swimmer Tracy Caulkins and golfer Elizabeth Rawls are inducted into the International Women's

Sports Hall of Fame. Only one other living woman (Australian tennis champion Margaret Court) is among the six athletes so honored this year.

September 30 / President Reagan signs H.R. 4421 into law (Public Law 99–425), thus enacting Congress's reauthorization of several major social service programs targeted on low-income households, including Low-Income Home Energy Assistance, Community Service Block grants, Head Start, and dependent care. The last, for which $20 million a year over four years is authorized, provides information and referral on available child care services, and establishes before- and after-school child care centers in existing facilities. This so-called "latchkey" element of the dependent care program has been a major priority for Rep. Sala Burton and other members of the Congressional Caucus for Women's Issues.

October 22 / The Tax Reform Act of 1986 is signed into law (P.L. 99–514). Provisions that should be particularly welcome to low-income working women supporting families on their own include an increase in the standard deduction for single heads of household, an expanded Earned Income Tax Credit for low-income working families with children, and an increased personal exemption. All are indexed to compensate for the effect of inflation. In combination, these provisions should ensure that poor and near-poor workers with children will not have to pay federal income tax.

The new law also increases the standard deduction for single filers and for married couples filing jointly, both of whom will benefit from the increased personal exemption. The two-earner deduction is, however, repealed.

October 29 / The National Organization for Women (NOW) is 20 years old today.

November 3 / Ruling in *Babbitt v. Planned Parenthood,* the

Supreme Court affirms a decision by the U.S. Court of Appeals for the 9th Circuit finding unconstitutional a 1980 provision of Arizona law that barred grants of state funds that year to any groups that "offer[ed] abortions, abortion procedures, counseling for abortion procedures, or abortion referrals."

November 4 / Election day brings two historic firsts for women when Maryland elects Barbara Mikulski to the U.S. Senate and Nebraska elects Kay Orr governor. Mikulski is the first Democratic woman elected to the Senate who was not preceded in Congress by a spouse. Orr is the first Republican woman elected governor in the U.S. Both Mikulski and Orr beat female major-party opponents.

November 4 / San Francisco, California, voters approve amending the city charter to require pay equity for city workers.

November 5 / The Census Bureau reports that more than one-quarter of the 33.4 million American families with children were headed by a single parent in 1985. The percentage for black families was more than 60 percent.

November 6 / The U.S. District Court in Minnesota holds unconstitutional a Minnesota law requiring women under age 18 either to notify both parents or to obtain judicial approval before getting an abortion. The case, *Hodgson v. the State of Minnesota,* is the first in which the court has had before it the evidence of the actual effects on teenagers and their families of the parental notification requirement.

November 12 / For the first time, the Supreme Court hears oral argument in a case (*Johnson v. Transportation Agency, Santa Clara County* [California]) involving the legality of affirmative action preferences favoring women over men.

November 13 / The "White House Task Force Report on

the Family" is released. The task force, headed by Under-secretary of Education Gary Bauer, alleges that family life has been "frayed by the abrasive experience of two liberal decades" and urges that the federal government favor the traditional two-parent family.

December 9 / The National Academy of Sciences Panel on Adolescent Pregnancy and Childbearing, reporting on its two-year study of teenage pregnancies in the United States (of which there are more than one million each year), recommends increasing adolescents' access to contraceptives and "aggressive public education" to encourage teens to use them.

December 12 / The United States Air Force announces that it will open 1,645 more positions to women, bringing to 95 the percentage of all Air Force positions open to "qualified and interested women." Women will continue to be excluded from positions that would expose them to hostile fire and capture.

December 12 / The White House Domestic Policy Council team, detailed to carry out President Reagan's February order for a study of the U.S. welfare system, submits its report and recommendations. Rather than "top-down" structural changes in federal welfare programs, the group advocates allowing states and localities to conduct experimental and demonstration programs in which existing public assistance programs could be combined and altered, in order to discover how best to get people off welfare and into productive work. The team's specific proposals include requiring all able-bodied public assistance applicants to work and allowing local communities to set their own income-eligibility and benefit levels.

December 23 / "Voyager," co-piloted by Jeana Yeager

and Dick Rutan, lands at Edwards Air Force Base after just over nine days in the air. Voyager is the first airplane ever to have flown around the world without landing or refueling.

Compiled by ANNE J. STONE

Women
in
Brief

Women in Business

JOYCE VAN DYKE

THE PAST DECADE has seen extraordinary growth in the number of women business owners. Between 1974 and 1984, women went into business for themselves at a rate three times that of men, and the number of self-employed women grew by 74 percent—twice the rate at which women entered the labor force during the same period.

As of 1983, according to the U.S. Small Business Administration (SBA), out of a total of 11.8 million nonfarm small businesses in this country, women owned 3.3 million (up from 1.9 million in 1977). SBA's figure is an estimate, based on data provided by the Internal Revenue Service (IRS). Unfortunately, IRS distinguishes ownership by sex only in the case of sole proprietorships, of which, according to the IRS, women owned 28 percent in 1983. Although, as discussed below, women-owned businesses include partnerships and corporations as well as sole proprietorships, a recent census study (U.S. Bureau of the Census, 1986) found that the latter account for most (92 percent) of women-owned businesses. (It should be noted, however, that the census did not collect data regarding corporations).

The rapid growth of women in business is partly a result of improvements in women's economic and legal status in recent decades, thanks to the anti-discrimination laws of the 1960s and 1970s covering employment, pay, education, and credit. More women have moved into business ownership during a period in which more women have acquired managerial experience. Women held 33 percent of all managerial jobs in 1985, up from 14 percent in 1965.

A spur to self-employment may be persistent discrimination faced by managerial women in the male-dominated corporate world, the argument being, "if you can't join 'em, beat 'em." A 1985 *Harvard Business Review* study which surveyed male and female executives found that while male executives' attitudes toward women have changed greatly in 20 years, women still perceive resistance to their advancement. Only 33 percent of the women respondents (compared to 58 percent of the men) thought that women had equal opportunity for advancement in their particular companies; only 18 percent thought women had equal opportunity in business in general (Sutton and Moore, 1985).

Like other women in the workforce, self-employed women are likely to be in the service sector. Since this sector is expected to create most of the new jobs in the next decade, women should be well-positioned for future business growth. According to the president's 1985 report on small business, 91 percent of women-owned sole proprietorships were either in personal, business, recreational, medical, professional, or other services, or in retail trade, finance, insurance, and real estate (*The State of Small Business,* 1985: 289).

But some of the highest annual growth rates for women in business have been in nontraditional areas, including agricultural services, forestry and fishing, mining, security brokerages and dealerships, general building contracting, and legal services.

An area in which women-owned firms are severely underrepresented is federal contracting. Women's businesses receive less than one percent of all federal prime contracts, the contracts awarded directly by a federal agency to a business. However, the value of contracts awarded to women-owned firms has risen significantly in recent years: in 1984, women-owned firms received $1.1 billion in federal prime contracts, a 195 percent increase since 1980. In 1986, the federal goal for prime contract awards to women-owned businesses was $1.3 billion.

In assessing receipts generated by women-owned businesses, a lack of comprehensive data has again been a problem. IRS data, which, as noted above, distinguish ownership by sex only in the case of sole proprietorships, show that the 28 percent owned by women accounted for only 11.5 percent ($53 billion) of the $465 billion in gross receipts generated by sole proprietorships in 1983. In part, the lower receipts of women-owned firms are predictable because such a high proportion of these firms are in services and retailing, types of businesses that tend to have lower revenues than manufacturing or construction.

Women entrepreneurs' receipts have, however, been growing more rapidly than men's: receipts from women-owned sole proprietorships increased by 26 percent from 1982 to 1983, compared to a six percent increase for all sole proprietorships.

But, again, it should be stressed that although sole proprietorships account for the substantial majority of businesses owned by women, they are by no means the only types of women-owned businesses. A 1984 survey of its membership by the National Association of Women Business Owners (NAWBO) found that a majority of member-respondents were co-owners of partnerships or corporations. The average yearly company revenue reported in the NAWBO survey was $425,000 (compared to IRS's average of $13,333 for female-owned sole proprietorships) ("Women-owned Businesses . . . ," 1985).

Another indicator of larger earnings by women-owned businesses comes from *Savvy* magazine's yearly round-up of the top 60 businesses run by women. In 1986, the "Savvy 60" included only those businesses with annual sales of at least $20 million (the 1985 cut-off was $15 million). Fifty-four of the 60 exceeded $20 million, with Estée Lauder's cosmetics company at the top, with $1.2 billion. Some of the others that made the list were in advertising, auto sales, fashion, oil and gas, publishing, computer systems, pistons, cookie stores, travel, building materials, and baseball (the Cincinnati Reds, owned by Margaret Rose Schott) (Walker, 1986).

Finally, women business owners are increasing their opportunity to contribute to economic and business policy. They are gaining more seats on economic development and small business councils, such as the U.S. Chamber of Commerce Small Business Council, which is currently chaired by a woman. Women made up almost one-third of the delegates to the 1986 White House Conference on Small Business (compared to 16 percent at the 1980 Conference), where they had a forum for discussing a wide range of business and economic issues.

Legislative initiatives to improve conditions for women in business have been introduced in Congress, including a bill to ban discrimination in commercial lending. While the Equal Credit Opportunity Act of 1974 outlawed sex discrimination in consumer credit, not all of its provisions were extended to cover commercial credit. The proposed legislation would forbid lenders to ask a commercial-loan applicant questions about marital status, and would require an explanation of the reasons for rejected loan applications.

Another encouraging development is the recent effort by the federal government to collect and publish comprehensive information about women-owned businesses. Improved data should make them—their achievements and particular problems—more visible to public policymakers. Clearly, women-owned businesses are becoming more important in the national economy. With better data, policymakers will be better able to estimate the needs of women-owned businesses and their impact on the economy.

Women in the Military

CAROLYN BECRAFT

IN THE PAST DECADE women's participation in the U.S. military has increased dramatically. By the end of Fiscal Year 1986, the total number of women in the active U.S. Armed Forces is projected to exceed 216,000: 81,600 women in the U.S. Army (including 11,600 officers); 52,100 women in the Navy (including 7,100 officers); 72,900 women in the Air Force (including 11,900 officers); and 10,189 women in the Marine Corps (including 689 officers) (Women's Equity Action League [WEAL], 1986). Military women today have access to education and training opportunities in a system that assures not only equal pay for equal work but also pay equity. And many serve in jobs that can clearly be considered nontraditional.

Women's participation in the military is not just a recent phenomenon. American women have served in every war that our nation has fought. However, until World War II, most women, except nurses, served in an auxiliary capacity.

Over 350,000 American women served in World War II, many in the European, African, and Pacific war zones. Seventy-seven American servicewomen were taken prisoner of war in the Philippines and were incarcerated for over three years; five women captured on Guam were imprisoned in Japan (Holm, 1982). At war's end, most of the women who had served in the military were discharged and sent home without ceremony.

Following World War II, Congress and the Armed Forces began to assess the contributions of military women and the possibility of continuing to use women in the peacetime services. In 1948, Congress passed the Women's Armed Services Act establishing in law the right for women to be included as permanent (as opposed to auxiliary or temporary) members of the military. While the act provided permanent status for women, it also placed restrictions on their numbers and on the ranks and types of jobs that women could hold.

At the same time, Congress passed two combat exclusion laws that limited the kinds of duties to which servicewomen could be assigned: 10 U.S.C.S. 8549 states that female members of the Air Force, except nurses and other professionals such as attorneys and physicians, "may not be assigned to duty in aircraft engaged in combat missions"; and 10 U.S.C.S. 6015, further amended in 1978, prevents the secretary of the Navy from assigning women permanently to "combat" vessels. (It should be noted that there is no law excluding women from combat in the Army. 10 U.S.C.S. 3012 provides that the secretary of the Army may assign, detail, and prescribe the duties of members of the Army. The Army has, however, determined its policies regarding the role of women by attempting to remain consistent with the "intent of Congress" when combat exclusion laws were enacted for the Navy and the Air Force.)

Throughout the 1950s and 1960s, women accounted for approximately 1.5 percent of military personnel, and women's roles were severely limited. Even during the Vietnam conflict, when the numbers of military nurses increased dramatically, the military's female proportion did not exceed two percent.

In 1973, the opportunities for women in the military

began to change with the end of the male draft and the
beginning of the All Volunteer Force. Faced with having to
recruit individuals to fill military jobs from a shrinking pool
of young men, military force planners began to view women
as a resource.

"In the past decade, women's participation in the military has increased
dramatically." Charlie Company, shown here, was the first Marine Corps
company to include women in its twenty-one week training program.
© *Eddie Adams / Contact / Woodfin Camp & Associates*

Concurrently, opportunities for women in general in our
society were enhanced by the passage of the Civil Rights Act
and Title IX of the Education Amendments. In addition,
many of the legal impediments that had previously limited
women's participation in the military were removed by court
decisions and legislation. *Crawford* v. *Cushman* (531 F.2d
114 [2d Cir., 1976]), established the right of military women
who bear children to remain in the service; *Frontiero* v. *Rich-
ardson* (411 U.S. 677) assured military women the same enti-

tlements for their dependents as military men; P.L. 94–106 opened the military service academies to women; and P.L. 95–485 allowed women to serve on certain categories of ships.

During the late 1970s, with the active encouragement of then-Secretary of Defense Harold Brown, the numbers of and opportunities for military women increased dramatically. Women were aggressively recruited into the mainstream of the services. Women were trained as pilots in the Army, Air Force, and Navy. Air Force women entered the missile field. Navy women exercised their newly won legal right to serve on ships. The Women's Army Corps was disbanded, and Army women were integrated into all job categories except those which were classified as "close combat" jobs. By 1980, the percentage of women in the military had increased to 8.5.

Opportunities for military women in the 1980s have continued to increase in spite of a rocky period (1980–84) when the Army attempted to restrict the role of women. Military women now hold such nontraditional jobs as truck driver, communications specialist, flight mechanic, military police officer, intelligence specialist, and aircraft mechanic. Defense Department data show that women are promoted at a faster rate than men. Thousands of military women are ready to move into positions that serve as steppingstones to policy positions in the Department of Defense. In 1986, 12 women held the rank of Brigadier General or Rear Admiral.

Yet even now, job and promotion opportunities for many military women continue to be curtailed because of combat exclusion laws and policies based on the outdated World War II definition of "combat" as occurring on a static battlefield with fixed lines. Today's war zone is acknowledged by military experts to be fluid, with no defined "front line." In fact, military strategists theorize that the first strikes of battle will

be targeted on the rear of the battlefield to knock out the
supply line; thus, the personnel—women and men—who
provide combat *support* are likely to be among the early casu-
alties.

Furthermore, the military has frequently redefined "combat" in order to utilize women personnel where needed.
Therefore, while today women make up 10 percent of the
total active military force, women's upward mobility continues to be hampered by a combination of military tradition
and changing interpretations of combat exclusion laws and
policies.

Nevertheless, although military women still face outdated
stereotypes about women's roles, their continued advancement throughout this decade and beyond is likely to be assured by the following:

1. The declining birth rates of the late 1960s and 1970s
have greatly diminished the number of 18-year-old males
from which the military draws its recruits every year. By the
year 1995, it is expected that if the services are to be maintained at their current sizes and proportions of males, one out
of every three males of military age would have to be recruited
into the military. This is a level that has never been approached with volunteers; consequently, the military is certain to consider the pool of 18-year-old females a vital recruiting resource.

2. Women have been one of the keys to the success of the
All Volunteer Force. Not only has the education level of
female recruits been consistently higher than that of males,
but the female proportion of the active duty force has grown
from two percent in 1973 to 10 percent in 1986. In the late
1970s and early 1980s the services had difficulty in reaching
their quotas for male recruits. In order to maintain their

forces at the numerical levels attained in the late 1970s and early 1980s without recruiting women, they would have been forced to reintroduce the draft. The same situation will apply in the late 1980s and 1990s. Currently there is no public sentiment to return to the draft.

3. In an effort to retain talented personnel in the mid-levels, the military is increasingly taking steps to assure career progression for them. As women progress through the ranks, the military will almost certainly continue to reevaluate its classification of combat jobs in order to assure continued career progression for women.

4. As large numbers of women enter and succeed in non-traditional jobs throughout our society, the military's rationale for prohibiting the assignment of women to certain categories of jobs becomes harder to justify. Although military tradition is slow to change, it is bound to adjust to the reality that women are succeeding—and earning public support and respect—as astronauts, politicians, athletes, business executives, firefighters, aviators, ambassadors, and clergy, and in myriad other jobs once thought inappropriate for women.

Women in Science

BETTY M. VETTER

THE STATUS OF WOMEN IN science today, and their prospects for the future, are better understood when viewed against a brief historical background.

Women's colleges were the major source of science baccalaureate education for women in the late nineteenth century, although some other private and public universities admitted women, both as undergraduates and as graduate students. Although women's representation in science education was small, by the 1920s women were earning substantial proportions of doctorates awarded in all the science fields, including 16 percent of those in the life sciences, eight percent of those in the physical sciences, and 17 percent of those in the social sciences. However, steady increases in the numbers of women in science ended in 1929, and their proportion of doctorate awards fell off during the Depression. A slight increase during World War II was followed by an abrupt drop beginning in the mid-1940s, when veterans returned home, armed with the G.I. bill, to fill the nation's colleges to overflowing.

Many educational opportunities for women were closed off in the post-war years. Higher admissions standards for women than for men were established to assure room for the veterans, and many of the best universities had quotas for women that eliminated even those who met the higher admissions standards. The proportion of women among new doctoral scientists dropped steadily, reaching a twentieth century low in the 1950s, when women earned less than four percent of the doctorates awarded in the physical sciences, and only nine percent and 11 percent in the life and social sciences, respectively.

The beginnings of the women's movement in the 1960s, coupled with a gradual understanding by girls and young women that they needed to prepare themselves for the world of work, brought increasing numbers of women into college, and into science fields. From 1960 to 1984, women earned almost 56,000 doctorates in science and an additional 1,000 in engineering; 36,100 of these degrees were awarded between 1974 and 1984. Women's share of all doctorates awarded in science increased from about eight percent in 1960 to 17 percent in 1974, and to 29 percent in 1984. However, during this period there has been little shift in field selection for women, who continue to show highest representation in the social and life sciences.

Most of the increase in science degrees can be attributed to an increase in the proportion of women among students completing degrees at all levels and in all fields. Women's share of science degrees—although lagging behind their share of degrees in all fields—increased markedly between 1973 and 1983: from 33 to 45 percent of bachelors' degrees; from 25 to 39 percent of masters' degrees; and from 16 to 29 percent of Ph.D.s.

Despite laws and executive orders requiring nondiscrimination, differential treatment of women and men did not immediately disappear, and equality of opportunity does not yet exist, even for students. Nevertheless, both the educational climate and employment opportunities for women scientists have certainly improved over the past 15 years, and continued improvement probably will result from efforts by

Biologist Roxie Laybourne of the Smithsonian Institution. Today, nearly one in four scientists is a woman, up from one in seven a decade ago.
© *Kenneth Garrett / Woodfin Camp, Inc.*

universities to attract good students from a shrinking population of college-age students.

Even with improved opportunities, however, there is serious doubt that the proportion of women entering science and engineering will continue to grow. Recent evidence indicates that although women are earning their proportionate half of bachelors' and masters' degrees overall, their rate of increase in earning science degrees is leveling off or even turning down. The announced plans of freshman women show a decline over the past two years in the percentage planning majors in computer science, physical science, and biological science, so that the numbers of women completing degrees in those fields may shrink faster than the total graduating classes over the next decade (Vetter and Babco, 1986). Because of the length of the educational pipeline, the proportion of women earning Ph.D.s in science should continue to increase for a few more years, but as current graduate students complete their highest degrees, the proportion of women in succeeding student groups probably will remain stable or drop slightly.

The increase in the number of women entering the science labor force has been sufficient to change the gender ratio among scientists from one in seven a decade ago to one in four today. Nevertheless, women have by no means yet reached equality with men having similar credentials. Some of the differential is attributable to sex differences in field choices, or to the more recent entry of women into the labor force. However, even when such factors as field, years of experience, employment sector, and degree level are controlled, differences remain, and all of them are negative for women. For example, women have higher unemployment rates than men in every field of science, at every degree level, and at every experience level. In 1984, women accounted for 42 percent of involuntarily unemployed scientists, even though, as noted above, their proportion in the science labor force overall was 25 percent.

In each of the seven biennial surveys of the population with doctoral degrees in science conducted by the National Research Council since 1973, unemployment rates for women have been found to be two to five times higher than for men, with some variation by field. Generally, the higher the unemployment rate for men, the wider the gap between the unemployment rates of men and women, an indication that women may have more difficulty than men in finding jobs in a tight job market.

Among employed scientists, women continue to fare less well than men in terms of status or rank, tenure or other job security, salary, and promotion, regardless of employment sector.

Women were 21 percent of all scientists employed at colleges and universities in 1985, but their proportion of faculty positions, tenured positions, and tenure-track positions is well below this figure. They were, for example, slightly less than 18 percent of all academically employed doctoral scientists in 1985, but more than 31 percent of those were neither tenured nor in a tenure-track. Although proportions differ by field, a gap exists in every field.

Even with tenure, women move up the professorial ranks more slowly than tenured men. Among academically employed scientists who earned their doctorates during the 1960s, more than 70 percent of the men but only about 42 percent of the women had reached the rank of professor as of 1983.

In industry, men are considerably more likely than

women with similar levels of experience to be engaged in research and development and in higher-paying management, while women are more likely than men to list their principal activity as reporting/computing or production/inspection.

Women earn less than men in every field of science, in every employment sector, at every degree level, and at every level of experience, although there is some recent evidence that this may be changing for women who have entered the labor force in the past decade. Beginning salaries of male and female science graduates with recent bachelors' degrees are more nearly in balance than at any later career stage. In 1985, salary offers to women with new bachelors' degrees in mathematics averaged nearly 99 percent of offers to their male peers; the ratio was nearly 90 percent for graduates in the biological sciences. But salary differences between men and women increase with additional years of experience, regardless of degree level, field, or type of employer. For example, in 1985, the ratio of women's to men's salaries among medical scientists with Ph.D.s widened from 94 percent at five or fewer years since the degree was awarded, to less than 73 percent 21 to 25 years afterward (National Research Council, pre-publication data provided to the author).

Despite the evidence of continuing inequality for women in the science community, women have nevertheless made real strides in increasing their participation in science over the past decade at every degree level and in every field and employment sector. Fifty-one women were members of the National Academy of Sciences in 1986, representing 3.5 percent of the total membership of 1,477. Only 60 women have been elected since the academy's founding in 1863, but three of the 59 new members elected in 1986 were women. Several of the major scientific societies, including the American Association for the Advancement of Science and the American Chemical Society, now have or recently had women presidents.

Continued gains for women in science are not assured, however, and even some gains of the past decade may be lost. Progress so far has occurred in a positive policy climate of legalized opportunities for equal educational access, supportive changes in society's view of the role of women, and favorable political backing. A change in this climate from supportive to hostile, or even to neutral, might be expected to dampen further growth in the participation of women in science, as well as their continued reach toward equality.

Women in Broadcasting

SALLY STEENLAND

TWENTY YEARS AGO, so few women appeared regularly on television and radio network news programs that they could almost be counted on the fingers of one hand: Barbara Walters, Marlene Sanders, Nancy Dickerson, Pauline Frederick, Liz Trotta, and very few others made up the entire group. Today, most viewers and listeners can reel off the names of at least a dozen well-known network news-women: Jane Pauley, Diane Sawyer, Leslie Stahl, Connie Chung, Joan Lunden, Ann Compton, Susan Stamberg, Judy Woodruff, and more.

The increase in the number of celebrated media women is the visible—and audible—evidence of the considerable progress women have made over the last two decades in gaining jobs in the broadcast industry, behind, as well as in front of, the camera or mike. Exact figures are hard to gather in an industry that employs so many people but keeps no centralized, standard employment records. Nevertheless, it is clear that overall, the employment picture for women in broadcasting is better today than it was even 10 years ago, although much of the progress did occur during the 1970s, largely in response to affirmative action regulations, pressure from women's organizations, and lawsuits.

Women have also made inroads in the major Hollywood production studios as writers, directors, and producers; have started their own production companies; and have created jobs as freelancers working for all three networks. This article, however, focuses on women employed in news at both the networks and local commercial stations across the country; it also looks briefly at the general employment profile for women at commercial television and radio stations.

Women in Network News

The most highly prized jobs in the broadcasting industry are the anchors of the evening news at the three major commercial television networks (ABC, CBS, NBC). Together, these programs command a viewing audience of more than 47 million American viewers. The anchors themselves are highly compensated, famous, and powerful; in fact, a few of them, such as Walter Cronkite, have become veritable American institutions. And all of them are male.

Except for a short time in the mid-1970s when Barbara Walters briefly co-anchored the ABC evening news program, every anchor at all three networks since the advent of network nightly news programs has been a man. And since all three current anchors are relatively young men, that situation is not likely to change for the next decade or two.

Just below the anchors in prestige and prominence are the network reporters who appear on the news each night from locations all over the country and around the world. The Washington bureau correspondents are preeminent and receive the most air time. In 1985, out of a total of 91 Washington bureau correspondents for all three networks, only 16 (18 percent) were women (Flander, 1985).

Moreover, women network reporters, both in Washington and elsewhere, appear on the air much less often than their male counterparts. A 1986 study conducted by the NOW Legal Defense and Education Fund (NOWLDEF) Media

"While upper-echelon broadcasting executives . . . are still white males, the number of women of all races in key positions in broadcasting is no longer insignificant." (c) LeRoy Woodson / Woodfin Camp, Inc.

Project found that stories filed by women correspondents accounted for less than 15 percent of all on-air stories at all three networks during the month of March (NOWLDEF, 1986). This represents an increase of only five percent over the decade; a 1977 report by the U.S. Commission on Civil Rights found that stories filed by women accounted for about 10 percent of the on-air stories that year (U.S. Commission on Civil Rights, 1977).

The picture is even bleaker for minority women reporters. The Media Project study found that stories filed by women of color represented only nine-tenths of one percent of all on-air stories in March 1986.

Women in Local News

The picture looks brighter for women in local news. In 1982, 36 percent of the local television news anchors were women, up from 11 percent in 1972. Moreover, 92 percent of all TV stations had a female anchor for at least one of their regular news programs (Stone, 1985).

There are also more women working in television and radio news jobs behind the scenes. In 1985, 31 percent of television and radio news staffers were women (26 percent were white women, five percent women of color), in occupations ranging from support staff to technical positions to management roles. Women accounted for 11 percent of local television news directors—the people who decide which stories get on the air each night—up from less than one percent in 1972. They were also 20 percent of radio news directors, up from four percent in 1972 (Stone, 1985).

These statistics are evidence of progress; they are also evidence that women still have a long way to go. While there are more women reporters than there used to be, they receive relatively little air time compared to their male peers. Minority female news correspondents, in particular, are rarely seen on the television screen. And although women have increased their share of news-management jobs, they have yet to attain decisionmaking positions in significant numbers.

Lest one think that such goals are impossible to achieve, consider National Public Radio (NPR), a national news network with critically acclaimed reporting, good ratings, and extreme fan loyalty. Half of NPR's reporters are female, as are many of its anchors, broadcast executives, and producers. In fact, not only is NPR staffed primarily by women in both on-air and off-air positions, but women correspondents at NPR cover all topics, including politics and crime, long considered the exclusive territory of male reporters. When "experts" are interviewed for a news piece at NPR, they are more likely to be female than at other networks, and the NPR news pieces themselves have broken down artificial barriers between "women's stories" and general interest news stories. NPR has developed a cadre of seasoned professional reporters and has won many awards for its news programs.

It must be noted, however, that public radio—like public television—pays salaries far below those paid by commercial stations; members of the NPR news staff, acclaimed though they may be, earn far less than their counterparts in commercial broadcasting (where, it should also be noted, women typically earn less than their male counterparts).

Women at Commercial Television and Radio Stations

In the broadcasting industry as a whole, the employment picture for women has changed little over the past five years. Since 1981, about one-third of all employees in commercial broadcasting have been women; of the some 170,000 commercial broadcasting employees in 1985, 37 percent were female. Almost 22,500 of these women worked in commercial television; 21,200 worked in commercial radio; and 8,800 worked at broadcast headquarters (ABC, CBS, NBC, and the corporate headquarter offices of other stations [National Association of Broadcasters, 1985]).

The National Association of Broadcasters (NAB), the trade association that represents TV and radio broadcasters, has also looked at women's representation in the various job categories in broadcasting. It has ranked four of these categories "top" in terms of salary and decisionmaking power. These are: (1) officers and managers (general manager, station manager, sales manager, etc.); (2) professionals (announcers, writers, on-air presenters, reporters, anchors, etc.); (3) technicians (engineers, camera operators, etc.); and (4) sales personnel (account executives, sales representatives, etc.). Not surprisingly, although women have made some gains in penetrating the top jobs, they still lag behind men. In 1985, 94 percent of the men employed in commercial broadcasting were found in the four top job categories, compared to 64 percent of the women. (Women, however, accounted for 88 percent of all office/clerical job positions in commercial broadcasting, according to in-house materials prepared by the Federal Communications Commission in 1985.)

The very top positions at TV and radio stations are the station officers and managers and the professionals. In 1985, women accounted for 28 and 29 percent, respectively, of all officers and managers of TV and radio stations. In both media, most (84 percent) of the women in these top managerial positions were white. In TV, nine percent were black, five percent were Hispanic, and two percent were Asian. Minority representation among women in top radio management was slightly lower (one percentage point less than in TV for each minority group).

Thirty-six percent of all TV professionals were female in 1985, as were 21 percent of radio professionals. About one in five of these female professionals was a minority woman (the breakdown was virtually identical for women in both media: 12 percent black, five percent Hispanic, and one to two percent Asian).

Women have the smallest representation in the technical job categories, which are still considered "nontraditional" work for women. In 1985, women held only 14 percent of these jobs in commercial television and eight percent in radio. Among those women in technical jobs, however, minorities were rather well-represented: in TV, 14 percent were black, six percent were Hispanic, and two percent were Asian. In radio, 23 percent were black, eight percent Hispanic, and one percent Asian (National Association of Broadcasters, 1985).

Among the top four categories, women have the highest representation in sales. In 1985, they constituted 41 percent of the sales force in commercial television, and 46 percent in radio. About nine of every 10 of the women in sales in both media were white: the racial/ethnic breakdown among women in television sales showed very low representation by minorities—four percent black, four percent Hispanic, and less than one percent Asian—and the breakdown for radio sales was virtually identical.

Conclusion

While upper-echelon broadcasting executives—those who earn the most money and make the most important decisions—are still white males, the number of women of all races in key positions in broadcasting is no longer insignificant. Many of these women are in small rather than large markets and very few earn salaries comparable to men's, but this should change as women increasingly gain experience, earn promotions, and demonstrate ambition. As noted above, NPR women are highly regarded by listeners, and a recent Nielsen ratings study in Chicago showed that television stations with women news anchors were more popular with viewers than stations with all-male news teams. Further research indicated that the public preferred hearing the news from women. Enlightened management, strong enforcement of equal employment laws and regulations, and assertive women employees are certainly necessary to help women continue to make gains in broadcasting, but in the long run it is the approval and confidence of the viewing/listening public that will ensure women's success.

Women and Sports

WENDY LAWRENCE

IN 1971, THE YEAR WHEN most of this year's high school sophomores were born, Susan Hollander, a student in Connecticut, wanted to compete in cross-country running. Because there was no girls' cross-country team at her high school, she sought to join the boys' team. She qualified for the team, but was later barred from competing because the Connecticut Interscholastic Athletic Conference (CIAC) rules forbade coed sports. Susan Hollander challenged the CIAC in court (*Hollander* v. *Connecticut Conference, Inc.*), but she lost. In upholding the CIAC rule, the judge stated: "Athletic competition builds character in our boys. We do not need that kind of character in our girls, the women of tomorrow."

Because there was no legal remedy against it, that kind of thinking not only discouraged women from trying their hand at sports, but also barred them from access to athletic facilities, coaching, teams, and athletic scholarships in the United States until 1972. In the 1970–71 school year, for example, approximately 295,000 girls (or just 7.5 percent of all high school girls) took part in high school sports, compared to 3.5 million boys. Just two years later, the number of girls in high school athletics had risen to 1.3 million—a participation rate of nearly 25 percent—while the rate for boys remained roughly unchanged. The numbers are just as impressive in intercollegiate athletics, discussed in Margaret Dunkle's article in this book.

The undisputed cause of these dramatic changes was the enactment of Title IX of the Education Amendments of 1972. This law forbade sex discrimination in federally aided education programs, including sports. Title IX was the tool women needed to gain access to sports facilities and training from elementary school to college—and they used it.

To assess the status of women in sports in the United States today, one must look at the difference Title IX has made. (It is important to note that Title IX was not directed exclusively at sports programs, however.) "I do not believe we would have made significant progress without Title IX," says Christine Grant, director of women's athletics at the University of Iowa. "In 1969, I came to the States [from Scotland] anticipating terrific opportunities for women," she recalls. "I was totally taken aback. . . . The discrepancies [between men's and women's programs] were appalling" with respect not only to the lack of funding for women's sports but also to social attitudes (*Christian Science Monitor*, July 28, 1985: 23). With the enactment of Title IX, the women's sports revolution began, and its effects can be seen in all areas of women's sports today—among amateurs, including those who participate in informal sports activities on an individual or team basis; among collegiate athletes; and among professional athletes.

The majority of women who participate in sports in the United States do not play on an organized team or through a school program. Rather, most take part in some sort of physical activity or sport on their own or with friends. Jogging, tennis, swimming, cycling, and aerobic dance, according to the Women's Sports Foundation, are the most popular sports for women, and they are usually enjoyed on an individual and informal level. In any case, experts agree that athletic skills must be encouraged and developed at an early age if peak performance is to be achieved in any sport.

When Title IX forced American schools, colleges, and universities to broaden their women's programs (and to provide equal stipends for team travel, uniforms, and equipment, among other things), women were, for the first time, not only widely encouraged to try sports but also provided with resources to help them develop athletic skills. Almost immediately women began to grasp the advantages that Title IX afforded them.

Not only are more and more women participating in sports at all levels, but they are no longer restricted, or restricting themselves, to traditionally acceptable "women's" or co-ed sports, such as gymnastics or tennis. They have ventured into sports that used to be considered either unhealthy for women, or unfeminine, or both. For the first time in Olympic history, the 1984 Games included a marathon for women. It had long been believed that a run of 26.2 miles would be too demanding for women, but 44 women (88 percent of those who started) finished the marathon at the Los Angeles Games. Women are now competing in such sports as auto racing (where Shirley Muldowney holds a number of national track records), bodybuilding, wrestling (16-year-old America Morris made California history when she pinned a varsity boy wrestler in a high school wrestling match), polo, and competitive cycling.

And women's professional sports are no longer the small potatoes they used to be: women are succeeding in getting corporate sponsors to underwrite major tours and competitions in tennis, golf, skating, and skiing. In 1985, for example, the total prize money on the Ladies Professional Golf Tour was $9 million, up from $1.7 million just ten years earlier. The ratio of the prize money for the women's tour to the prize money for the men's tour narrowed as well. However, a large disparity remains: prize money for the men's tour was more than $25 million in 1985.

This disparity is only one of the many that remain for women in sports; although there have been tremendous gains, women's athletics have not yet approached parity with men's by any measure. Although it seems unlikely that the enormous progress women have made in sports at all levels can be reversed, further progress could be halted or severely slowed by the Supreme Court's interpretation of Title IX in

Stanford University pre med student Debi Thomas wins world skating championship in Geneva, March 1986.
AP / Wide World Photos

Grove City College v. *Bell*. On February 24, 1984, the Supreme Court ruled that the receipt of federal money by one department in a college did not necessarily mean that Title IX applied to the entire institution. The *Grove City* ruling, overturning the broad application of Title IX that had prevailed since its enactment, effectively ended the law's usefulness in forcing equality of access to and opportunity in sports. According to Brooklyn College's Linda Carpenter, who has written extensively on Title IX's impact on athletics: "Once the teeth were gone, the spirit, and feeling that 'we'll do right by you' were gone. There is no Title IX in college sports anymore because [college sports] do not have federal support" (*The Seattle Times*, June 8, 1986: C-1).

Already, educational institutions are relaxing their efforts to comply with the spirit of Title IX. Less than a year after the *Grove City* decision, according to Eva Auchincloss, executive director of the Women's Sports Foundation, 23 sex discrimination cases aimed at enforcing compliance with Title IX in educational athletic programs had been dropped (*Chronicle of Higher Education*, August 29, 1984: 31–32). The Reagan administration, which had argued for a narrow interpretation of Title IX, has dropped hundreds of complaints that had been brought before the Justice Department's Office of Civil Rights, the office responsible for investigating Title IX violation complaints.

Will schools and colleges continue to fund women's sports programs voluntarily now that they are no longer required by federal law to do so? Many believe not. Although "mini-Title IXs" have been enacted in some states, enforcement efforts in others have been relaxed since *Grove City*. Legislation (the Civil Rights Restoration Act) has been intro-

duced in the U.S. Congress to put the teeth back into Title
IX (which, it must again be stressed, is by no means relevant
only to athletics), but, as of this writing, the bill is stalled by
controversy over access to abortion. Many fear that, as a
result, the momentum toward equal access to school and
college sports will be stalled as well.

Women in Intercollegiate Sports

MARGARET C. DUNKLE

WOMEN'S ATHLETIC PROGRAMS have undergone profound changes since 1972, when Title IX of the Education Amendments of 1972 was enacted. While no law, by itself, could have propelled all of the enormous changes in programs and attitudes that have occurred in the past 15 years, Title IX provided the legal and symbolic fuel for this progress.

In the preceding article, Wendy Lawrence quotes a judge who, in 1971, expressed the view that participation in competitive athletics was inappropriate for girls. Today, however, most Americans have egalitarian attitudes towards men's and women's sports. For example, six out of seven people (86 percent) believe that participation in sports is important for girls while they are growing up; only slightly more people— 95 percent—believe that sports are important for boys (Miller Brewing Company, 1983: 14, 17).

The 1984 Olympic Games in Los Angeles provided a showcase for the athletic skills of the first generation of post-Title IX female athletes. At these Olympics, U.S. women outperformed U.S. men when it came to winning medals. Women from the United States won 45 percent of all gold medals and 33 percent of all medals awarded to women. U.S. men won a more modest 38 percent of gold medals and 26 percent of all medals awarded to men (Women's Sports Foundation, 1984a: 21).

For the first time in history, and largely because of Title IX, athletic scholarships had financed the college education of many of the women members of the U.S. Olympic team: all 12 members of the gold-medal women's basketball team had athletic scholarships, as did 11 of the 13 members of the volleyball team, 26 of the 42 members of the track and field team, 12 of the 15 players of team handball, and seven of the 16 members of the field hockey team (Women's Sports Foundation, 1984b: 1).

As the following statistics show, the achievements of U.S. female superstars in the 1984 Olympics symbolize the dramatic growth in sports participation and opportunities for women across this country since the early 1970s. In 1971–72, women accounted for 16 percent of all varsity athletes at institutions in the National Collegiate Athletic Association (NCAA). By 1983–84, when NCAA institutions had more than 273,000 varsity athletes, the female proportion of the total had nearly doubled to 31 percent (NCAA, 1974: 5, 13; NCAA, 1984). Women were somewhat better represented among varsity athletes attending the typically smaller institutions belonging to the National Association of Intercollegiate Athletics (NAIA), where the female proportion was 35 percent (National Association of Intercollegiate Athletics, 1984). Overall, of the roughly five percent of all college undergraduates who participate in intercollegiate athletics, about one-third are women (Atwell, 1980: 1).

Most of these female college athletes are white and most come from middle- or upper-income families: close to 80 percent come from families where the father is a professional or manager (Coakley and Pacey, 1984: 233). In 1978, when black women accounted for 12 percent of all female college students, they made up only eight percent of women collegiate athletes (Murphy, 1980: 80). However, the proportion of black women participating in college athletics and receiving athletic scholarships is increasing. Only nine percent of all freshmen women receiving athletic financial aid in 1977 were black, but by 1982 this figure had increased to 15 (Bartell et al., 1984: 2–12).

Far more women have received athletic scholarships in recent years than in the past, but most athletic scholarships continue to go to males. A 1982 study of the highly competitive NCAA Division I institutions found that only 28 percent of the freshmen students receiving athletic financial aid were women. This represents an improvement over 1977, when the comparable percentage was 20 percent. Similarly, less than one percent of all female students—compared to three percent of all male students—received athletic scholarships in 1982.

The situation with respect to funding college athletic programs for women is similar. Although it is a lot better than it used to be, it is not nearly on a par with spending for men's athletics.

In considering budgets for college athletic programs, it should be noted that very few of them, either men's or women's, are self-supporting. For example, 69 percent of the men's programs at NCAA colleges lost money in 1981, with an average deficit of over $250,000 (Raiborn, 1982: 8, 40, 42).

College athletic budgets for women have grown substantially since 1972, when they were estimated to account for one to two percent of the total sports budget (Hanford, 1974: 50). Less than 10 years later (1980–81), the women's share of athletic budgets ranged from 11 to 24 percent of the total, depending on the type of college. Women received the lowest budget percentages at colleges with large football programs (Raiborn, 1982: 23, 46).

The expansion of college athletic programs for women that these increases reflect has not been at the expense of men's athletic programs. According to NCAA figures, men's athletic programs have continued to receive the lion's share of increases in collegiate sports budgets. Between 1978 and 1981, from two-thirds to four-fifths of the budget increases for college sports went to men's programs, regardless of the size or intensity of the athletic program. The disparity was greatest at the institutions with highly competitive (Division I) football teams: here, men's sports received an average of 81 percent of the added sports dollars (ibid.).

Another troubling trend is the disappearance of women coaches. The percentage of women coaching women's athletics actually decreased between 1978 and 1984 in every sport except crew and sailing. Indeed, almost half (46 percent) of all women's teams had male coaches in 1983–84, and in the same year, only 17 percent of women's intercollegiate athletic programs had female athletic directors (Acosta and Carpenter, 1984).

In short, while legal protections (now uncertain) and changed public attitudes have produced both tangible advances for women's athletics and a more receptive climate, the gender gap in sports remains wide.[1]

Women in Unions

ANNE NELSON

A MEDIA OUTCRY was raised in 1985 with the publication of the AFL-CIO's study, *The Changing Situation of Workers and Their Unions*, which drew national attention to declining union membership and asked what could be done about it. Graphs and tables in the national press told the story of the decline: union membership had dropped from 35 percent of the workforce in 1954 to less than 19 percent in the 1980s (AFL-CIO, 1985).

But another tale lies behind these reports. As America's industrial profile has changed with the growth of the service sector and the decline, or at least stagnation, of the heavy manufacturing sector, so too have the profiles of America's workforce in general and its organized workforce in particular. Both have become more female. While job losses in giant "rust-belt" industries have hurt labor's traditional organized base, predominantly male, the percentage of women who have joined labor unions has increased.

Women now constitute 41 percent of the membership in the nation's unions and labor associations, a dramatic increase from 25 percent 10 years ago. This overall proportion has largely escaped attention, in part because occupational segregation is reflected in specific unions (for example, teachers' unions tend to be largely female, steelworkers' to be overwhelmingly male). Nevertheless, women's voices are being heard, and women's issues are receiving attention

throughout the labor movement. And there is growing awareness that the future of organized labor in this country may
depend heavily on its ability to organize large numbers of
women in the workforce. That means organizing white collar
workers and those in the rapidly growing service and retail-
wholesale trades.

Does the proportion of women in union leadership begin
to approximate the proportion of women among the rank
and file? No, but inroads have been made. "Expanding Wom-
en's Role in Unions" reports that in 1979 an estimated 16
percent of all national professional staff positions were filled
by women. "Today," the experts say, "we double that estimate" (Baden, 1986).

And women are gaining key positions. In recent years, the
AFL-CIO has named Dorothy Shields as its Director of Education, making her the first woman to head an AFL-CIO
department, and Cynthia McCaughn coordinates a new
Women's Affairs section. Women lawyers are found in legal
departments at local, district, and national union levels, and
more women sit at the bargaining table as members of nego-
tiating committees—a rare occurrence in the past.

In 1985, Deborah Bell was appointed Director of Research and Negotiation by the huge union representing New
York City's public employees, District Council 37 of the
American Federation of State, County and Municipal Employees (AFSCME). The foremost female staff appointment
in an arena long regarded as male territory, organizing, was
that of Vicki Saporta, named Director of Organizing for the
International Brotherhood of Teamsters in September 1983.

Women are less often found in elective positions than in
appointive staff posts. The 35-member AFL-CIO Executive
Council, in a brave departure from custom, elected its first

woman, Joyce Miller, in 1980, and its second, Barbara Hutch-
inson, in 1982. (In so doing, the council set aside an informal
requirement that all council members be presidents of national unions.)

Four national unions boasted women presidents in 1986:
the National Education Association, the Association of Flight
Attendants, Actors' Equity Association, and the Screen Actors' Guild. At local levels, the number of women elected to
union office is increasing rapidly. A 1985 poll by AFSCME
found that 45 percent of its local union offices were held by
women, as were 33 percent of its local presidencies. The New
York Metro Area Postal Union, the largest postal union local
in the country with 25,000 members, is currently headed by
Josie McMillian. Sandra Feldman was recently elected president of the 91,000-member New York City United Federation of Teachers. In the fall of 1985, Betty Tianti was chosen
to lead Connecticut's AFL-CIO.

"A new chapter in trade union history" was how the
AFL-CIO NEWS (May 10, 1986) characterized the election
of Shirley Carr as president of the Canadian Labor Congress.
As the NEWS pointed out, Carr is "the first woman to head
a national labor body in the western world." Although not
a U.S. triumph, it is close to home.

Too little is known about the routes to success of union
women who are acquiring leadership roles, either elective or
appointed, and it can be difficult even to find out how many
women there are. Unfortunately, as of 1980, the Bureau of
Labor Statistics stopped publishing its *Directory of National
Unions and Employee Associations*, where data on female membership and national officeholders were presented. The government no longer even requests such information on the
national level, and never has requested it from regional or
local unions.

"Women's voices are being heard . . . throughout the labor movement."
Pictured here is a 1986 demonstration of Janitors Local #47 of the Service
Employees International Union, Cleveland, Ohio. *Courtesy SEIU*

The publications and activities—the very growth—of the Coalition of Labor Union Women (CLUW) are strong evidence of the vitality of labor women's desire not only to have women's issues raised but also to give women a strong voice within the leadership. From its original 10 chapters and 5,000 members in 1974, CLUW has grown to today's 75 chapters and 18,000 members. Women's concerns are also given special attention by the AFL-CIO's Department of Professional Employees (DPE), which for 10 years has had a Committee on Salaried and Professional Women. The committee has focused on the progress of technical and professional women, and furthered the development of union staff women. It is the only official women's committee of the AFL-CIO, and both it and CLUW work directly with rank-and-file women members through conferences and education programs.

The efforts of CLUW, the DPE Committee on Salaried and Professional Women, and the national, regional, and local women's committees of unions and employee associations have provided the major vehicles for publicizing the concerns of working women. Their conferences and publications draw the attention of union executive board members, and extend the outreach of union women to others. They create the conditions for legislative alliances.

University labor education, provided at most of the nation's land grant schools, builds the self-confidence and information women need to advance to leadership posts. Annual regional summer schools extend regular education programs for union women. Now in their eleventh year, they are sponsored by the University and College Labor Education Association in cooperation with the AFL-CIO. Fourteen years ago Cornell University pioneered in credit studies for women unionists. The George Meany Center for Labor Studies offers national leadership programs.

What do women unionists cite as the issues they care most about? Pay equity is number one. Job discrimination and sexual harassment are high on the list. Dependent care is of increasing importance. The effect of office technology is receiving new attention, and with it comes concern about the growth of the part-time workforce made possible by computer routinization of work. Two-thirds of all part-time workers are female and 30 percent of them are involuntary part-timers. Almost 18 percent of the country's workforce is composed of part-time employees in jobs characterized by low pay, poor benefits, and lack of promotion opportunities.

Pay equity has union-wide endorsement, supported by a convention vote of the AFL-CIO. AFSCME has led the way; it and the Service Employees International Union (SEIU) have both successfully bargained pay equity contracts in California. AFSCME litigation in the state of Washington has received the greatest notice, from the 1983 decision of Judge Jack Tanner supporting equity remedies to the final out-of-court settlement in 1986. In Minnesota, AFSCME also succeeded in getting support for a phased restructuring of wages. So far, the pay equity campaign has been directed largely at public employers. Can it succeed in the corporate sector? It is too soon to tell, but publicity accompanying successful pay equity drives appears to have prompted positive thoughts among private employers. Business Week reported that companies are reexamining their pay scales for men and women, and are quietly evening up the disparities (Bernstein, 1986: 52).

In many ways, the ultimate issue confronting women's leadership in labor organizations is to increase the number of women carrying union cards, for unions are political organizations. In 1985, the median weekly wages of union women were 32 percent higher than those of non-union women, but collective bargaining has not always ensured equal employment opportunities for women. Unions, for their part, have not concentrated on organizing the predominantly female occupations. Today, labor is trying to change that pattern and to learn how to appeal to the traditionally difficult-to-organize woman worker.

A promising approach is exemplified by the evolution of the office workers' network launched by Karen Nussbaum in 1975. Begun as a series of caucuses where office workers could exchange advice and plan strategy, it became 9 to 5, the National Association of Working Women (of which Nussbaum is president). This pre-union form of organization led to later union affiliation by some chapters with the SEIU and formation of SEIU's District 925. Such innovative and non-rigid combinations of "union and non-union" organizations may provide the key to drawing substantial numbers of women workers into the labor movement.

Women in Higher Education

DONNA SHAVLIK *and*
JUDITH G. TOUCHTON

THE ISSUE FOR women in higher education—administrators, faculty, staff, and students—is not whether they have made progress over the last 15 years; they certainly have. Rather, the issue is whether gains for women have been coming as fast as they should have, and whether they will accelerate as time goes on.

In 1975, when the Office of Women in Higher Education of the American Council on Education began to collect data on women chief executive officers (CEOs) at institutions of higher learning, only 148 such institutions, five percent in all, were headed by women. By 1985 that number had risen to over 300; about eight percent of these were minority women. A doubling of the number of college presidents over the decade undoubtedly represents progress, but the current rate of increase in the proportion of women CEOs will not produce parity with men until the year 2070. Women are still rarely viewed as leaders; governing boards continue to allow themselves to say that "our institution or our community is not ready for a woman"; and women, more than men, still seem to compare themselves to ideals of leadership rather than to the current set of leaders. Those women who are presidents do enjoy a high degree of respect, and in those instances where the term applies, have dealt effectively with being "first." In a recent study of college and university presidencies, *Presidents Make a Difference* (1984), Clark Kerr stated: "I was impressed particularly by the high quality of a number of women presidents who probably had a tougher road getting to the top." As Kerr's and other statements confirm, women possess the ability, the preparation, and the interest to assume academic leadership positions. When this is more widely recognized, the rate of growth in the numbers of women college and university presidents should begin to accelerate.

Women have also increased their proportion among senior administrators other than presidents, i.e., vice presidents, provosts, and deans, in the last 10 years. In 1975, there were 1,625 such women throughout all the 2,689 accredited institutions of higher education in the United States. This worked out to an average of 0.6 per institution. By 1983 the total number of senior women administrators had reached 3,084, an average of 1.1 for each of the, by then, 2,824 accredited institutions. Again, undeniable progress was made, but, assuming that second-level administrative positions require less administrative experience than college presidencies, this progress might have been expected to be more dramatic than it actually was.

Of the more than 400,000 full-time faculty members on college and university campuses in the fall of 1983, women accounted for 27.3 percent, up from 22.3 percent in 1972. This is another clear gain, yet it should be stressed that the proportion of women full-time faculty members today doesn't approach what it was more than a century ago (36.4 percent in 1879). Moreover, even though the total number of full-time and part-time women faculty has grown steadily since 1974, the percentage of women at the full professor level has

changed very little since then. In 1972, women constituted
9.8 percent of all full professors; by 1983, the women's share
of these positions had risen only to 10.7 percent. One reason
for such slow growth is that a greater proportion of women
were promoted to full professorships in the 1940s, and, now
that those women are retiring, newly tenured women are not
moving as quickly as men into the most senior faculty ranks.

Data on minority female faculty and administrators are
not readily available for the comparative years, but it is important to note that minuscule advancement was made by Hispanic, Asian Pacific, and American Indian women in both
administrative and faculty positions from 1979 to 1981. Black
women, however, experienced slight declines in both positions during this period.

Women students constituted 52 percent of all college
students in 1984, compared to only 46 percent in 1974. They
were slightly more likely than men to attend part time in both
years. Women have been proportionately represented among
college students in recent years; that is, they account for 52
percent of all. In 1982, of the 6.4 million college women, 15
percent were members of minority groups, and among blacks,
American Indians, and Hispanics, women's enrollment exceeded that of men. Only among Asian Pacific students did
men outnumber women (Melandez and Wilson, 1985).
Among graduate students, however, men accounted for the
larger proportion—51 percent in 1984.

Not all students in higher education earn degrees; however, women are increasing their share of degrees at every
level of post-secondary education. In 1974, women were
awarded 45 percent of all bachelors' degrees; in 1980, their
share was up to 50 percent, and, in 1982, it reached 51
percent. (Earned-degree data for minority women are availa-

ble only for 1980, when they constituted 14 percent of women earning bachelors' degrees.) Similar gains occurred among master's degree recipients, of which the female proportion—45 percent in 1974—was 50 percent in both 1980 and 1982. Minority women accounted for 12 percent of females awarded masters' degrees in 1980. Women are making slower, but very steady, progress at the doctoral level. Among all recipients of doctorates, women accounted for 21 percent in 1974, 31 percent in 1980 (0.3 percent were earned by minority women), and 33 percent in 1982. The increase in the proportion of women among the recipients of first professional degrees (e.g., law and medicine) increased from 12 percent to 30 percent between 1974 and 1982.

One more important development that should not be overlooked is the tremendous growth in the availability and dissemination on college and university campuses of knowledge about women. Women's studies courses, which 15 years ago were few in number and found on few campuses, have multiplied to thousands of courses on hundreds of campuses today.

Women's achievements at all levels of higher education are encouraging, but they are not cause for complacency. Often, progress appears significant largely because women's representation started so dismally small. Not only time but continuing effort will be needed to ensure that America's colleges and universities give full representation to, and take full advantage of, women's talents, perspectives, and strengths.

The Classroom Climate
for Women

BERNICE R. SANDLER

THE OBVIOUS BARRIERS that for so many years stood between women and equal educational opportunity are largely gone. Today, female students can enter academic institutions and fields of study of which their mothers and grandmothers could only dream. Yet, like society as a whole, the academic world is still infected with attitudes that can militate against achievements by women. Thus, although women may now attend most of the same colleges and universities that men do, and be taught in the same class by the same faculty, the female student's classroom experiences are likely to be less positive than her male peer's.

The problem is that although most faculty want—and, indeed, try—to be fair, faculty of both sexes tend to treat female students quite differently from male students. In a variety of subtle ways (often so subtle that neither the professor nor the student notices that anything untoward has occurred), faculty behavior can convey to every student in the room the implication that women are not as worthwhile as men and that they are not expected to participate as fully as men in class, in college, or in life.

These findings were reported in 1982, when the first comprehensive report on the classroom climate for women students was published by the Project on the Status and Education of Women (PSEW) at the Association of American Colleges. Based on a review of the literature, as well as campus and individual reports, the paper, entitled *The Classroom Climate: A Chilly One for Women?* by Roberta Hall and the present author, identified over 30 ways in which faculty treated female students differently from male students. Following the publication of the report, some campuses began to pay attention to this issue by disseminating the paper to their faculty, conducting seminars and workshops, and undertaking related research. Nevertheless, both formal and informal information relayed to PSEW indicate that this remains a major problem across the country.

Some of the behaviors observed in the study are so small that they might be considered trivial. They do not happen in every class, nor do they happen all the time, and as isolated incidents, they may have little effect. But when they occur repeatedly, their cumulative effect can damage women's self-confidence, inhibit their learning and classroom participation, and lower their academic and career aspirations. (See, for example, El-Khawas, 1980.)

The behaviors fall into two categories: ways in which female students are singled out and treated differently, and ways in which they are ignored. Some examples:

• Professors tend to make more eye contact with men than with women, so that male students are more likely to feel recognized and encouraged to participate in class.

• Professors are more likely to nod and gesture, and, in general, to pay attention when male students are talking. When women talk, faculty are less likely to be attentive; they may shuffle papers or look at their watches.

- Professors interrupt female students more than male students, thus communicating, at least in part, that what women have to say is less important than what men have to say. Moreover, when a male student is interrupted, the purpose is generally to expand on what the student is saying. Faculty interruptions of a female student, however, often consist of remarks unrelated to what the student has been saying—such as comments on her appearance—that have the effect of bringing her discussion to a halt.

- Female students are not called upon as frequently as male students, even when the women are clearly eager to participate in classroom discussion, again suggesting that what men have to say is more important than what women have to say.

- Male students are called by name more often than female students, as if men had more individual identity than women.

- Women are more likely to be asked questions that require factual answers (e.g., "*When* did the revolution occur?"), while men are more likely to be asked higher-order questions (e.g., "*Why* did the revolution occur?"). Such behavior may subtly communicate a presumption that women are less capable of independent analysis than men.

- Male students are "coached" more than female students by faculty probing for a more elaborate answer (such as, "What do you mean by that?"). This gives male students an advantage, since probing not only encourages students to speak and develop their ideas, but also implies that they know the answer if they will just explain it more fully.

- Faculty are more likely to respond extensively to men's comments than to women's comments. Women's comments are more likely to be ignored or to receive an ambiguous "uh-huh." Often, when a point made by a female student elicits no response, the same point made subsequently by a male student elicits a positive response from the professor, who gives the male student approval and credit for the point as if it had not been raised previously. Thus, men receive much more reinforcement than women for intellectual participation.

Why should these behaviors occur? Many certainly have their origins in patterns and attitudes established long before students and faculty reach the college classroom. A major underlying reason is that throughout our society, what women do tends to be seen as less valuable than what men do.

Numerous experiments have demonstrated that devaluation of women occurs. (See, for example, Paludi and Bauer, 1983; Paludi and Strayer, 1985.) A typical experiment involves two groups of people. Each group is presented with several items, such as articles, works of art or résumés, and asked to evaluate them. The items shown to each group are identical, but those items ascribed to women for one group are ascribed to men for the other. The results of these experiments are remarkably consistent: if people believe a woman was the creator, they will rank the item lower than if they believe it was created by a man. Both men and women devalue those items ascribed to females. Studies of how people view success shows a similar pattern: both men and women tend to attribute males' successes to talent, females' successes to luck. (See, for example, Erkut, 1979.)

Thus, female students can be just as well prepared, just as articulate, and just as willing to participate in discussion as their male peers, and still receive considerably less attention and less reinforcement from faculty than do male students. No wonder women students generally participate less in class than men!

The subtle behaviors described above are by no means the only factors that chill the classroom climate for women. Faculty remarks that overtly disparage women are still surprisingly prevalent. PSEW staff continually receive reports of such remarks. So is sexual harassment, which is experienced by 20 to 30 percent of all female students. The campus surveys in PSEW's files confirm these figures. The relatively small percentage of women on most faculties means that female students typically have fewer role models, less opportunity to benefit from mentoring, and less opportunity for informal talk with faculty (male faculty are more likely to engage in those conversations with male students). And there is a widespread lack of structural support for women's concerns: on many campuses there is no women's center at all; on many others the centers are inadequately funded. There are too few programs for reentry students (among whom women substantially predominate); there are still too few women's studies courses, and those that exist too often receive only limited support, if not denigration. All of these factors communicate to female students that although they have been allowed inside the gates, women are still outsiders in the academic world.

Women in Theatre

JOYCE VAN DYKE

WOMEN in theatre include actors, playwrights, directors, choreographers, literary managers, stage managers, producers, designers (usually of costumes, less often of sets or lighting), lyricists, composers, casting agents, and business managers.

Theatre is an art form, but as a communal and publicly created art form, it is closely tied to the marketplace. So it is not surprising that the picture of women in theatre has many features in common with that of women in other occupations and industries.

One of these features is that there aren't many women at the top, especially on Broadway, unless they are appearing on stage. (Even then, most plays have more parts for men than for women.) Of approximately 30 plays on Broadway in the 1983–84 season, only two (or about 6.6 percent) were by women playwrights. Women directors on Broadway are even scarcer: a 1984 study of directors and scenic designers by the League of Professional Theater Women found that out of 261 plays produced on Broadway in the five seasons from 1977 to 1982, only nine productions (3.4 percent) were directed by women. Female scenic designers were similarly underrepresented on Broadway, and nearly all of those surveyed said they felt excluded from "old-boy networks."

The 1985–86 season showed a similar pattern, although women writers were better represented. Out of approximately 35 shows that opened on Broadway, four were written by women. Two of those writers not only directed their own

shows, but were the only women to direct on Broadway during the season. Emily Mann directed her play, *Execution of
Justice,* and Jane Wagner directed the "kozmic soup opera"
she wrote for Lily Tomlin, *The Search for Signs of Intelligent Life
in the Universe.*

Still scarce in commercial theatre, women are concentrated in the not-for-profit theatre: off-Broadway, off-off Broadway, and regional theatres, small theatres, and experimental
theatres across the country. Most of the theatre-members of
the Theatre Communications Group (the national service
organization for the not-for-profit professional theatre) have
at least one woman in a major staff position. But the women
are usually found on the business side (managing director, or
director of marketing or development), rather than in the top
artistic positions such as artistic director or producing director. However, some of the major regional theatres, including
Washington, D.C.'s Arena Stage and Houston's Alley
Theatre, as well as over 30 off-Broadway and off-off-Broadway
theatres in New York, have female artistic directors or co-
directors.

The founder and artistic director of the Manhattan
Theatre Club, Lynne Meadow, has said: "I definitely think
the situation is changing. . . . When I was at the Yale Drama
School in the late 1960s, I was the only woman in my class;
there were no women directors in the class ahead of me and
no women in the class behind me" ("Women Directing More
Plays . . . ," 1984).

In off-Broadway productions, women artists are more numerous. If one-act plays are included, women wrote over 25
and directed over 25 of the more than 150 off-Broadway
shows in 1985–86. (About ten plays in each category—writing and directing—were one-act plays.)

Across the country during the same season, women's

theatres and theatre groups were active. One of the oldest of these is the Women's Interart Theatre in New York. Founded in 1969, it has about 300 members and promotes the work and interaction of women artists in as many media as possible. Like other small theatres in New York, Women's Interart is currently struggling to hang on to affordable quarters in the neighborhood which, during its long tenancy, it has helped to make more valuable.

Another women's theatre group is the Women's Project at the American Place Theatre in New York. With about 100 director-members and 100 writer-members, it produces both plays and rehearsed readings each season. In March 1986, the Project produced *Women Heroes*, a series of six one-act plays about historical and imaginary characters.

In Boston in 1986, the Women in Theatre Festival (in its second year) drew theatre women from California, Oregon, Nebraska, Indiana, Minnesota, Maryland, New York, New England, and England. Among the companies represented were Thunder Thighs from Baltimore, At the Foot of the Mountain from Minneapolis, and Spiderwoman from New York City—three groups that work as collectives and that presented improvised works without formal plots. (Only seven of the 20 pieces presented at the festival were plays.) As one commentator summed up the festival: "Characters and heroines were created to struggle in an unjust world: some did, others got stuck, still others died. And despite the [festival's] attempts to be apolitical, it is clear that there is something astir in feminism which is being reflected, rather than healed, in our theatre" (Kingsbury, 1986).

Women in theatre are still fighting for freedom, which includes, in the words of playwright-director Maria Irene Fornes, "the freedom to deal with themes other than gender" (Fornes, 1985: 15).

Women and Reproduction

RACHEL BENSON GOLD *and*
CORY L. RICHARDS

BEARING CHILDREN AND raising a family are central to the aspirations of most American women. Equally important is the ability to do so under the best possible circumstances. Over the course of a woman's "childbearing years" (roughly, between the ages of 15 and 44), she faces a series of reproductive options and opportunities, but also a series of challenges and obstacles.

Since most American women want to have only a few children, the challenge they face for most of their childbearing years is avoiding an unintended pregnancy. Of the 55 million women of reproductive age in the United States in 1982, the most recent year for which data are available, one-third were pregnant, seeking to become pregnant, infertile or not in a sexual relationship, but the remaining two-thirds, 36 million women, were at risk of an unintended pregnancy. (Unless otherwise indicated, all data are from the Alan Guttmacher Institute.)

More than 90 percent of these women used some method of contraception. Nearly one-third of them reported that either they or their partners had been sterilized, making surgical sterilization the most common form of contraception. Nearly 29 percent of users relied on oral contraceptives, and 23 percent used a barrier method such as the diaphragm, condom, or foam. Seven percent reported using an intrauterine device (IUD), although the number of women using IUDs will likely drop dramatically, since virtually all IUDs have been removed from the U.S. market as a result of the crisis in liability insurance. The remaining contraceptive users relied on periodic abstinence, withdrawal, or other methods.

The kind of contraceptive a woman uses typically varies with her age, marital status, race, and socioeconomic status. Oral contraceptive use is the most common method among teenagers, and use of the pill peaks at ages 20 to 24. Sterilization is the most common method for women over 30. Poor women and white women are most likely to rely on contraceptive sterilization, and nonwhite women are more likely than white women to use oral contraceptives.

Not all women, however, are protected from risk of unintended pregnancy by contraceptive use. Teenagers are less likely than women in any other age group to use contraception: one-fifth of all sexually active teenagers use no method of contraception at all. Unmarried women and black women are also less likely to be contraceptive users than their married or white counterparts. The reasons why women do not use contraception are complex and varied. Cost is clearly one important factor. The average first-year cost for oral contraceptives is nearly $200, and the cost of using a diaphragm with spermicide is over $150. Obtaining an IUD usually costs well over $100. While historic differentials in contraceptive-use patterns between rich and poor women and black and white women in the United States have narrowed significantly, the gap is far from closed. Although nearly five million women are able to receive family planning services through federally subsidized clinics, more than four in 10 of the low-income and teenage women in need of subsidized contraceptive care do not receive medically supervised family planning services. In addition, some women are deterred from using the most effective methods of contraception because they misunderstand the risks (and underestimate or are unaware of the benefits) or because they feel that the currently available methods of contraception are too intrusive or otherwise "inappropriate" for their lifestyles.

Partially because contraceptive use is not universal and partially because even the most effective methods of contraception are not foolproof, some three million plus American women still become pregnant unintentionally each year. Among American teenagers, unintended pregnancy is twice as likely as it is in France, Canada, and Great Britain, three times as likely as it is in Sweden, and seven times as likely as

More than 125,000 women and men participate in the March for Women's Lives in Washington, D.C., March 9, 1986. *AP / Wide World Photos*

it is in the Netherlands. Black women in the United States are 2½ times more likely than white women to become pregnant unintentionally. Similarly, unmarried women are more likely than married women to do so.

While 13 percent of all unintended pregnancies end in miscarriage, 46 percent, or about 1.5 million, are terminated by abortion each year. Eight in 10 abortions are obtained by unmarried women, who are seven times more likely than married women to obtain one. Black women confronted with unintended pregnancies choose abortion in roughly the same proportion as white women; however, since more black women than white women are faced with unintended pregnancies, black women are more than twice as likely as white women to have abortions.

Not all women who need abortions are able to obtain them: poor women, teenagers, and women in non-urban areas have the greatest difficulty in obtaining abortions. Public funding for abortion is available in only 14 states and the District of Columbia, and even there only to the very poor, i.e., those eligible for Medicaid. And, even though nearly half of all metropolitan areas have no abortion provider, abortion services are highly concentrated in urban areas. Nearly 90 percent of all nonmetropolitan areas, where more than a quarter of all women of reproductive age live, have no abortion provider at all. Furthermore, the later in pregnancy an abortion is needed, the more difficult it is for any woman, but particularly for young and rural women, to find abortion providers. Fewer than one-third of all abortion providers will perform procedures past the end of the first trimester of pregnancy.

About 3.6 million women gave birth in 1982. Even when joyously anticipated, pregnancy and childbirth can be a financial strain. The cost of even an uncomplicated delivery averages $5,000 nationwide, and the cost in some areas may be considerably higher. Although most families can defray at least some of the cost of childbirth through either public or private insurance, nearly one in five women of reproductive age has no insurance coverage.

Although no data are available at this time to link lack of insurance coverage directly to an inability to obtain adequate prenatal care, it is known that the same groups of women who are likely not to have insurance coverage are the same groups of women who are most likely to receive either late prenatal care or no care at all during pregnancy. Failure to obtain adequate prenatal care is closely tied to poor birth outcomes, and especially with low birthweight, a major factor associated with infant mortality. Although some women may forgo prenatal care because of financial constraints, most pregnant women are able to gain hospital admission for deliveries. However, they may not be able to pay for the care if they have no insurance coverage. One study found that patients admitted for delivery accounted for 37 percent of all surgical patients who received care for which the hospital was not compensated (Sloan, Valvana, and Mullner, 1984).

For yet another group of women the problem is neither avoiding pregnancy nor affording pregnancy-related care but rather becoming pregnant. Approximately 15 percent of all married couples in the United States are estimated to be infertile for various reasons. Treatment for infertility is expensive, frequently not covered by health insurance, and uncertain to produce favorable results. For those couples whose infertility problems cannot be solved through either corrective surgery or drug therapy, artificial insemination and *in vitro* fertilization are sometimes viable options, depending on the cause of the infertility problem. However, neither of these options is widely available in the United States, and both have significant price tags.

In short, American women may have greater reproductive options, both legally and technologically, now than ever before, but exercising those options in the context of real life is another matter. For a variety of reasons, some of which are understandable, American women—and particularly American teenagers—seem to have less success in controlling their fertility than their counterparts in most other developed countries. At least insofar as the prevention of unintended pregnancy is concerned, this appears to be true for American women as a whole, not just for minorities and the disadvantaged. Still, minority status and poverty, as well as residence in a rural area, are important factors. In the United States today, a woman who is likely to be disadvantaged in making and effecting one reproductive choice at one point in her life runs a high risk of being disadvantaged in making and effecting other reproductive choices at other points along the 30-year continuum of her reproductive life.

Images of Black Women

ALGEA O. HARRISON

How BLACK MEN AND their relationships with black women are portrayed has been the subject of considerable public debate since the release of *The Color Purple*, a movie based on Alice Walker's novel of the same name. Defenders of the film stress that it is fiction: that it is a story about particular individuals and their unique experiences. Nevertheless, controversy still rages over whether the film's generally unsympathetic black male characters will encourage negative stereotypes of black men.

Far less public, but no less significant, is the controversy in the social science community about how black families, and black women in particular, have traditionally been perceived—and portrayed—by social scientists. A case in point is the image of black women that emerges from years of social science literature, wherein black women's personality traits have been characterized as anti-feminine, their behavior described as impacting negatively on their families, and their social roles explained as major determinants of oppressive conditions in the black community.

This image has been synthesized from studies that, in the eyes of many social scientists, were seriously flawed. Critics have charged, for example, that studies of black families and black women have been distorted by serious methodological problems, cultural bias, failure to consider the pervasive effects of racism and sexism, and failure to consider the mores, norms, and proscriptions of black culture. (See, for instance, Staples and Mirandé, 1980.)

Many scholars now advocate alternative conceptual frameworks for the study of black families, on the grounds that the black family cannot be explained and interpreted in reference to "norms" that are based essentially on whites' idealized values and whites' experiences (Myers, 1981).

Underlying traditional research on black families, these scholars believe, were assumptions—explicit or implicit—based on a white middle-class idea of what a "good," "healthy" family ought to be like: in particular, this ideal family should have two parents, with the husband able to earn enough to support the family, including his nonworking wife.

To the extent that families conformed to this image, social scientists tended to judge them as healthy, stable families. To the extent that they differed from the image, they tended to be judged as deviant and producers of social instability and other social ills. Black families have historically often differed —have had to differ—from the middle-class ideal. For example, because black fathers have so often been able to find only low-wage and/or uncertain work, black mothers have always been likely to combine income-producing work outside the home with family responsibilities.

Thus, when black families were included in scientific studies, they were generally used as a comparison group to presumably "normal" white, middle-class families for purposes of illustrating deviance; the deviance was perceived as responsible for social problems in the black community. Furthermore, because the personality traits and behavior of women who were seen as fostering the "traditional" family were considered the norms for femininity, behavior that was contrary to or different from that of white, middle-class females was considered anti-feminine, deviant, and inappropriate. It was from this point of view that black families and black women were examined by social scientists.

The multiple roles necessarily assumed by many black women to ensure their families' survival were singled out as a determinant of the social problems in the black community. It was speculated that the way in which black women carried out their roles as wives and mothers had the effect of depreciating black men, negating the development of appropriate sex-role identity among children, and hampering their children's academic achievement, thereby causing the destabilization of family life and creating social ills in the community. In contrast, women—most typically, white women—whose roles were confined to those of wife and mother, were portrayed as fostering wholesome socioemotional development among their children. They were viewed as welcomed and needed helpmates for their husbands, thus enhancing the general welfare of their families, communities, and nation. In short, black families were labeled matriarchal and deviant since the behavior and personality traits of black women differed from the "norms" of white women.

Even when, perhaps in response to the growing feminist movement, social scientists began to reexamine women's social roles and consider the impact of sexism, black women were included only peripherally for the interactional effect of sexism and racism. Furthermore, not everyone accepted the stark reality that black women were at the bottom of the pyramid in comparison to white women and men of both races in income, occupation, and employment. (Black women were somehow perceived as having some advantage over black men and white women.) In the period of affirmative action programs, black working women were believed to be contributing to the unemployment and underemployment of black men (since they were seen as competing with black men for jobs) and causing delinquency among their children.

Moreover, the current interpretation of the incidence of teenage pregnancy, increasing for both races, differs for black and white females. The increase among black teenagers is interpreted as an indication of modeling their mothers' behavior—loose morals, contributing to the breakdown of families, destabilizing the black community, etc. This perspective was reflected in the CBS television program *The Vanishing Family* with Bill Moyers (January 25, 1986, 9:00–11:00 P.M.). On the other hand, the increase in teenage pregnancy among whites is often attributed to a failure of the health care delivery system, and outdated attitudes regarding sex education and birth control.

The potential for change in the treatment of black women in the social science literature emerged generally from two sources—the works of Hoffman (1974) and Hetherington and colleagues (1979)—and the reexamination of black family life by social scientists sensitive to black culture. Hoffman's examination of the effects on children of having a mother who worked outside the home helped remove some of the stigma traditionally attached to mothers who went out to work. Although very few black women were included in the Hoffman research, a large percentage of black women have always been employed in the paid labor force, and Hoffman's findings that children suffer no ill effects from a mother's employment outside the home alleviated some of the guilt for black women and some of the finger-pointing by the majority culture. Likewise, Hetherington's work on the effect of divorce, concluding that it is more harmful for children to live in conflictual families than in single-parent families, is important, even though this study, too, failed to include a representative number of blacks. Both studies, in effect, support caution in attributing social problems in the black community to the incidence of female-headed households, divorce, and employed mothers. Indeed, one cannot generalize all findings from the white community to the black community. Nevertheless, suspicion is called for when phenomena in the black community are interpreted very differently from similar phenomena in the white community.

More recently, there has been a trend toward reexamining the lives of black families for an accurate, sensitive description and explanation of their lifestyles. This has increased the potential for a similar reexamination of black women. From such studies personality traits specific to the experiences of black women should be investigated for differences within the black community. The outcome would be much more meaningful than studies examining black women's traits largely in reference to those that are increasingly understood to be specific to the experiences of white middle-class women (e.g., fear of success). Eventually, research on black women will be conducted along the lines that are already widely understood to be accurate and telling with respect to white women: examination of internal and personal factors and the interactional effects of the cultural milieu. Using this approach, it must be hoped that a picture of black women will come into focus that is far more truthful than the one that has prevailed for so long in the social science literature. The result will be felt far beyond the social science community. Once the information finds its way into the popular consciousness, it could greatly affect the perceptions of policymakers, and, ultimately, our public policy as well.

Latinas in the United States

RUTH E. ZAMBRANA

THE EXPERIENCES OF Latin women in the United States have received relatively little scholarly attention. ("Latina" is the word of choice for many Hispanic and Spanish-origin women to describe their ethnicity. In this article, "Latina" is used in specific reference to women of Mexican-American and Puerto Rican origin. It is important to note, however, that Latinas from both Cuba and Central America also represent an increasingly integral sector of American society.) What research has been conducted has tended to focus on the effects of poverty, the costs of lack of education, the deterioration of the nuclear family, and the rise of single-parent families.

It is true that, as depicted by basic demographic and socioeconomic data, the status of Hispanic women (and men) is rather dismal. As a whole, Hispanics in the United States have lower educational attainment, lower wages, and lower family incomes than whites of non-Spanish origin. In a sense, these minorities appear not to have achieved what the dominant culture defines as success.

Generalized statistics, however, may conceal significant differences among the various subgroups that make up the Hispanic population. For example, while 43 percent of Spanish-origin women overall have completed high school, the proportion of high school graduates ranges from 36 and 39 percent for Mexican-American and Puerto Rican women, respectively, to more than 50 percent for Cuban women and women of "other" Spanish origin. In fact, although Cubans and "other" Latinos make up only 1.7 percent of the total Latino population in the United States, their educational, occupational, and income distributions greatly distort the overall data and mask the very different conditions of Mexican-Americans and Puerto Ricans.

Despite evidence to the contrary, there has been a tendency to treat Hispanics as a homogeneous group. By acknowledging their heterogeneity, researchers can then move beyond analyses of the consequences of being "unsuccessful" —however that is defined—to the more important study of why certain groups succeed or do not succeed, e.g., how certain features of the social structure may have or may have not contributed to achieving success or upward mobility. Success can be defined as the product (or outcome) of a broad spectrum of choices and opportunities that may or may not be available to certain individuals. If these opportunities— most notably, access to education—can be identified, it may be possible to extend their availability. Here research is notably deficient. At present, it is important to find out what choices are open to Latinas, and to identify the barriers that impede Latinas' access to social and economic opportunities. Perhaps answers to these questions will pave the way for others.

In the case of Latin women, work, family life, education, occupational status, and health have typically been circumscribed by race and class, as well as gender. These factors, too long overlooked by researchers, may restrict their options. Moreover, Latinas, even more than other women, have traditionally been viewed by researchers and others as homemakers, and their contributions in other areas have been ignored. The last 10 years, however, have seen some changes, as documented in this article. The changes are largely due to the efforts of the cadre of Latinos who entered the universities in small but historically significant numbers in the 1960s and 1970s. These "insider-outsider" experts bring a qualitatively different approach to the study of the status of Latinas.

In the past decade a number of social scientists (e.g., Maxine Baca-Zinn, Lea Ybarra, Margarita Melville, Mario Barrera, and Maria Chacon) have challenged cultural explanations of failure. The work of these and other researchers has initiated a reassessment of the factors that affect the life experiences of Latinas in the United States. From their groundbreaking theoretical and empirical work, other studies have been generated.

For example, in response to the lack of knowledge and understanding of the work, family life, and educational experiences of Latinas, the National Network of Hispanic Women has completed a nationwide survey of 303 Latina respondents who were in management positions and/or who owned small businesses in 1985. Both professional and entrepreneurial women were included. The data obtained will provide information on work and occupational history, marital and family roles, and health. In addition, the present author has completed a cross-sectional study of factors that have influenced the success of Mexican-American women in higher education. The purpose of this inquiry was to identify their family-of-origin, and record elementary and secondary school experiences, higher education barriers, their mental and physical health, stressful educational events, and academic sources of support.

In New York, the Puerto Rican Studies Center at Hunter College has completed oral histories of female Puerto Rican garment workers, as well as a national directory of Puerto Rican professional women, including those in higher education. The center also plans a study of the experiences of Puerto Rican women in higher education. These projects by Latino investigators are unprecedented efforts to describe the quality of life of Latinas in America in the areas of work, education, and family welfare.

Although there are a number of Hispanic research centers in the country, few have shown much interest in the experiences of women. In 1985, however, the Tomas Rivera Center for Educational Policy in Claremont, California, organized several working conferences to discuss the educational experiences of Latinas. A monograph is being published which discusses research and policy implications for Hispanic women in education. On the East Coast, the Institute for Puerto Rican Policy in New York is preparing a monograph on the *Condition of Latinas in the U.S. Today*. This publication, expected to be available in early 1987, will summarize current census data on Latinas.

A significant number of Latina students and professionals all over the country and in diverse fields are conducting small and large studies of Latinas. Such independent studies, however, generally go unnoticed unless there is some personal contact between the researchers involved and other scholars. To remedy this situation, the Center for Research on Women at Memphis State University has developed a Clearinghouse for Research on Women of Color and Southern Women. Its computer-based data set, which includes published works, unpublished works, works in progress, and a human resources file, will enable investigators to identify the studies being conducted on the Latina experience in the United States.

In all areas of research on Hispanic populations, several basic premises should underlie and guide the inquiry:

1. Socioeconomic status, occupational history, barriers to

access to institutional services or programs, and psychosocial issues such as level of stress and sources of social support must be taken into account in designing the research.

2. The tremendous diversity among the Hispanic population must be considered. This diversity is related to such factors as class position, cultural differences deriving from different countries of origin, generational differences in the United States, and regional/geographic distribution. Generalizations based on national data must be made with caution and a clear understanding of the areas of diversity.

3. Research teams should include at least one Hispanic researcher who is knowledgeable about the cultural, class, and regional characteristics of the population under study. Interpretation of the data cannot be meaningful without a conceptual understanding of these issues (Becerra and Zambrana, 1985).

Although the 1980s have been designated "The Decade of the Hispanic," the publicity has far outrun the actual commitment to develop and support Latino scholars and scholarship. Enrollment of minority students in graduate programs has actually decreased in recent years, and there are still very few minority scholars in institutions of higher learning. As a result, the Ford Foundation has decided to reinstitute its minority fellowship program—a positive step. But a far deeper and more widespread commitment to promoting research by and on Hispanics in the United States is essential. Unless the origins of problems that beset low-income Latinas, in particular, are well-understood, no solutions to these problems will be found.

Women Among Immigrants to the United States

MARION F. HOUSTOUN *and*
ROGER G. KRAMER

THE CONVENTIONAL WISDOM that immigrants to the United States are primarily young economically motivated males has been recently overturned, at least as far as legal immigrants are concerned. A recent study by the U.S. Department of Labor (Houstoun et al., 1984) found that for the last half-century (1930–79), more than half of all newcomers settling in the United States each year have been female. Indeed, two-thirds have been women or children. Before 1930, the proportion of females arriving each decade varied from a low of 30.4 percent in the peak decade of the 1900s, when some 8.2 million immigrants, principally young males, arrived on U.S. shores, to a high of 43.8 percent in the 1920s, when numerical limits on immigration were first enacted. After 1930, the percentage of females among the newcomers varied from a high of 61.2 in the 1940s to a low of 53.0 in the 1970s, when some 4.3 million immigrants were admitted to this country.

Why have females dominated legal immigration to the United States for so many years? There are two main reasons: one is that American males have been far more likely than American females to marry abroad. The second is that U.S. immigration policy gives high priority—a priority that has grown stronger as immigration has been increasingly regulated after the 1920s—to unifying the nuclear family. Moreover, from the 1920s until 1952, when the Immigration and Nationality Act was amended to eliminate sex discrimination in the rights of U.S. residents to sponsor admission of their foreign spouses, the law itself directly favored the admission of women because it gave greater preferential treatment to the spouses of U.S. males.

The two traditional male sex roles of breadwinner and warrior have been significant factors in determining the sex distribution of immigration to the United States. When the quota laws imposed limits on immigration half a century ago, the flood of male immigrant workers was reduced to a trickle. The remaining immigrant flow was dominated by women and children migrating to reunite, or to form families, with earlier-arriving immigrant workers. By the 1940s, however, it was U.S.-born males who generated large flows of immigrant women and children. Hundreds of thousands of young U.S. servicemen assigned to Europe and Asia in the 1940s, to Korea in the 1950s, and to Vietnam in the 1960s and 1970s, married foreign brides.

Current U.S. immigration policy is based primarily on the humanitarian principles of family reunification and refugee resettlement. Spouses, unmarried minor children, and parents of U.S. citizens are exempt from the numerical limits that otherwise restrict immigration to an annual worldwide ceiling of 270,000 and per-country ceilings of 20,000. Immigrants admitted under these ceilings are selected on the basis of a six-class preference system that strongly favors other kinds of relatives of U.S. citizens, but the system also provides for the admission of new spouses and children of earlier-arriving immigrants, and some needed workers and their families. Refugees are not subject to the preference system, or to those numerical ceilings. Instead, refugee admissions are annually set by the president after consultation with the Congress.

Under current policy, females have continued to outnumber males. In recent years, immigrant wives of U.S. citizens substantially outnumbered immigrant husbands; these wives alone accounted for 10 percent of all immigrants admitted in fiscal years 1972–79. Wives immigrating to join U.S. permanent resident aliens also strongly outnumbered husbands, and constituted three percent of all recent immigrants. Together, these foreign brides accounted for nearly 90 percent of the sex differential among newcomers to the United States.

In addition, more mothers than fathers of U.S. citizens settled here, a reflection of both women's longer life expectancies and a greater tendency of widows than of widowers to reunite with their children. U.S. citizens also adopted significantly more girls than boys from overseas. Preliminary inquiries indicate that not only are more girls available for adoption from abroad, but American parents strongly prefer adopting female children.

While the predominance of females in recent immigration to the United States could in theory stem from a large number of women emigrating from a few countries, the Labor Department study found that, in fact, women dominated the majority of all flows from countries that sent significant numbers of immigrants to the United States. However, some interesting sex differentials emerged by region. Women dominated most immigration from Europe, Southeast Asia, the more developed countries of Oceania (i.e., Australia and New Zealand), and nearly all countries in the Western Hemisphere. Men dominated immigration from Africa, Middle

South Asia (e.g., India, Pakistan, Bangladesh), the Middle East, and the less developed countries of Oceania (e.g., Fiji, Tonga).

Mexico, the largest single source of recent immigration to the United States (15 percent), is also the largest single source of foreign brides of U.S. citizens. However, significant numbers of foreign brides emigrated from countries with a substantial peacetime U.S. military presence (the Philippines, Korea, Germany, the United Kingdom, Thailand, and Japan). Though there are few data available, the National Committee Concerned with Asian Wives of U.S. Servicemen recently estimated that 200,000 Asian-born wives of American servicemen live in the United States. This suggests that U.S. national security interests affect the national origin, as well as the sex distribution and number, of recent immigrants to this country.

Not surprisingly, given the emphasis on family reunification in U.S. immigration law and the fact that many U.S. men marry abroad, immigrant women are a great deal more likely to be married than are their U.S. sisters. (Of all immigrant women admitted in 1972–79, 71 percent were married, as compared to 58 percent of all U.S.-born women in 1980.) Perhaps because most immigrant women are married, they are substantially less likely than immigrant men to report an occupation when they arrive, since they may identify themselves as housewives. Just over one-third of all working-age immigrant women reported an occupation at entry, compared with more than three-fourths of their male counterparts. Like their U.S. sisters, most of them reported sex-segregated occupations. Eight of the 10 occupations employing most women in the United States were also most often reported by immigrant women: secretary, bookkeeper, waitress, registered nurse, teacher, private household worker, typist, and nursing aide—marketplace versions of the traditional nurturing or maintenance roles of women. However, like recent immigrants in general, immigrant women were significantly more likely than their U.S. peers to report occupations at either the very top or the bottom of the occupational ladder. Though immigrant women were almost twice as likely as U.S. women to report professional or technical occupations, they were more than five times as likely to report employment as private household workers.

Women immigrants are generally considered to suffer from the double disability of being both female and foreign (Intergovernmental Committee on Migration, 1981). Notwithstanding that the bulk of all immigrants admitted to the United States since 1930 have been female, studies of the status and role of women immigrants in this country are woefully few. Though researchers are becoming aware of this lacuna, much remains to be learned about the impact of women immigrants on the United States—and the impact of the United States upon them.

Appendices

American Women Today:
A Statistical Portrait

Highlights of Tables and Figures

Table 1.   *Persons in the United States by Race and Sex, 1980*
 As of 1980, the latest year for which detailed break-
downs are available, there were 116.5 million females in
the United States and 110 million males; 19.8 million
were nonwhite women and 18.4 million were nonwhite
men. Blacks are by far the largest minority group, and
American Indians a distant second.

Figure 1.   *Age Pyramids for the United States by Race, 1986*
 The shapes of population pyramids for whites,
blacks, and "all others" in the United States reflect
substantial differences in age distribution. Minorities of
both sexes are, on the whole, younger than whites, as
evident in the higher percentage of minority females
and males who are under age 25. Among all races,
women are overrepresented at the upper (65 and above)
ages.

Figure 2.   *Persons of Spanish Origin by Type of Spanish Origin and Sex, 1980*
 Persons of Mexican origin predominate among the
Spanish-origin population in the United States. (*Note:*
persons of Spanish origin may be of any race.) In 1980,
females of Mexican origin accounted for just under 30
percent of the total Spanish-origin population; males
of Mexican origin accounted for another 30 percent.

Puerto Rican and Cuban females were 7.1 and 2.9 percent, respectively, of the United States population of Spanish origin.

Table 2.   *Average Life Expectancy at Birth by Sex and Race, Selected Years, 1950–1984*

The number of elderly in the United States is on the rise, and one factor contributing to this increase is an improvement in life expectancy. Estimated female life expectancy at birth—78.3 years—was 7.2 years greater in 1984 than it had been in 1950. In contrast, males at birth can expect to live only 71.1 years, an increase of 5.5 years since 1950. Blacks of both sexes have lower life expectancies than their white counterparts.

Table 3.   *Leading Causes of Death by Sex and Race, 1983*

Although death rates vary substantially by sex and race, major cardiovascular diseases (e.g., heart attack, stroke) are the leading cause of death for all Americans. Cancer is the number two killer; among women, death rates for digestive, breast, and respiratory cancers rank highest.

Figure 3.   *Sex Ratio of the Population by Age and Race, 1986*

Differences in life expectancy affect the male-female balance, or sex ratio. There is a slight excess of males over females from birth up to age 24 or so, after which the balance begins to tip the other way. Among the elderly (65 and older), there are only about 67 men for every 100 women.

Table 4.   *Median Age at First Marriage by Sex, Selected Years, 1900–1984*

Today's young women are marrying later than their mothers. As of 1984, the median age at first marriage was 23 for women, nearly three years higher than it had been in the 1950s and 1960s.

Table 5.   Marital Status of Persons Age 15 and Over by Sex, Race, and Spanish Origin, March 1985

While a majority of Americans over the age of 15 are married and living with their spouses, differences by sex are pronounced. Women are both less likely than men to be single (never married) and less likely than men to be married and living with a spouse. (An exception involves persons of Spanish origin, among whom the percentage of married women living with their husbands slightly exceeds the percentage of married men living with their wives.) Women are more likely than men to be currently divorced or currently widowed.

Figure 4.   Marital Status of Persons Age 15 and Over, and Age 65 and Over, by Sex, March 1985

Age and sex combine to have a significant impact on marital status. The proportion of the population that has never married drops sharply among the aged (65 and over). However, older women are only about half as likely as older men to be living with a spouse, and nearly four times as likely as men in the upper ages to be currently widowed.

Figure 5.   Divorced Persons per 1,000 Married Persons with Spouse Present, by Sex, Race, and Spanish Origin, 1960, 1970, 1980, and 1984

One measure of the change in marital stability is the divorce ratio, which is the number of currently divorced persons per 1,000 currently married persons who live with their spouses. Among whites and blacks of both sexes the divorce ratio in 1984 was about 3½ to four times higher than it had been just 24 years earlier. However, the divorce ratio among women is far higher than it is among men, regardless of race or Spanish origin.

Table 6.   Births to Unmarried Teenage Mothers by Race, 1984

Pregnancy among unmarried teenagers is an issue of enormous concern to policymakers, educators, women's

advocates, and the like. Three-quarters of a million babies were born to unmarried females under the age of
20 in 1984. Not surprisingly, the younger the mother,
the less likely she is to be married: 83 percent of all
15-year-olds, and 48 percent of all 18- and 19-year-olds,
who gave birth in 1984 were unmarried.

Table 7.   *Family Type by Race and Spanish Origin, 1970, 1980, 1984, and
1985*

While the percentage of female-headed and male-
headed families is well above its 1970 level, married-
couple families still predominate. Four out of five U.S.
families (80 percent) are married-couple families.
Among blacks, the percentage of married-couple families actually rose somewhat between 1984 and 1985.

Figure 6.   *Family Type by Race and Spanish Origin, 1985*

No longer is the married-couple family with a stay-
at-home wife the norm for U.S. families. As of 1985, the
most common family type was the married-couple family with the wife in the paid workforce. Such families
accounted for more than 43 percent (two in every five)
of all families in the United States. This overall figure,
however, obscures significant differences by race and
Spanish origin. Among blacks, the female-headed family is the most common family type (42 percent), while
among persons of Spanish origin, the married-couple
family with a wife who does not work for pay has a slight
edge.

Figure 7.   *Living Arrangements of Children Under Age 18 by Marital Status
of Parents, Race, and Spanish Origin, March 1984*

Marital status and family type naturally affect the
living arrangements of children. The majority of white
children and children of Spanish origin live with both
parents (82 percent and 72 percent, respectively); somewhat less than half (44 percent) of all black children do.

Table 8.   *Educational Attainment of Persons Age 25 and Over by Sex, Race, and Spanish Origin, March 1985*

Although male-female differences in educational attainment are not great, women over age 25 are more likely than men to have ended their formal education with graduation from high school.

Table 9.   *First Professional Degrees Awarded in Selected Fields, 1964–1965, 1973–1974, and 1983–1984*

Women are earning a significantly larger share of advanced degrees than they used to. As of 1964–65, very few of the first professional degrees in dentistry, medicine, and law went to women, but in 1983–84, women received almost 20 percent of such degrees in dentistry, 28 percent in medicine, and 37 percent in law.

Table 10.   *Women Graduates of the United States Service Academies, 1986 and 1980–1986*

Women are also becoming a presence in the United States service academies: they accounted for at least one in every ten 1986 graduates of West Point, the Air Force Academy, and the Coast Guard Academy. However, women were only six percent of the Naval Academy's graduating class of 1986.

Table 11.   *Persons Age 16 and Over in the Civilian Labor Force by Sex, Race, and Spanish Origin, Selected Years, 1950–1985 and April 1986*

Few trends over the past 35 years have been as pronounced as the increase in female labor force participation. As of April 1986, 51.7 million women were in the civilian labor force (i.e., working or looking for work), an increase of 180 percent since 1950. Unfortunately, historical data do not always distinguish race and ethnic group; the data that are available, however, show increasing labor force participation on the part of black women and women of Spanish origin, as well as white women.

Figure 8.   Civilian Labor Force Participation Rates for Persons Age 16 and
Over by Sex, Race, and Spanish Origin, Selected Years, 1950–
1985 and April 1986

The number of women in the labor force translated
into an overall female participation rate of 54.6 percent
in April 1986. Black women had the highest participation rate (56.9 percent) among women, followed by
white women (54.3 percent), with women of Spanish
origin third (49.6 percent). As the female labor force
participation rate has increased, that of males—chiefly
white men—has declined.

Table 12.   Civilian Labor Force Participation Rates by Age and Sex, Selected
Years, 1950–1985 and April 1986

The increase in female labor force participation is by
no means confined to young women: the participation
rates are well above their 1950 levels for women of all
ages except the oldest (65 and above). As of April 1986,
seven out of 10 women in the prime childbearing and
childrearing years (20 to 44) were in the labor force.

Table 13.   Unemployment Rates for Persons Age 16 and Over by Sex, Race,
and Spanish Origin, Selected Years, 1950–1985 and April 1986

Although employed women were more immune
than men to the recession of 1981–82, female unemployment rates are usually higher than those of men.
Among blacks, however, the opposite tends to be true.

Figure 9.   Persons at Work in Nonagricultural Industries by Sex, Marital
Status, and Full- or Part-time Status, April 1986

Regardless of marital status, women are more likely
than men to work part time. Nonetheless, full-time
work is by far the most common employment status for
workers of both sexes.

Figure 10.   Percent of Children with Mother in the Labor Force by Age of
Children, Selected Years, 1970–1984 and March 1985

Today, the majority of children under 18—57.5 percent in 1985—have mothers in the labor force. Younger

children's mothers are more likely to stay at home, but even among children under six, nearly half—49 percent—have mothers who are in the labor force.

Figure 11. *Children with Mother in the Labor Force by Family Type, 1970 and 1984–1985*

Whether they are in two-parent or female-headed families, the percentage of children with mothers in the labor force has increased dramatically since 1970. The increase has been most pronounced for children under the age of six in two-parent families. As of 1985, almost 51 percent of such children had mothers who were working or looking for work, up from just under 28 percent in 1970.

Figure 12. *Labor Force Participation Rates of Women Between the Ages of 18 and 44 Who Have Had a Child in the Preceding 12 Months, June 1976 and June 1980–June 1985*

Even infants are increasingly likely to have working mothers. As of 1985, nearly half of all women between the ages of 18 and 44 who had had a child in the preceding 12 months were in the labor force.

Figure 13. *Occupational Distribution of All Employed Men and of Employed Women by Race, Age 16 and Over, April 1986*

Employed women of all races are heavily concentrated in a few occupations: in April of 1986, one out of two (48 percent) was either a service or administrative support (a category that includes clerical) worker.

Table 14. *Proportion Female Workers in Selected Occupations, 1975 and 1985*

Despite continuing and sometimes growing job segregation in many occupations (e.g., elementary school teaching, nursing, social work), women's representation in a number of nontraditional jobs is on the rise. Women now account for 18 percent of all lawyers and judges, up from seven percent in 1975; 11 percent of architects, versus four percent in 1975; and 35 percent of economists, as opposed to 13 percent in 1975.

Table 15.   *Women-owned Businesses, 1982*

Women owned nearly 12.1 million businesses—24 percent of all businesses—in 1982. Yet women-owned firms generated only 10 percent of all receipts generated by America's businesses in that year.

Figure 14.   *Distribution by Industry of Women-owned Businesses, 1982*

Of all businesses owned by women, nearly half (49 percent) were in the service industry; one-fourth were in the wholesale and retail trade. Very few—two percent or less—were in either construction, manufacturing, or transportation.

Table 16.   *Women in Elective Office, Selected Offices, 1975–1987*

Increasing numbers of women are running for public office and getting elected, at least at the state level. The percentage of women in Congress, however, has shown little change since 1975.

Table 17.   *Women in the Judiciary, 1985 and 1986*

By the mid-1980s, women were only eight percent of all federal judges and seven percent of the judges on state benches.

Table 18.   *Historical Data on the Number of Women Directors on Fortune Boards During the Last 17 Years*

The absolute number of women on corporate boards is on the rise, as is the number and proportion of corporations with female board members. Nonetheless, the increase is not as impressive as it might appear at first glance. In 1979, for example, 361 directorships in 316 Fortune companies were held by women, for a ratio of 1.14 female directors per company. By 1986, there were 576 female-held directorships in 439 companies—a ratio of 1.31.

Table 19.   Median Income of Families by Family Type, Race, and Spanish
             Origin, 1985

     Working wives contribute substantially to family in-
come. In 1985, married-couple families in which the
wife was in the paid labor force had a median income
of $36,431, some 50 percent higher than the median
($24,556) for families in which the wife stayed at home.
Among black couples, family income nearly doubled if
the wife went off to work. Not surprisingly, the financial
status of female-headed families is far more precarious
than that of married couples or male-headed families.
Families headed by women had a median income of
only $13,600 in 1985.

Figure 15.   Median Income of Persons Age 15 and Over by Age, Sex, and
             Year-round, Full-time Employment Status, 1985

     As would be expected, year-round, full-time workers
report incomes well above the incomes of all persons of
the same age and sex. This is true for both women and
men; however, the median income of year-round, full-
time women workers was just over $16,000 in 1985, in
contrast to their male counterparts' median of almost
$25,000.

Table 20.   Selected Sources of Income for Persons Age 15 and Over by Sex,
             Race, and Spanish Origin, 1984

     Over half of all women 15 and older reported wage
or salary income in 1984; differences by race or Spanish
origin were slight. However, the percentages of women
reporting income from property or interest were somewhat higher among whites than among minority
women. (It should be noted that these figures reveal
nothing about the amount of income received from
such sources, and it might have been low.)

Figure 16.   Ownership of Selected Assets by Type of Household, 1984

     Married-couple households not only have consider-
ably higher median incomes than households headed by

females or males, they are also, not surprisingly, more likely to own such property as automobiles, homes, stocks, savings accounts, and other assets. Male householders fare better than their female counterparts with respect to almost all assets except home ownership. Female heads of households report home ownership more frequently than do male householders, perhaps because they are more likely than men to obtain the house in a divorce settlement, but also because a great many of them are widows who inherited the house. Still, fewer than half (49 percent) of all female householders own their homes.

Figure 17. *Poverty Rates of Families by Family Type, Race, and Spanish Origin, 1985*

Poverty is a major problem among female-headed families, especially among those whose heads are black or of Spanish origin. Among these minority families, poverty rates exceeded 50 percent in 1985.

Table 21. *Trends in Poverty Rates of Persons by Family Type, Race, and Spanish Origin, 1960–1985*

Poverty rates, after declining for some years, began to climb again in 1978–80. They then began to fall once again for most persons beginning in 1984. This recent decline, however, has not been as pronounced for persons in female-headed families; their poverty rates, depending on race or Spanish origin, are 2½ to 3½ times as high as those of persons living in other types of families.

Table 22. *Percent of Poor Children Living in Female-headed Households by Race and Spanish Origin, Selected Years, 1960–1985*

The poverty rates of children in female-headed families, particularly those headed by blacks, are exceptionally high. As of 1985, over half (54 percent) of all children in female-headed families, but over three-fourths of those in black female-headed families, were living below the poverty level.

The Tables and Figures

Table 1 • PERSONS IN THE UNITED STATES BY RACE
AND SEX, 1980 (numbers in thousands)

Race	Female		Male	
	Number	Percent	Number	Percent
White	96,686	83.0	91,685	83.3
Black	13,976	12.0	12,519	11.4
American Indian	691	0.6	674	0.6
Eskimo	21	*	22	*
Aleut	7	*	7	*
Japanese	380	*	321	*
Chinese	398	*	408	*
Filipino	400	*	374	*
Korean	207	*	148	*
Asian Indian	174	*	187	*
Vietnamese	126	*	136	*
Hawaiian	84	*	82	*
Guamanian	16	*	16	*
Samoan	21	*	21	*
Other	3,305	2.8	3,453	3.1
Total	116,492	100.0	110,053	100.0

*Less than one-half of one percent.

Source: U.S. Bureau of the Census, Census of the Population, Vol. I, PC80-1-B1, 1983, Table 38.

Figure 1 • AGE PYRAMIDS FOR THE UNITED STATES BY RACE, 1986[1]

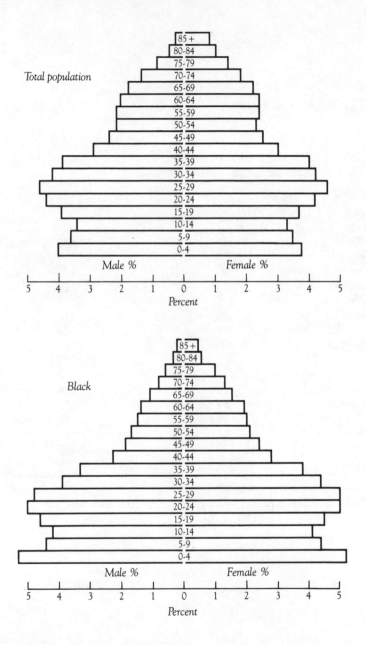

[1]1984 Census Bureau projections for 1986.

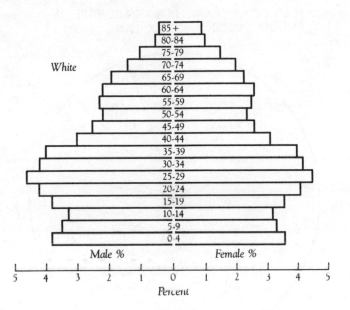

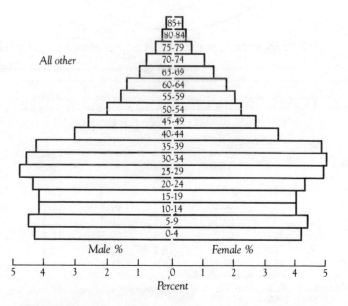

Source: U.S. Bureau of the Census, Current Population Reports, Series P-25, No. 952, 1984, Table 6 (middle series).

Figure 2 • PERSONS OF SPANISH ORIGIN BY TYPE OF
SPANISH ORIGIN AND SEX, 1980

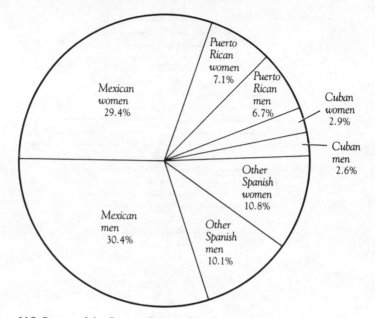

Source: U.S. Bureau of the Census, Census of the Population, Vol. I, PC80-1-B1,
1983, Table 39.

Table 2 • AVERAGE LIFE EXPECTANCY AT BIRTH BY SEX
AND RACE, SELECTED YEARS, 1950–1984

Year	All races		White		Black	
	Female	Male	Female	Male	Female	Male
1950	71.1	65.6	72.2	66.5	NA	NA
1960	73.1	66.6	74.1	67.4	NA	NA
1970	74.7	67.1	75.6	68.0	68.3	60.0
1975	76.6	68.8	77.3	69.5	71.3	62.4
1980	77.4	70.0	78.1	70.7	72.5	63.8
1984 (est.)	78.3	71.1	78.8	71.8	73.7	65.5

Source: National Center for Health Statistics, *Monthly Vital Statistics Report,* Vol. 33,
No. 13, 1985, Table 7.

Table 3 • LEADING CAUSES OF DEATH¹ BY SEX AND RACE, 1983 (rate per 100,000 in specified group)

All races		White		Black	
Female	Male	Female	Male	Female	Male
Major cardiovascular diseases: 406.3 (heart diseases: 305.7)	Major cardiovascular diseases: 432.9 (heart diseases: 354.1)	Major cardiovascular diseases: 426.3 (heart diseases: 321.5)	Major cardiovascular diseases: 451.2 (heart diseases: 370.9)	Major cardiovascular diseases: 336.0 (heart diseases: 248.1)	Major cardiovascular diseases: 367.6 (heart diseases: 288.5)
Cancers: 170.1 (digestive, peritoneum: 45.0) (breast: 31.6) (respiratory: 29.8)	Cancers: 209.6 (respiratory: 74.0) (digestive: 52.5) (genital: 22.5)	Cancers: 177.9 (digestive: 45.5) (breast: 33.3) (respiratory: 31.5)	Cancers: 213.8 (respiratory: 75.9) (digestive: 52.9) (genital: 22.0)	Cancers: 140.7 (digestive: 40.6) (breast: 24.4) (respiratory: 22.3)	Cancers: 210.5 (respiratory: 72.6) (digestive: 55.4) (genital: 30.9)
Accidents: 23.8 (motor vehicle: 10.4)	Accidents: 56.2 (motor vehicle: 28.1)	Pneumonia and influenza: 25.0	Accidents: 55.6 (motor vehicle: 28.5)	Diabetes mellitus: 24.8	Accidents: 63.1 (motor vehicle: 25.2)
Pneumonia and influenza: 23.1	Chronic obstructive pulmonary diseases: 37.9	Accidents: 24.0 (motor vehicle: 10.8)	Chronic obstructive pulmonary diseases: 41.1	Accidents: 23.6 (motor vehicle: 7.6)	Homicide and legal intervention: 51.4
Chronic obstructive pulmonary diseases: 19.2	Pneumonia and influenza: 24.6	Chronic obstructive pulmonary diseases: 21.2	Pneumonia and influenza: 25.1	Perinatal conditions: 18.2	Perinatal conditions: 25.6

(continued on next page)

Table 3 (continued)

	All races		White		Black	
	Female	Male	Female	Male	Female	Male
	Diabetes mellitus: 17.9	Suicide: 19.2	Diabetes mellitus: 17.3	Suicide: 20.6	Pneumonia and influenza: 13.8	Pneumonia and influenza: 24.0
	Chronic liver disease, cirrhosis: 8.1	Chronic liver disease, cirrhosis: 15.4	Chronic liver disease, cirrhosis: 7.9	Chronic liver disease, cirrhosis: 15.2	Kidney diseases: 12.0	Chronic obstructive pulmonary diseases: 21.2
	Kidney diseases[2]: 8.1	Homicide and legal intervention: 13.6	Kidney diseases: 7.6	Diabetes mellitus: 12.7	Homicide and legal intervention: 11.3	Chronic liver disease, cirrhosis: 18.3
	Perinatal conditions: 6.9	Diabetes mellitus: 12.9	Suicide: 5.9	Homicide and legal intervention: 8.6	Chronic liver diseases, cirrhosis: 9.8	Diabetes mellitus: 16.0
	Septicemia: 5.8	Perinatal conditions: 9.7	Septicemia: 5.5	Kidney diseases: 7.8	Septicemia: 9.0	Kidney diseases: 12.4

[1]Deaths from "symptoms, signs, and ill-defined conditions" and "all other diseases," with rates higher than some listed, have not been included in this table.

[2]Excludes deaths from kidney infections.

Source: National Center for Health Statistics, Monthly Vital Statistics Report, Vol. 34, No. 6, Supplement (2), 1985, Table 9.

Figure 3 • SEX RATIO[1] OF THE POPULATION BY AGE
AND RACE, 1986[2]

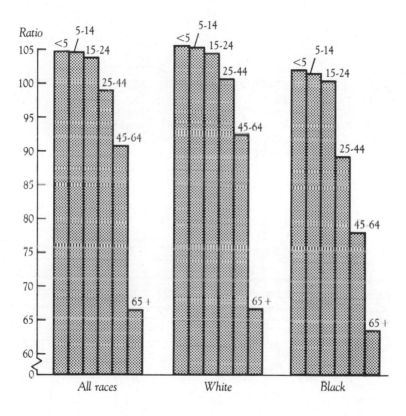

[1]Number of men per 100 women in the particular age group.
[2]1984 Census Bureau projections for 1986.
Source: U.S. Bureau of the Census, Current Population Reports, Series P-25, No.
952, 1984, Table 6 (middle series).

Table 4 • MEDIAN AGE AT FIRST MARRIAGE BY SEX,
SELECTED YEARS, 1900–1984

Year	Women	Men
1900	21.9	25.9
1910	21.6	25.1
1920	21.2	24.6
1930	21.3	24.3
1940	21.5	24.3
1950	20.3	22.8
1960	20.3	22.8
1970	20.8	23.2
1980	22.0	24.7
1984	23.0	25.4

Source: U.S. Bureau of the Census, Current Population Reports, Series P-20, No. 399, 1985, Table A.

Table 5 • MARITAL STATUS OF PERSONS AGE 15 AND
OVER BY SEX, RACE, AND SPANISH ORIGIN,
MARCH 1985 (in percentages)

Marital status	White		Black		Spanish origin[1]	
	Women	Men	Women	Men	Women	Men
Single (never married)	20.7	28.2	36.9	43.4	26.0	36.6
Married, spouse present	56.6	61.3	31.2	38.9	51.9	50.6
Married, spouse absent	2.8	2.2	8.5	7.2	7.5	5.8
Widowed	11.8	2.3	13.3	3.5	7.2	2.1
Divorced	8.0	6.0	10.2	7.0	7.4	4.9
Total percent	100.0	100.0	100.0	100.0	100.0	100.0
Number (in thousands)	81,603	75,487	11,092	9,141	5,967	5,809

[1]Persons of Spanish origin may be of any race.

Source: U.S. Bureau of the Census, Current Population Reports, unpublished data for 1985.

Figure 4 • MARITAL STATUS OF PERSONS AGE 15 AND OVER, AND AGE 65 AND OVER, BY SEX, MARCH 1985

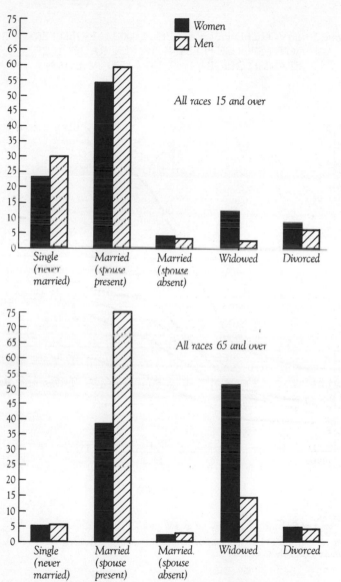

Source: U.S. Bureau of the Census, Current Population Reports, unpublished data for 1985.

Figure 5 • DIVORCED PERSONS PER 1,000 MARRIED PERSONS
WITH SPOUSE PRESENT, BY SEX, RACE, AND
SPANISH ORIGIN, 1960, 1970, 1980, AND 1984

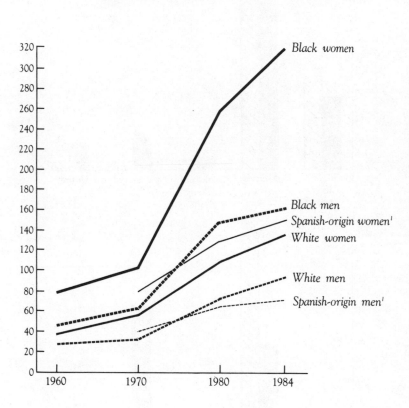

[1]Persons of Spanish origin may be of any race.

Source: U.S. Bureau of the Census, Current Population Reports, Series P-20, No. 399, 1985, Table C.

Table 6 • BIRTHS TO UNMARRIED TEENAGE MOTHERS
       BY RACE, 1984

	Total live births to teenage mothers	Total births to unmarried teenagers	Births to unmarried mothers as percent of total births in age group
ALL RACES			
Under 15	9,965	9,075	91.1
15–19	469,682	261,104	55.6
15	24,142	19,945	82.6
16	53,178	38,763	72.9
17	89,424	56,647	63.3
18–19	302,938	145,749	48.1
WHITE			
Under 15	3,959	3,193	80.6
15–19	320,953	133,275	41.5
15	12,869	9,032	70.2
16	32,529	19,267	59.2
17	59,618	29,681	49.8
18–19	215,937	75,295	34.9
BLACK			
Under 15	5,720	5,634	98.5
15–19	134,392	119,742	89.1
15	10,637	10,386	97.6
16	19,158	18,415	96.1
17	27,112	25,261	93.2
18–19	77,485	65,680	84.8
ALL OTHERS			
Under 15	286	248	86.7
15–19	14,337	8,087	56.4
15	636	527	82.9
16	1,491	1,081	72.5
17	2,694	1,705	63.3
18–19	9,516	4,774	50.2

Source: National Center for Health Statistics, Monthly Vital Statistics Report, Vol. 35, No. 4, Supplement, 1986, Tables 17 and 18.

Table 7 • FAMILY TYPE BY RACE AND SPANISH ORIGIN,
1970, 1980, 1984, AND 1985 (in percentages)

Family type	1970	1980	1984	1985
ALL RACES				
Married-couple families	86.7	81.7	80.3	80.1
Wife in paid labor force	NA	(50.2)	(53.5)	(54.0)
Wife not in paid labor force	NA	(49.8)	(46.5)	(46.0)
Female householder, no husband present	10.9	15.1	16.2	16.1
Male householder, no wife present	2.4	3.2	3.6	3.8
Total percent	100.0	100.0	100.0	100.0
Total number of families (in thousands)	51,237	60,309	62,706	63,558
WHITE				
Married-couple families	88.6	85.1	83.9	83.5
Wife in paid labor force	NA	(49.3)	(52.5)	(52.9)
Wife not in paid labor force	NA	(50.6)	(47.5)	(47.1)
Female householder, no husband present	9.1	11.9	12.8	12.9
Male householder, no wife present	2.2	3.0	3.3	3.6
Total percent	100.0	100.0	100.0	100.0
Total number of families (in thousands)	46,022	52,710	54,400	54,991
BLACK				
Married-couple families	68.0	53.7	51.2	53.2
Wife in paid labor force	NA	(59.6)	(64.0)	(64.1)
Wife not in paid labor force	NA	(40.4)	(36.0)	(35.9)
Female householder, no husband present	28.2	41.7	43.7	41.5
Male householder, no wife present	3.7	4.6	5.1	5.3
Total percent	100.0	100.0	100.0	100.0
Total number of families (in thousands)	4,774	6,317	6,778	6,921
SPANISH ORIGIN[1]				
Married-couple families	NA	73.1	71.7	70.4
Wife in paid labor force	NA	(46.2)	(49.1)	(49.1
Wife not in paid labor force	NA	(53.8)	(50.9)	(50.9
Female householder, no husband present	NA	21.8	23.0	23.3
Male householder, no wife present	NA	5.1	5.3	6.3
Total percent		100.0	100.0	100.0
Total number of families (in thousands)	NA	3,235	3,939	4,206

[1]Persons of Spanish origin may be of any race.

Source: U.S. Bureau of the Census, Current Population Reports, Series P-20, No. 218, 1971
Table 6; Series P-60, No. 127, 1981. Table 1; Series P-60, No. 149, 1985, Table 1; Series P-60
No. 154, 1986, Table 1.

Figure 6 • FAMILY TYPE BY RACE AND SPANISH ORIGIN,
1985 (percent of total families)

☐ Married couple, wife in paid labor force
▥ Married couple, wife not in paid labor force
▨ Female householder, no husband present
■ Male householder, no wife present

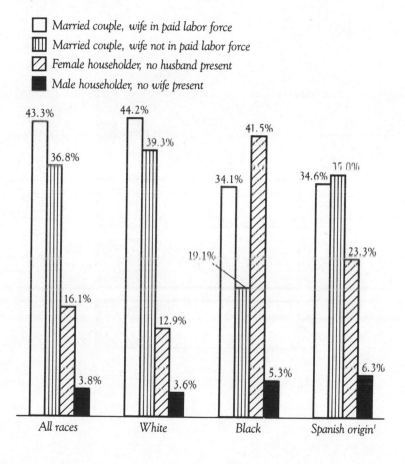

¹Persons of Spanish origin may be of any race.
Source: U.S. Bureau of the Census, Current Population Reports, Series P-60, No. 154, 1986, Table 1.

Figure 7 • LIVING ARRANGEMENTS OF CHILDREN UNDER
AGE 18 BY MARITAL STATUS OF PARENTS,
RACE, AND SPANISH ORIGIN, MARCH 1984

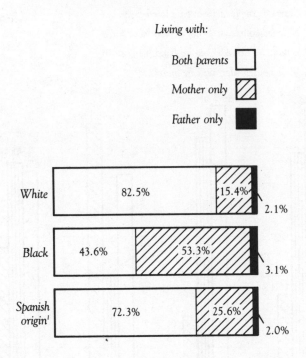

¹Persons of Spanish origin may be of any race.

Source: U.S. Bureau of the Census, Current Population Reports, Series P-20, No. 399, 1985, Table 9.

Table 8 • EDUCATIONAL ATTAINMENT OF PERSONS AGE 25 AND OVER BY SEX, RACE, AND SPANISH ORIGIN, MARCH 1985 (in percentages)

Years of school completed	All races		White		Black		Spanish origin[1]	
	Women	Men	Women	Men	Women	Men	Women	Men
Elementary, 0–8	13.6	14.1	12.8	13.2	19.5	22.9	38.0	37.6
High school, 1–3	12.9	11.4	12.1	10.8	19.6	18.7	14.7	13.9
High school, 4	41.3	34.8	42.4	35.3	35.5	31.9	29.5	27.2
College, 1–3	16.2	16.5	16.4	16.7	14.3	15.3	10.6	11.5
College, 4	10.0	12.5	10.1	13.0	6.9	6.9	4.5	5.2
College, 5 or more	6.0	10.5	6.2	11.0	4.1	4.2	2.8	4.5
Total percent	100.0	100.0	100.0	100.0	100.0	100.0	100.0	100.0
Total number (in thousands)	75,768	67,755	65,500	59,405	8,266	6,554	4,392	4,063

[1]Persons of Spanish origin may be of any race.

Source: U.S. Bureau of the Census, Population Division, unpublished data from the Current Population Survey.

Table 9 • FIRST PROFESSIONAL DEGREES AWARDED IN SELECTED FIELDS, 1964–1965, 1973–1974, AND 1983–1984

Field	1964–65			1973–74			1983–84		
	Both sexes, total	Women		Both sexes, total	Women		Both sexes, total	Women	
		Number	Percent		Number	Percent		Number	Percent
Dentistry	3,135	23	0.7	4,440	85	1.9	5,353	1,051	19.6
Medicine	7,347	478	6.5	11,355	1,263	11.1	15,813	4,454	28.2
Veterinary medicine	NA	NA	NA	1,384	155	11.2	2,269	963	42.4
Law	11,792	395	3.3	29,325	3,340	11.4	37,012	13,630	36.8

Source: U.S. Department of Education, Office of Educational Research and Improvement, unpublished data.

Table 10 • WOMEN GRADUATES OF THE UNITED STATES SERVICE
ACADEMIES, 1986 AND 1980–1986[1]

	Class of 1986		Classes of 1980–1986	
Academy	Total number of women	Women as percent of 1986 graduates	Total number of women	Women as percent of all graduates
Air Force	106	11.0	700	10.8
Coast Guard	16	11.8	101	8.6
Military (West Point)	92	10.4	530	8.0
Naval	65	6.3	434	6.2

[1]The class of 1980 was the first to include women.

Source: Data provided to the Women's Research and Education Institute by the United States Air Force Academy Activities Group, the United States Coast Guard Academy, the United States Military Academy, and the United States Naval Academy, June 1986.

Table 11 • PERSONS AGE 16 AND OVER IN THE CIVILIAN LABOR
FORCE BY SEX, RACE, AND SPANISH ORIGIN, SELECTED
YEARS, 1950–1985 AND APRIL 1986 (numbers in thousands)

	All races		White		Black		Spanish origin[1]	
Year	Women	Men	Women	Men	Women	Men	Women	Men
1950	18,389	43,819	—	—	—	—	—	—
1955	20,548	44,475	17,888	40,197	—	—	—	—
1960	23,240	43,388	20,172	41,743	—	—	—	—
1965	26,200	48,255	22,737	43,400	—	—	—	—
1970	31,543	51,228	27,521	46,035	—	—	—	—
1975	37,475	56,299	32,508	50,324	4,247	5,016	1,625	2,580
1980	45,487	61,453	39,127	54,473	5,253	5,612	2,208	3,494
1985	51,050	64,411	43,455	56,472	6,144	6,220	2,902	4,546
1986[2]	51,665	64,651	43,926	56,602	6,255	6,324	3,204	4,987

[1]Persons of Spanish origin may be of any race.

[2]Rates for April 1986 are not seasonally adjusted.

Source: U.S. Department of Labor, Bureau of Labor Statistics, Handbook of Labor Statistics, 1985, Table 4; Employment and Earnings, January 1986, Tables 3 and 39; May 1986, Table A-4; and unpublished BLS data.

Figure 8 • CIVILIAN LABOR FORCE PARTICIPATION RATES FOR
PERSONS AGE 16 AND OVER BY SEX, RACE, AND
SPANISH ORIGIN, SELECTED YEARS, 1950–1985 AND
APRIL 1986

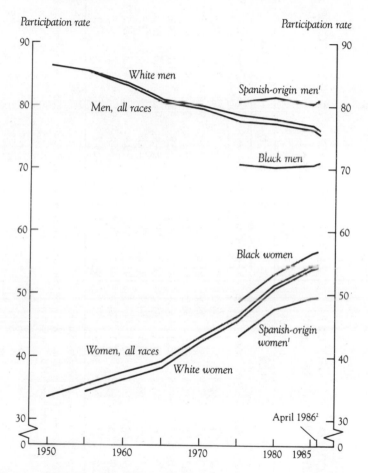

[1]Persons of Spanish origin may be of any race.

[2]Rates for April 1986 are not seasonally adjusted.

Source: U.S. Department of Labor, Bureau of Labor Statistics, *Handbook of Labor Statistics*, 1985, Table 5; *Employment and Earnings*, January 1986, Tables 3 and 39; May 1986, Table A-4; and unpublished BLS data.

Table 12 • CIVILIAN LABOR FORCE PARTICIPATION RATES BY AGE AND SEX, SELECTED YEARS, 1950–1985 AND APRIL 1986

	Age and sex												
	16–19		20–24		25–34		35–44		45–54		55–64		65 and over	
Year	Women	Men	Women	Men	Women	Men	Women	Men	Women	Men	Women	Men	Women	Men
1950	41.0	63.2	46.0	87.9	34.0	96.0	39.1	97.6	37.9	95.8	27.0	86.9	9.7	45.8
1955	39.7	58.9	45.9	86.9	34.9	97.6	41.6	98.1	43.8	96.4	32.5	87.9	10.6	39.6
1960	39.3	56.1	46.1	88.1	36.0	97.5	43.4	97.7	49.9	95.7	37.2	86.8	10.8	33.1
1965	38.0	53.8	49.9	85.8	38.5	97.2	46.1	97.3	50.9	95.6	41.1	84.6	10.0	27.9
1970	44.0	56.1	57.7	83.3	45.0	96.4	51.1	96.9	54.4	94.3	43.0	83.0	9.7	26.8
1975	49.1	59.1	64.1	84.5	54.9	95.2	55.8	95.6	54.6	92.1	40.9	75.6	8.2	21.6
1980	52.9	60.5	68.9	85.9	65.5	95.2	65.5	95.5	59.9	91.2	41.3	72.1	8.1	19.0
1985	52.1	56.8	71.8	85.0	70.9	94.7	71.8	95.0	64.4	91.0	42.0	67.9	7.3	15.8
1986¹	50.2	53.0	70.4	83.4	71.3	94.1	72.7	94.6	65.7	91.0	41.8	67.1	7.4	16.1

¹Rates for April 1986 are not seasonally adjusted.

Source: U.S. Department of Labor, Bureau of Labor Statistics, *Handbook of Labor Statistics*, 1985, Table 5; *Employment and Earnings*, January 1986, Table 3; and May 1986, Table A-4.

Table 13 • UNEMPLOYMENT RATES FOR PERSONS AGE 16
AND OVER BY SEX, RACE, AND SPANISH
ORIGIN, SELECTED YEARS, 1950–1985 AND
APRIL 1986

	All races		White		Black		Spanish origin[1]	
Year	Women	Men	Women	Men	Women	Men	Women	Men
1950	5.7	5.1	—	—	—	—	—	—
1955	4.9	4.2	4.3	3.7	—	—	—	—
1960	5.9	5.4	5.3	4.8	—	—	—	—
1965	5.5	4.0	5.0	3.6	—	—	—	—
1970	5.9	4.4	5.4	4.0	—	—	—	—
1975	9.3	7.9	8.6	7.2	14.8	14.8	13.5	11.4
1980	7.4	6.9	6.5	6.1	14.0	14.5	10.7	9.7
1985	7.4	7.0	6.4	6.1	14.9	15.3	11.0	10.2
1986[2]	6.9	7.0	5.9	6.0	14.1	15.2	10.7	10.1

[1]Persons of Spanish origin may be of any race.

[2]Rates for April 1986 are not seasonally adjusted.

Source: U.S. Department of Labor, Bureau of Labor Statistics, *Handbook of Labor Statistics*, 1985, Table 27; *Employment and Earnings*, January 1986, Table 39; May 1986, Table A-4; and unpublished BLS data.

Figure 9 • PERSONS[1] AT WORK IN NONAGRICULTURAL
INDUSTRIES BY SEX, MARITAL STATUS, AND
FULL- OR PART-TIME STATUS, APRIL 1986[2]

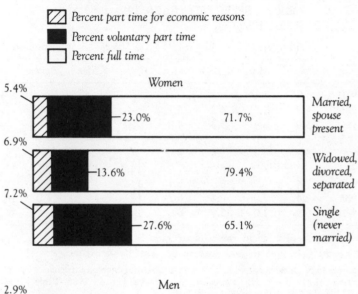

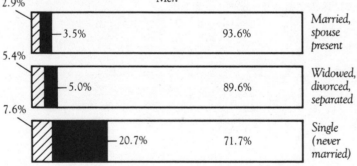

[1]Persons 16 years of age and older.

[2]Data are not seasonally adjusted.

Source: U.S. Department of Labor, Bureau of Labor Statistics, *Employment and Earnings,* May 1986, Table A-30.

Figure 10 • PERCENT OF CHILDREN WITH MOTHER IN THE
LABOR FORCE BY AGE OF CHILDREN, SELECTED
YEARS, 1970–1984 AND MARCH 1985

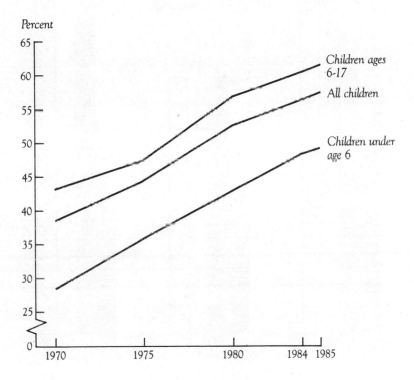

Source: U.S. Department of Labor, Bureau of Labor Statistics, *Handbook of Labor Statistics,* 1985, Table 55; U.S. Department of Labor, *News,* September 19, 1985.

Figure 11 • CHILDREN WITH MOTHER IN THE LABOR FORCE
BY FAMILY TYPE, 1970 AND 1984–1985[1]
(percent with mother in the labor force)

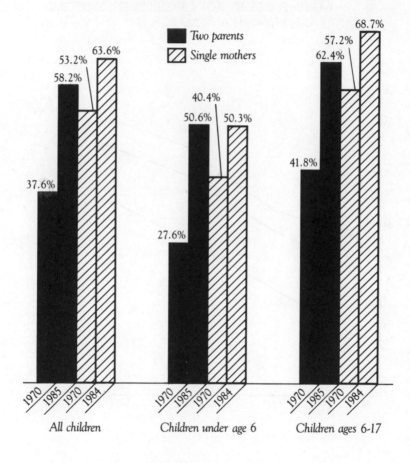

[1]Data for children living with mother only were not available for 1985.

Source: U.S. Department of Labor, Bureau of Labor Statistics, *Handbook of Labor Statistics*, 1985, Table 55; U.S. Department of Labor, *News*, September 19, 1985.

Figure 12 • LABOR FORCE PARTICIPATION RATES OF
WOMEN BETWEEN THE AGES OF 18 AND 44 WHO
HAVE HAD A CHILD IN THE PRECEDING 12
MONTHS, JUNE 1976 AND JUNE 1980–JUNE 1985

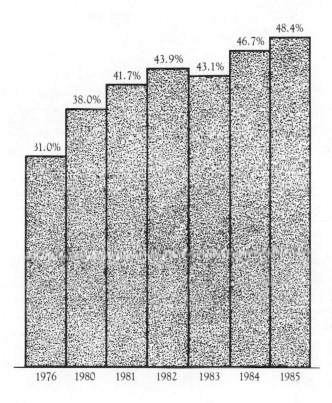

Source: U.S. Bureau of the Census, Current Population Reports, Series P-20, No.
406, 1986, Table C.

Figure 13 • OCCUPATIONAL DISTRIBUTION OF ALL
EMPLOYED MEN AND OF EMPLOYED WOMEN BY
RACE, AGE 16 AND OVER, APRIL 1986[1]

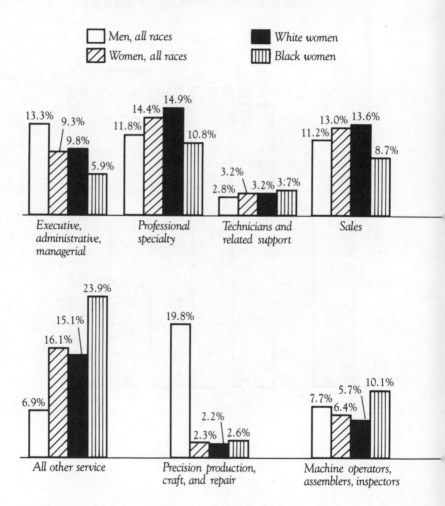

[1]Data are not seasonally adjusted.

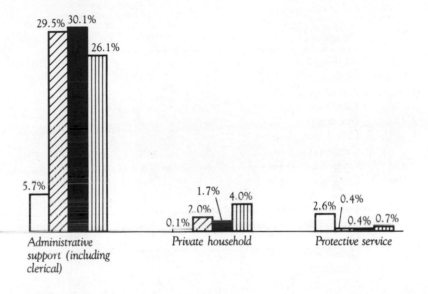

29.5% 30.1%
26.1%
5.7%
1.7% 4.0%
2.0%
0.1%
2.6% 0.4%
0.4% 0.7%

Administrative   Private household   Protective service
support (including
clerical)

6.8%
0.9%
0.9% 1.2%

6.4%
1.3%
1.4% 2.0%

4.8% 1.0%
1.1% 0.4%

Transportation and   Handlers, equipment   Farming, forestry,
material moving   cleaners, helpers,   fishing
                        laborers

Source: U.S. Department of Labor, Bureau of Labor Statistics, *Employment and Earnings*, May 1986, Table A-23.

Table 14 • PROPORTION FEMALE WORKERS IN
SELECTED OCCUPATIONS, 1975 AND 1985

Occupation	Women as percent of total employed	
	1975	1985
Airline pilot	—	2.6
Architect	4.3	11.3
Auto mechanic	0.5	0.7
Bartender	35.2	47.9
Bus driver	37.7	49.2
Cab driver, chauffeur	8.7	10.9
Carpenter	0.6	1.2
Child care worker	98.4	96.1
Computer programmer	25.6	34.3
Computer systems analyst	14.8	28.0
Data entry keyer	92.8	90.7
Data-processing equipment repairer	1.8	10.4
Dentist	1.8	6.5
Dental assistant	100.0	99.0
Economist	13.1	34.5
Editor, reporter	44.6	51.7
Elementary school teacher	85.4	84.0
College/university teacher	31.1	35.2
Garage, gas station attendant	4.7	6.8
Lawyer, judge	7.1	18.2
Librarian	81.1	87.0
Mail carrier	8.7	17.2
Office machine repairer	1.7	5.7
Physician	13.0	17.2
Registered nurse	97.0	95.1
Social worker	60.8	66.7
Telephone installer, repairer	4.8	12.8
Telephone operator	93.3	88.8
Waiter/waitress	91.1	84.0
Welder	4.4	4.8

Source: U.S. Department of Labor, Bureau of Labor Statistics, *Employment and Earnings*, January 1976, Table 2, and January 1986, Table 22.

Table 15 • WOMEN-OWNED BUSINESSES, 1982[1]

Industry	Total number	Number owned by women	Percent owned by women	Percent of receipts generated by women-owned businesses
Total (all industries)	12,059,950	2,884,450	23.9	10.2
Construction	1,324,793	61,665	4.7	4.9
Manufacturing	314,219	49,727	15.8	9.1
Transportation	499,656	40,596	8.1	8.2
Wholesale and retail trade	2,866,187	761,940	26.6	11.7
Finance, insurance, real estate	1,703,321	263,734	15.5	5.4
Services	4,723,771	1,401,776	29.7	12.3
Other	628,003	305,012	48.6	12.2

[1]Excluding corporations with more than 25 shareholders. (Ninety-two percent of the women-owned businesses are individual proprietorships.)

Source: U.S. Bureau of the Census, 1982 Economic Censuses, 1986, Table E.

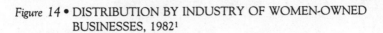

Figure 14 • DISTRIBUTION BY INDUSTRY OF WOMEN-OWNED
BUSINESSES, 1982[1]

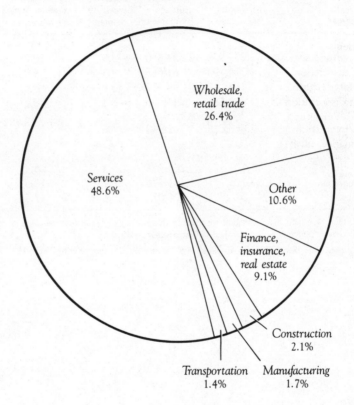

[1]Excluding corporations with more than 25 shareholders. (Ninety-two percent of the
women-owned businesses are individual proprietorships.)

Source: U.S. Bureau of the Census, *1982 Economic Censuses*, 1986, Table E.

Table 16 • WOMEN IN ELECTIVE OFFICE, SELECTED
OFFICES, 1975–1987

Elected officeholders	Percentage female							Number of women	
	1975	1977	1979	1981	1983	1986	1987	1986	1987
Members of U.S. Congress	4	3	3	3	4	5	5	25	25
Statewide elective officials	10	8	11	11	13	14	14	42	43
Members of state legislatures	8	9	10	12	13	15	16	1,101	1,156

Source: Center for the American Woman and Politics. *Women in Elective Office*, May 1986, and unpublished data.

Table 17 • WOMEN IN THE JUDICIARY, 1985 AND 1986

	Total women	Women as percent of all judges
Women on the Federal Bench[1]	64	8.5
Supreme Court	1	11.1
Circuit Courts of Appeal	18	10.7
District Courts	44	7.6
Court of International Trade	1	NA
Women on State Benches[2]	873	7.4
Courts of last resort	23	6.8
Intermediate appellate courts	46	6.5
Other full-time courts	804	7.3

[1]Active "Article III" judges as of August 20, 1986.
[2]Full-time, law-trained judges as of September 1, 1985.

Source: Data on federal judges provided to the Women's Research and Education Institute by the Administrative Office of the United States Courts, 1986. Data on state judges from Fund for Modern Courts, Inc., 1985.

Table 18 • HISTORICAL DATA ON THE NUMBER OF WOMEN
DIRECTORS ON FORTUNE BOARDS DURING THE
LAST 17 YEARS

Year	Total number of women directors	Number of directorships held by women	Number of companies with women on their boards	Percentage of companies with women on their boards
1969	46	NA	NA	NA
1976	147	NA	175	13
1977	204	NA	228	18
1979	262	361	316	24
1980	317	461	378	29
1981	336	490	398	30
1982	336	499	405	31
1983	367	527	427	33
1984[1]	313	455	364	36
1985[1]	339	511	407	41
1986[1]	395	576	439	44

[1]The statistics are based on the new Fortune 1000 classification rather than the former Fortune 1350 classification and thus appear to have declined; figures for this year, however, actually reflect a proportionate increase.

Source: Reproduced by permission of Catalyst, 250 Park Avenue South, New York, New York 10003. © Catalyst 1986.

Table 19 • MEDIAN INCOME OF FAMILIES BY FAMILY TYPE,
RACE, AND SPANISH ORIGIN, 1985 (in dollars)

	All races	White	Black	Spanish origin[1]
Married couple	31,100	31,602	24,570	22,269
Wife in paid labor force	36,431	36,992	30,502	28,132
Wife not in paid labor force	24,556	25,307	15,129	17,116
Male householder, no wife present	22,622	24,109	16,416	19,773
Female householder, no husband present	13,660	15,825	9,305	8,792

[1]Persons of Spanish origin may be of any race.

Source: U.S. Bureau of the Census, Current Population Reports, Series P-60, No. 154, 1986, Table 1.

Figure 15 • MEDIAN INCOME OF PERSONS AGE 15 AND OVER
    BY AGE, SEX, AND YEAR-ROUND, FULL-TIME
    EMPLOYMENT STATUS, 1985

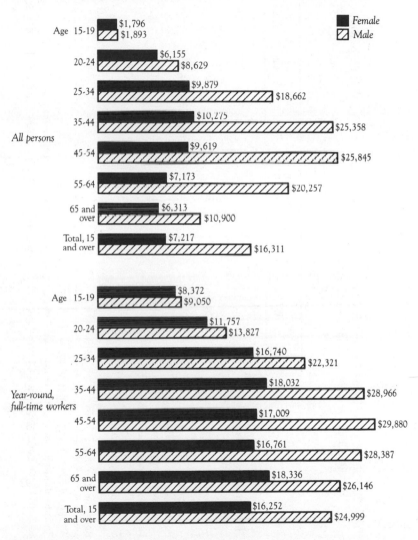

Source: U.S. Bureau of the Census, Current Population Reports, Series P-60, No. 154, 1986, Table 10.

Table 20 • SELECTED SOURCES OF INCOME FOR PERSONS AGE 15 AND OVER BY SEX, RACE, AND SPANISH ORIGIN, 1984 (percentage receiving income from source)

Source	Women				Men			
	Total	White	Black	Spanish origin[1]	Total	White	Black	Spanish origin[1]
Wage or salary	55.4	55.4	55.2	50.5	70.8	71.7	64.1	73.6
Nonfarm self-employment	3.5	3.8	1.0	2.1	8.2	8.8	2.9	5.0
Property income[2]	55.7	60.3	23.3	30.0	56.4	60.5	24.2	30.1
Interest	54.1	58.6	22.2	28.8	54.6	58.6	23.4	28.6
Social security or railroad retirement	19.9	20.8	15.7	9.8	15.6	16.1	14.0	8.9
Public assistance and supplemental security income	6.2	4.4	19.9	12.4	2.5	1.9	6.7	4.3
Public assistance and welfare income	4.0	2.6	13.7	9.1	1.2	0.9	2.9	1.9
Supplemental security income	2.5	1.9	6.7	3.8	1.4	1.1	4.0	2.5
Retirement and annuities	5.2	5.6	2.9	1.6	9.4	9.9	5.7	3.2

[1]Persons of Spanish origin may be of any race.

[2]Includes dividends, interest, net rental income, income from estates or trusts, and net royalties.

Source: U.S. Bureau of the Census, Current Population Reports, Series P-60, No. 151, 1986, Table 35.

Figure 16 • OWNERSHIP OF SELECTED ASSETS BY TYPE OF HOUSEHOLD, 1984[1]

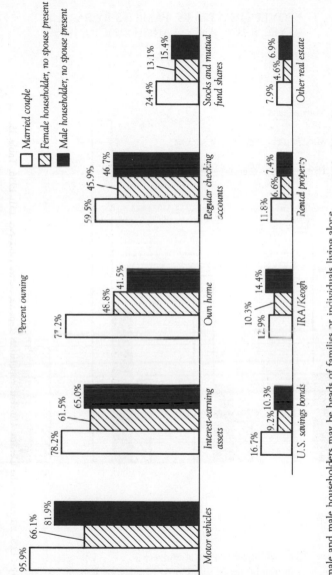

Legend:
☐ Married couple
▨ Female householder, no spouse present
■ Male householder, no spouse present

Percent owning

Motor vehicles: 95.9%, 81.9%, 66.1%
Interest-earning assets: 78.2%, 61.5%, 65.0%
Own home: 77.2%, 46.8%, 41.5%
Regular checking accounts: 59.5%, 45.9%, 46.7%
Stocks and mutual fund shares: 24.4%, 13.1%, 15.4%

U.S. savings bonds: 16.7%, 9.2%, 10.3%
IRA/Keogh: 12.9%, 10.3%, 14.4%
Rental property: 11.8%, 6.6%, 7.4%
Other real estate: 7.9%, 4.6%, 6.9%

[1]Female and male householders may be heads of families or individuals living alone.

Source: U.S. Bureau of the Census, Current Population Reports, Series P-70, No. 7, 1986. Table 1.

Figure 17 • POVERTY RATES OF FAMILIES BY FAMILY
TYPE, RACE, AND SPANISH ORIGIN, 1985

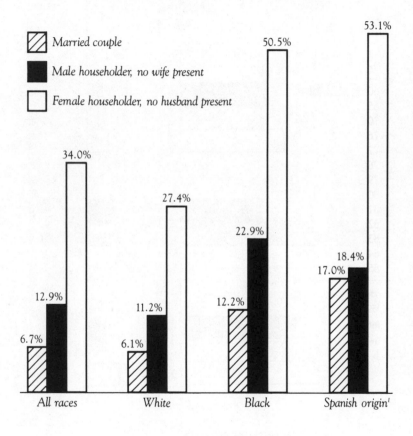

¹Persons of Spanish origin may be of any race.

Source: U.S. Bureau of the Census, Current Population Reports, Series P-60, No. 154, 1986, Table 15.

Table 21 • TRENDS IN POVERTY RATES OF PERSONS BY
FAMILY TYPE, RACE, AND SPANISH ORIGIN,
1960–1985

	All races		White		Black		Spanish origin[1]	
Year	Female-headed	All others	Female-headed	All others	Female-headed	All others	Female-headed	All others
1960	49.5	18.5	42.3	14.9	70.0[2]	50.7[2]	NA	NA
1965	46.0	13.2	38.5	10.3	65.1[3]	33.4[3]	NA	NA
1970	38.2	8.2	31.4	6.8	58.8	21.7	NA	NA
1976	34.4	7.1	27.3	6.0	54.7	16.9	54.3	17.9
1977	32.8	6.9	25.5	5.9	53.9	16.6	53.3	15.3
1978	32.3	6.6	24.9	5.7	53.1	15.1	53.3	14.6
1979	32.0	7.0	24.9	5.9	52.2	16.2	48.9	15.5
1980	33.8	8.0	27.1	6.9	53.1	17.9	52.5	18.5
1981	35.2	8.8	28.4	7.6	55.8	19.4	54.0	18.6
1982	36.2	9.8	28.7	8.7	57.4	20.0	57.4	22.0
1983	35.6	10.1	28.3	8.8	55.9	20.5	53.2	20.9
1984	34.0	9.3	27.3	8.2	52.9	19.1	54.3	20.9
1985	33.5	8.9	27.3	7.9	51.8	16.4	54.2	21.1

[1]Persons of Spanish origin may be of any race.
[2]1959.
[3]1966.
Source: U.S. Bureau of the Census, Current Population Reports, Series P-60, No.
154, 1986, Table 16.

Table 22 • PERCENT OF POOR CHILDREN[1] LIVING IN
FEMALE-HEADED HOUSEHOLDS BY RACE AND
SPANISH ORIGIN, SELECTED YEARS, 1960–1985

Year	All races	White	Black	Spanish origin[2]
1960	23.7	21.0	29.4[3]	NA
1965	31.7	27.1	44.1[4]	NA
1970	45.8	36.6	60.7	NA
1976	55.4	45.0	73.9	44.6
1977	56.4	45.3	74.9	48.9
1978	58.5	46.3	78.0	48.9
1979	56.4	44.5	77.1	44.4
1980	52.8	41.3	75.4	47.1
1981	52.2	42.0	73.2	48.5
1982	51.0	39.2	74.5	46.8
1983	50.2	39.7	74.6	45.2
1984	52.4	41.8	74.9	47.2
1985	53.8	43.0	78.4	49.6

[1]Refers to related children under age 18 in families.
[2]Persons of Spanish origin may be of any race.
[3]1959.
[4]1966.
Source: U.S. Bureau of the Census, Current Population Reports, Series P-60, No. 154, 1986, Table 16.

Chapter Notes

Introduction

1. Gerda Lerner, *The Grimké Sisters from South Carolina* (New York: Schocken, 1971), p. 189.

O N E Women in Twentieth Century America: An Overview

1. That housework itself was arduous and complex remained essentially unacknowledged, for housework was not really "work" in the manly sense of the term.
2. The longer-term consequences of a cohort shaped by its wartime experiences, like that of its predecessors seared by the Great Depression, can only be inferred, but its importance should not be underestimated. The mothers of the baby boom generation experienced a moment of independence and cultural validation (whether personally or vicariously) that may well have shaped the mixed messages they gave their daughters. It was their daughters who loudly proclaimed the rebirth of feminism two decades later, and politicized daily life once again with the slogan "the personal is political."

T W O Women and the Family

1. Sample surveys of divorced men and women are difficult to carry out, and Weitzman's efforts compare favorably with other small-scale studies. Her study is based upon a random sample of final decrees of dissolution granted in Los Angeles County between May and July 1977 (Weitzman, 1985: Appendix A). Nevertheless, Weitzman was forced to eliminate cases in which the parties had moved out of state. More important, she was able to locate only about 50 percent of the sample, and 17 percent of those who were located refused to be interviewed. These limitations may have produced the discrepancy between her estimates and those of the nationally representative PSID, which has involved annual interviews by professional interviewers from the Survey Research Center at the University of Michigan. For example, it may be that the minority who were still in California, more easily located and willing to cooper-

ate, differed in unknown ways from the majority of those who divorced in Los Angeles between May and July 1977 and who were not interviewed.

Moreover, in her calculations of post-divorce family income, Weitzman excludes the income of new spouses and permanent cohabitors (p. 327). This exaggerates the difference between men and women after divorce, because the addition of a new husband's (usually much higher) earnings typically raises a divorced woman's family income substantially. Thus, if a divorced woman in Weitzman's sample has remarried, her new husband is counted in assessing her needs as an extra person to be clothed and fed, but his income is assumed to be zero. As Weitzman notes, the exclusion of new spouses' earnings also will lead to an underestimate of remarried men's family income (because their new wives are assumed not to be earning money), but this procedure leads to a far greater underestimate of remarried women's family income because men earn more, on average, than women. The comparable figures on pre- and post-divorce income from the PSID, cited below in the text, come from Duncan and Hoffman (1985b), Tables 14.A.7 and 14.A.8 for all men and women and 14.A.9 and 14.A.10 for comparisons of those with pre-divorce incomes above and below the median level.

2. Weitzman (1985) cites even lower remarriage probabilities for women according to age at divorce, but her reference (p. 204) is to a government publication which does not present the information needed to calculate these probabilities. Moreover, she argues incorrectly that a much greater proportion of divorces occur to women married 15 years or more today than was the case 25 years ago (p. 187). Thus, she is led to pay disproportionate attention to the situation of older divorced women who have not remarried.

3. According to the criteria of the U.S. Bureau of the Census, a household consists of all persons living in a single housing unit, whether they are related or not. A family is defined as two or more persons who live in the same household and who are related by blood, marriage, or adoption. Social statisticians rarely consider the possibility that a family could extend over more than one household.

T H R E E **Women and the Economy**

1. Unless otherwise noted, data on employment and usual weekly earnings are from U.S. Bureau of Labor Statistics, *Employment and Earnings* (Washington D.C.: U.S. Government Printing Office, January 1986).

2. Unless otherwise noted, data on income and annual earnings are from U.S. Bureau of the Census, Current Population Reports, Series P-60, No. 149, *Money Income and Poverty Status of Families and Persons in the United States: 1984*, and Series P-60, No. 152, *Characteristics of the Popu-*

lation Below the Poverty Level: 1984 (Washington, D.C.: U.S. Government Printing Office, 1985 and 1986).

F O U R **The Women's Movement in Recent American Politics**

1. In particular, the legislation does not deal with issues such as integration (the practice of offsetting pension plan benefits by the amount of social security retirement benefits to which an employee is entitled) or vesting (the length of time a person must work to qualify for pension benefits at retirement age). Also, most women (and, for that matter, most men) do not receive private pension benefits; for many women, the protection of pension rights is therefore a moot issue.
2. Discrimination in insurance provided or sponsored by employers (unless the employer has fewer than 15 employees) is already prohibited under Title VII of the Civil Rights Act of 1964.
3. An exception was 1944, when many voting-age men were in the military.

Women in Intercollegiate Sports

1. This article is adapted from *The Sports Gender Gap: The Complete Do-It-Yourself Guide to Sex Equity in Intercollegiate Athletics*, which was developed under a grant from the U.S. Department of Education, Women's Educational Equity Act Program. The opinions expressed do not necessarily reflect the position or policy of the Department.

References

ONE **Women in Twentieth Century America: An Overview**

Addams, Jane. *Twenty Years at Hull House.* New York: Macmillan, 1910.

American Women: Report of the President's Commission on the Status of Women. Washington, D.C.: U.S. Government Printing Office, 1963.

Anderson, Karen. *Wartime Women: Sex Roles, Family Relations, and the Status of Women During World War II.* Westport, Connecticut: Greenwood Press, 1981.

Chambers, Clarke. *Seedtime of Reform: American Social Service and Social Action, 1918–1933.* Minneapolis: University of Minnesota Press, 1962.

D'Emilio, John. *Sexual Politics, Sexual Communities: The Making of a Homosexual Minority in the United States, 1940–1970.* Chicago: University of Chicago Press, 1983.

DuBois, Ellen Carol. *Feminism and Suffrage: The Emergence of an Independent Women's Movement in America, 1848–1860.* Ithaca, New York: Cornell University Press, 1978.

Evans, Sara M. *Personal Politics: The Roots of Women's Liberation in the Civil Rights Movement and the New Left.* New York: Knopf, 1979.

——— and Harry C. Boyte. *Free Spaces: The Sources of Democratic Change in America.* New York: Harper & Row, 1986.

Gavin, Nancy. "Women and the UAW in the 1950s." In *Women, Work and Protest: A Century of U.S. Women's Labor History,* edited by Ruth Milkman. Boston: Routledge & Kegan Paul, 1985.

Goodin, Joan M. "Working Women: The Pros and Cons of Unions." In *Women in Washington,* edited by Irene Tinker. Beverly Hills, California: Sage Publications, 1983.

Harrison, Cynthia E. "A 'New Frontier' for Women: The Public Policy of the Kennedy Administration." *Journal of American History* 67 (December 1980): 630–46.

Hartmann, Susan. *The Home Front and Beyond: American Women in the 1940s.* Boston: Twayne Publishers, 1982.

Horton, James. "Freedom's Yoke: Gender Conventions Among Antebellum Free Blacks." *Feminist Studies* 12 (Spring 1986): 51–86.

Jones, Jacqueline. *Labor of Love, Labor of Sorrow.* New York: Basic Books, 1985.

Kessler-Harris, Alice. *Out to Work: A History of Wage Earning Women in the United States.* New York: Oxford University Press, 1982.

Komarovsky, Mirra. *Blue Collar Marriage.* New York: Random House, 1962.

Look, October 16, 1956, 35.

Lora, Ronald. "Education: Schools as Crucible in Cold War America." In *American Democracy on Trial,* edited by Duane Leach and Monroe Billington. New York: McCutchan, 1968.

May, Elaine. *Explosive Issues: Sex, Women and the Bomb in Cold War America.* Unpublished paper presented at the American Historical Association, Washington, D.C., December 1984.

Milkman, Ruth. "Women's Work and the Economic Crisis: Some Lessons from the Great Depression." *Review of Radical Political Economics* 8 (Spring 1976): 73–97.

————. "Organizing the Sexual Division of Labor: Historical Perspectives on 'Women's Work' and the American Labor Movement." *Socialist Review* 10 (January–February 1980): 95–150.

Oppenheimer, Valerie. *The Female Labor Force in the United States: Demographic and Economic Factors Governing Its Growth and Changing Composition.* Berkeley: University of California Press, 1970.

Rosen, Marjorie. *Popcorn Venus: Women, Movies and the American Dream.* New York: Avon, 1974.

Rothman, Sheila. *Woman's Proper Place.* New York: Basic Books, 1978.

Rubin, Lillian. *Worlds of Pain: Life in the Working Class Community.* New York: Basic Books, 1976.

Saturday Evening Post, June 12, 1943, 55.

Scott, Anne Firor and Andrew MacKay Scott. *One Half the People: The Fight for Woman Suffrage.* Philadelphia: Lippincott, 1975.

Strom, Sharon Hartman. "Leadership and Tactics in the American Woman Suffrage Movement: A New Perspective from Massachusetts." *Journal of American History* 62 (September 1975): 296–315.

Swerdlow, Amy. "Ladies' Day at the Capitol: Women Strike for Peace Versus HUAC." *Feminist Studies* 8 (Fall 1982): 493–520.

Tax, Meredith. *The Rising of the Women: Feminist Solidarity and Class Conflict, 1880–1917.* New York: Monthly Review Press, 1980.

U.S. Bureau of the Census. *Statistical Abstract of the United States, 1967,* 88th Edition. Washington, D.C.: U.S. Government Printing Office, 1967.

Ware, Susan. *Beyond Suffrage: Women in the New Deal.* Cambridge: Harvard University Press, 1981.

Weiner, Lynn. *From Working Girl to Working Mother: The Female Labor Force in the United States, 1920–1980.* Chapel Hill: University of North Carolina Press, 1985.

T W O **Women and the Family**

Bacharach, Christine A. *Characteristics of Cohabiting Women in the United States: Evidence from the National Survey of Family Growth, Cycle III.* Paper presented at the annual meeting of the Population Association of America, Boston, 1985.

Bane, Mary Jo. "Household Composition and Poverty." In *Fighting Poverty: What Works and What Doesn't,* edited by Sheldon H. Danziger and Daniel H. Weinberg. Cambridge: Harvard University Press, 1986.

Bureau of National Affairs, Inc. *Work and Family: A Changing Dynamic.* Washington, D.C.: Bureau of National Affairs, Inc., 1986.

Cherlin, Andrew J. "Remarriage as an Incomplete Institution." *American Journal of Sociology* 84 (November 1978): 634–50.

———. *Marriage, Divorce, Remarriage.* Cambridge: Harvard University Press, 1981.

——— and Frank F. Furstenberg, Jr. *The New American Grandparent: A Place in the Family, A Life Apart.* New York: Basic Books, 1986.

——— and James McCarthy. "Remarried Couple Households." *Journal of Marriage and the Family* 47 (February 1985): 23–30.

Duncan, Greg J. *Years of Poverty, Years of Plenty.* Ann Arbor, Michigan: Institute for Social Research, 1984.

——— and Saul D. Hoffman. "A Reconsideration of the Economic Consequences of Marital Dissolution." *Demography* 22 (November 1985a): 485–97.

———. "Economic Consequences of Marital Instability." In *Horizontal Equity, Uncertainty, and Economic Well-Being,* edited by Martin David and Timothy Smeeding. Chicago: University of Chicago Press, 1985b.

Furstenberg, Frank F., Jr., Christine Winquist Nord, James L. Peterson, and Nicholas Zill. "The Life Course of Children of Divorce: Marital Disruption and Parental Conflict." *American Sociological Review* 48 (October 1983): 656–68.

——— and Jeanne Brooks-Gunn. "Teenage Childbearing: Causes, Consequences and Remedies." In *Applications of Social Science to Clinical Medicine,* edited by Linda H. Aiken and David Mechanic. New Brunswick, New Jersey: Rutgers University Press, 1985.

Hagestad, Gunhild O. "The Aging Society as a Context for Family Life." *Daedalus* 115 (Winter 1986): 119–39.

Koo, Helen P. and C.M. Suchindran. "Effects of Children on Women's Remarriage Prospects." *Journal of Family Issues* 1 (December 1980): 497–516.

Pleck, Joseph H. *Working Wives/Working Husbands.* Beverly Hills, California: Sage Publications, 1985.

Presser, Harriet B. and Virginia Cain. "Shift Work among Dual-Earner Couples with Children." *Science* 219 (February 18, 1983).

Preston, Samuel H. "Children and the Elderly in the U.S." *Scientific American*, December 1984, 44–49.

Uhlenberg, Peter and Mary Anne P. Salmon. "Change in Relative Income of Older Women, 1960–1980." *The Gerontologist* 26 (April 1986): 164–70.

U.S. Bureau of the Census. Current Population Reports, Series P-23, No. 124. *Child Support and Alimony: 1981.* Washington, D.C.: U.S. Government Printing Office, 1983a.

———. Current Population Reports, Series P-23, No. 129. *Child Care Arrangements of Working Mothers: June 1982.* Washington, D.C.: U.S. Government Printing Office, 1983b.

———. Current Population Reports, Series P-60, No. 144. *Characteristics of the Population below the Poverty Level: 1982.* Washington, D.C.: U.S. Government Printing Office, 1984.

———. Current Population Reports, Series P-20, No. 399. *Marital Status and Living Arrangements: March 1984.* Washington, D.C.: U.S. Government Printing Office, 1985.

Weitzman, Lenore J. *The Divorce Revolution: The Unexpected Social and Economic Consequences for Women and Children in America.* New York: Free Press, 1985.

Westoff, Charles F. "Marriage and Fertility in the Developed Countries." *Scientific American*, December 1978, 51–57.

THREE Women and the Economy

Barrett, Nancy S. "Obstacles to Economic Parity for Women." *American Economic Review* 72 (May 1982): 160–65.

———. "Part-time Workers." *Personnel Administrator*, December 1983, 94–104.

Beller, Andrea. "Occupational Segregation by Sex: Determinants and Changes." *Journal of Human Resources* 17 (Summer 1982): 371–92.

Bergmann, Barbara R. "Reducing the Pervasiveness of Discrimination." In *Jobs for Americans*, edited by Eli Ginsburg. The American Assembly. Englewood Cliffs, New Jersey: Prentice-Hall, Inc., 1976.

———. "The Economic Risks of Being a Housewife." *American Economic Review* 71 (May 1981): 81–85.

Bielby, William T. and James N. Baron. "Sex Segregation Within Occupations." *American Economic Review* 76 (May 1986): 43–52.

Blau, Francine. "Discrimination Against Women: Theory and Evidence." In *Labor Economics: Modern Views*, edited by William Darity. Boston: Martinus Nijhoff, 1984.

———— and Marianne A. Ferber. *The Economics of Women, Men, and Work.* Englewood Cliffs, New Jersey: Prentice-Hall, 1986.

———— and Lawrence Kahn. "Race and Sex Differences in Quits by Young Workers." *Industrial and Labor Relations Review* 34 (July 1981): 563–77.

Blinder, Alan. "Wage Discrimination: Reduced Form and Structural Estimates." *Journal of Human Resources* 8 (Fall 1973): 436–55.

Blumrosen, Ruth. "Wage Discrimination, Job Segregation, and Title VII of the Civil Rights Act of 1964." *University of Michigan Journal of Law Reform* 12 (Spring 1979): 397–502.

Burtless, Gary and Robert H. Haveman. "Policy Lessons from Three Labor Market Experiments." In *Employment and Training R & D: Lessons Learned and Future Directions.* Conference proceedings of the National Council on Employment Policy, January 26–27, 1985.

Dupnoff, Steven and Philip Kraft. *Gender Stratification in Computer Programming.* Paper presented before the Eastern Sociological Society, Boston, March 1984.

Flaim, Paul O. and Ellen Sehgal. "Displaced Workers of 1979–83: How Well Have They Fared?" *Monthly Labor Review* 108 (June 1985): 3–16.

Fleisher, Belton and George Rhodes. "Fertility, Women's Wage Rates, and Labor Supply." *American Economic Review* 69 (March 1979): 14–24.

Fox, Mary Frank and Sharlene Hesse-Biber. *Women at Work.* New York: Mayfield Publishing Company, 1984.

Kahn-Hut, Rachel, Arlene Daniels, and Richard Colvard (eds.). *Women and Work: Problems and Perspectives.* New York: Oxford University Press, 1982.

Kahne, Hilda and Andrew Kohen. "Economic Perspectives on the Roles of Women in the American Economy." *Journal of Economic Literature* 13 (December 1975): 1249–92.

Len, Carol and Robert W. Bednarzik. "A Profile of Women on Part-time Schedules." *Monthly Labor Review* 101 (October 1978): 10.

Lloyd, Cynthia B. and Beth T. Niemi. *The Economics of Sex Differentials.* New York: Columbia University Press, 1979.

McAdoo, Harriette Pipes. *Extended Family Support of Single Black Mothers.* Report to the National Institute of Mental Health, March 1983.

Mason, Karen Oppenheim, John L. Czajka, and Sara Arber. "Changes in U.S. Women's Sex-Role Attitudes, 1964–74." *American Sociological Review* 4 (August 1976): 573–96.

Mellor, Earl F. "Investigating Differences in Weekly Earnings of Women and Men." *Monthly Labor Review* 107 (June 1984): 17–28.

———— and Steven E. Haugen. "Hourly Paid Workers: Who They Are and What They Earn." *Monthly Labor Review* 109 (February 1986): 20–26.

Mincer, Jacob. "Labor Force Participation of Married Women: A Study of Labor Supply." In *Aspects of Labor Economics.* Princeton, New Jersey: Princeton University Press, 1962.

Norwood, Janet L. *The Female-Male Earnings Gap: A Review of Employment and Earnings Issues.* Report 673. Washington, D.C.: U.S. Government Printing Office, September 1982.

Randour, Mary Lou, Georgia L. Strasburg, and Jean Lipman-Blumen. "Women in Higher Education: Trends in Enrollments and Degrees Earned." *Harvard Educational Review* 52 (May 1982): 189–202.

Shapiro, David and Lois Shaw. "Growth in the Labor Force Attachment of Married Women: Accounting for Changes in the 1970's." *Southern Economic Journal* 50 (October 1983): 461–73.

Sieling, Mark S. "Staffing Patterns Prominent in Female-Male Earnings Gap." *Monthly Labor Review* 107 (June 1984): 29–33.

Simms, Margaret. "The Participation of Young Women in Employment and Training Programs." In *National Research Council, Youth Employment and Training Programs: The YEDPA Years.* Washington, D.C.: National Academy Press, 1986.

Smith, Ralph (ed.). *The Subtle Revolution: Women at Work.* Washington, D.C.: The Urban Institute, 1979.

Smith, Shirley L. "Work Experience Profile, 1984: The Effects of Recovery Continue." *Monthly Labor Review* 109 (February 1986): 37–43.

Steinberg, Ronnie and Alice Cook. *Women, Unions and Equal Employment Opportunity.* Albany, New York: Center for Women in Government, State University of New York at Albany, 1981.

U.S. Bureau of the Census. Current Population Reports, Series P-60, No. 149. *Money Income and Poverty Status of Families and Persons in the United States: 1984.* Washington, D.C.: U.S. Government Printing Office, 1985.

U.S. Civil Service Commission. *Equal Employment Opportunity Statistics.* Washington, D.C.: U.S. Government Printing Office, 1978.

U.S. Congressional Budget Office. *Demographic and Social Trends: Implications for Federal Support of Dependent-Care Services for Children and the Elderly.* Prepared for and released by the U.S. House of Representatives Select Committee on Children, Youth, and Families, Washington, D.C., March 1984.

U.S. Department of Labor, Bureau of Labor Statistics. *Employment and Earnings.* Washington, D.C.: U.S. Government Printing Office.

———. *Employment in Perspective: Women in the Labor Force.* (selected dates) Reports No. 712, 713, 715, 716, 719, 721, 725, 726. Washington, D.C.: U.S. Government Printing Office, 1984 and 1985.

———, Women's Bureau. *Facts on U.S. Working Women.* Fact Sheet No. 85-7. Washington, D.C.: U.S. Department of Labor, Women's Bureau, July 1985.

U.S. General Accounting Office. *Part-time Employment in Federal Agencies.* Washington, D.C.: U.S. Government Printing Office, 1976.
Vickery, Clair. "The Time-Poor: A New Look at Poverty." *Journal of Human Resources* 12 (Spring of 1977): 27–48.
Westat, Inc. *Impact on 1977 Earnings of New FY 1976 CETA Enrollees in Selected Program Activities.* Continuous Longitudinal Manpower Survey: Net Impact Report No. 1, prepared for the Office of Program Evaluation, Employment and Training Administration, U.S. Department of Labor. Rockville, Maryland: Westat, March 1981.

F O U R **The Women's Movement in Recent American Politics**

"Beneath the Enthusiasm for Women Candidates." *National Journal,* September 15, 1984, 1743.
Berry, Jeffrey M. *The Interest Group Society.* Boston: Little, Brown, 1984.
Center for the American Woman and Politics (CAWP). *Selected Statewide Races.* New Brunswick, New Jersey: CAWP, 1984.
———. *Women in Elective Office.* New Brunswick, New Jersey: CAWP, February 1983; April 1986.
"Changes in the Workplace." *Newsweek,* March 31, 1986, 57.
Friedan, Betty. *The Feminine Mystique.* New York: W.W. Norton & Co., 1963.
Gelb, Joyce and Marian Lief Palley. *Women and Public Policies.* Princeton, New Jersey: Princeton University Press, 1982.
———. *Women and Public Policies, Second Edition.* Princeton, New Jersey: Princeton University Press, 1987.
Hewlett, Sylvia Ann. *A Lesser Life.* New York: William Morrow, 1986.
Kamerman, Sheila. "Child Care Services: An Issue for Gender Equity and Women's Solidarity." *Child Welfare* LXIV (May–June 1985): 259–71.
Klein, Ethel. "The Gender Gap: Different Issues, Different Answers." *The Brookings Review,* Winter 1985, 33–37.
"The New York Times/CBS News Poll." *The New York Times,* November 8, 1984, A-19.
"Polls Suggest Women Support Democrats in '86 Races." *The New York Times,* May 11, 1986, A-22.
Pomper, Gerald. *Voters' Choice.* New York: Dodd Mead, 1975.
Poole, Keith and Harmon Zeigler. *Public Opinion and Politics.* New York: Longman, 1985.
Thom, Mary. "The All-Time Definitive Map of the Gender Gap." *MS.,* July 1984, 55–60.
Washington Social Legislation Bulletin 27 (August 23, 1982).
"Who Cast Their Votes for Reagan and Mondale?" *National Journal,* November 10, 1984, 2132.
"Women Gain in Statehouse." *National Journal,* November 17, 1984, 2220.

"The 'Women Problem' in Reagan's Approval Ratings." *National Journal*, August 21, 1982, 1459.

Women in Brief

Acosta, Vivian and Linda Jean Carpenter. *Percentage of Teams Coached by Women*. Unpublished data. Brooklyn, New York: 1984.

AFL-CIO. *The Changing Situation of Workers and Their Unions*. A Report by the AFL-CIO Committee on the Evolution of Work. Washington, D.C.: AFL-CIO, February 1985.

Atwell, Robert H., Bruce Grimes, and Donna A. Lopiano. *The Money Game: Financing Collegiate Athletics*. Washington, D.C.: American Council on Education, 1980.

Baden, Naomi. "Changing Women's Role in Unions." *Labor Studies Journal*, Winter 1986, 229–49.

Bartell, Ted, J. Ward Keesling, Linda LeBlanc, and Richard Tombaugh. *Study of Freshman Eligibility Standards: Technical Report*. Reston, Virginia: Advanced Technology, Inc., 1984.

Becerra, Rosina and Ruth E. Zambrana. "Approaches to Latino Research: Methodological Considerations." *Social Work Research and Abstracts*, Summer 1985, 42–49.

Bernstein, Aaron. "Comparable Worth: It's Already Happening." *Business Week*, April 28, 1986, 52.

Christian Science Monitor, July 28, 1985, 23.

Chronicle of Higher Education, August 29, 1984, 31–32.

Coakley, Jay J. and Patricia L. Pacey. "The Distribution of Athletic Scholarships Among Women in Intercollegiate Sport." In *Sport and the Sociological Imagination*, edited by N. Theberge and P. Donnelly. Fort Worth: Texas Christian University Press, 1984.

El-Khawas, Elaine H. *Differences in Academic Development During College. Men and Women Learning Together: A Study of College Students in the Late 1970s*. Providence, Rhode Island: Brown University, Office of the Provost, April 1980.

Erkut, Sumru. *Expectancy, Attribution, and Academic Achievement: Exploring Implications of Sex-Role Orientation*. Working Paper No. 27. Wellesley, Massachusetts: Wellesley College Center for Research on Women, 1979.

Flander, Judy. "Women in Network News." *Washington Journalism Review*, March 1985, 39–43.

Fornes, Maria Irene. "Women's Work." *American Theatre*, September 1985, 15.

Hanford, George (ed.). *A Report to the American Council on Education into the Need for and Feasibility of a National Study of Intercollegiate Athletics*, Vol. 1. Washington, D.C.: American Council on Education, 1974.

Hetherington, E.M., M. Cox, and R. Cox. "Family Interactions and the

Social, Emotional, and Cognitive Development of Children Following Divorce." In *The Family: Setting Priorities*, edited by V.C. Vaughn and T.B. Brazelton. New York: Science and Medicine Publishers, 1979.

Hoffman, Lois Wladis. "Effects of Maternal Employment on the Child— A Review of the Research." *Developmental Psychology* 10 (1974): 204–28.

Holm, Jeanne. *Women in the Military: An Unfinished Revolution.* Novato, California: Presidio Press, 1982.

Houstoun, Marion F., Roger G. Kramer, and Joan Mackin Barrett. "Female Predominance in Immigration in the United States Since 1930: A First Look." *International Migration Review* 18 (Winter 1984): 908–63.

Intergovernmental Committee on Migration Fifth Seminar on Adaptation and Integration of Permanent Immigrants. *Situation and Role of Migrant Women.* Geneva, Switzerland: Intergovernmental Committee, 1981.

Kingsbury, Marty. "Second Annual Theatre Festival." *Sojourner*, May 1986.

Melandez, Sarah E. and Reginald Wilson. *Minorities in Higher Education: Fourth Annual Status Report.* Washington, D.C.: American Council on Education, 1985.

Miller Brewing Company and Research and Forecasts, Inc. *The Miller Lite Report on American Attitudes Toward Sports.* Milwaukee, Wisconsin: Miller Brewing Company, 1983.

Murphy, Margaret Diane. *The Involvement of Blacks in Women's Athletics in Member Institutions of the Association of Intercollegiate Athletics for Women.* Ph.D. diss., Florida State University, 1980.

Myers, H.F. "Research on the Afro-American Family: A Critical Review." In *The Afro-American Family: Assessment, Treatment, and Research Issues,* edited by B. Bass, G. Wyatt, and G. Powell. New York: Grune and Stratton, 1981.

National Association of Broadcasters (NAB). *Broadcasting Facts,* October 1985.

National Association of Intercollegiate Athletics (NAIA). *Fact Sheet: 5 Year NAIA Varsity Participation Study.* Kansas City, Missouri: NAIA, 1984.

National Collegiate Athletic Association (NCAA). *Fact Sheet: 1983–1984 Participation Study—Women's Sports; Fact Sheet: 1983–1984 Participation Study—Men's Sports.* Mission, Kansas: NCAA, 1984.

———. *Sports and Recreational Programs of the Nation's Universities and Colleges, Report #4.* Mission, Kansas: NCAA, 1974.

NOW Legal Defense and Education Fund (NOWLDEF). *One Year Plus: Little Progress for Women in Network News.* NOWLDEF press release, April 9, 1986.

Paludi, Michele A. and William Bauer. "Goldberg Revisited: What's in an Author's Name." *Sex Roles,* 9, No. 3 (1983): 387–90.

———— and Lisa A. Strayer. "What's in an Author's Name? Differential Evaluations of Performance as a Function of Author's Name." *Sex Roles*, 12, Nos. 3–4 (1985): 353–61.

Presidents Make a Difference: Strengthening Leadership in Colleges and Universities. Washington, D.C.: Association of Governing Boards of Universities and Colleges, 1984.

Raiborn, Mitchell H. *Revenues and Expenses of Intercollegiate Athletic Programs.* Mission, Kansas: National Collegiate Athletic Association, 1982.

The Seattle Times, June 8, 1986, C–1.

Sloan, F.A., J. Valvana and R. Mullner. *Identifying the Issues: A Statistical Profile.* Paper presented at the conference, Uncompensated Hospital Care: Defining Rights and Assigning Responsibilities. Nashville, Tennessee: Vanderbilt University, April 6–7, 1984.

Staples, Robert and Alfredo Mirandé. "Racial and Cultural Variations among American Families: A Decennial Review of the Literature on Minority Families." *Journal of Marriage and the Family* 42 (1980): 157–73.

The State of Small Business: A Report of the President. Washington, D.C.: U.S. Government Printing Office, 1985.

Stone, Vernon A. "Survey Shows Little Change for Minorities or Women." *Communicator,* June 1985, 36–37.

Sutton, Charlotte Decker and Kris K. Moore. "Executive Women—20 Years Later." *Harvard Business Review,* September–October 1985, 42–66.

U.S. Bureau of the Census. *1982 Economic Censuses, Women-owned Businesses, 1982.* Washington, D.C.: U.S. Government Printing Office, April 1986.

U.S. Commission on Civil Rights (USCCR). *Window Dressing on the Set: Women and Minorities in Television.* Washington, D.C.: USCCR, August 1977.

Vetter, Betty M. and Eleanor M. Babco. *Professional Women and Minorities— A Manpower Data Resource Service.* Sixth Edition. Washington, D.C.: Commission on Professionals in Science and Technology, February 1986.

Walker, Kelly B. "The Savvy 60." *Savvy,* April 1986.

"Women Directing More Plays but Broadway is Still Elusive." *The New York Times,* January 16, 1984.

"Women-owned Businesses Found Stronger in Survey." *Washington Post,* January 14, 1985.

Women's Equity Action League (WEAL). "Recruitment Statistics and Policies: Women in the Active Armed Services." *WEAL Facts,* January 1986.

Women's Sports Foundation. *Fact Sheet: American Female Medal Winners, 1984 Los Angeles Olympics.* San Francisco: Women's Sports Foundation, 1984a.

————. *Fact Sheet: 1984 Women Olympians.* San Francisco: Women's Sports Foundation, 1984b.

American Women Today: A Statistical Portrait

NOTE: The Current Population Reports of the U.S. Bureau of the Census are listed in ascending order by series and publication numbers. Thus, a report in the P-20 series precedes a P-60 report.

Catalyst. *Historical Data on the Number of Women Directors on Fortune Boards During the Last 17 Years* (fact sheet). New York: Catalyst, 1986.

Center for the American Woman and Politics (CAWP). *Women in Elective Office* (fact sheet). New Brunswick, New Jersey: CAWP, May 1986.

————. *Women in State Legislatures 1986* (fact sheet). New Brunswick, New Jersey: CAWP, April 1986.

Fund for Modern Courts, Inc. *The Success of Women and Minorities in Achieving Judicial Office: The Selection Process.* New York: Fund for Modern Courts, Inc., 1985.

National Center for Health Statistics. "Annual Summary of Births, Marriages, Divorces, and Deaths, United States, 1984." *Monthly Vital Statistics Report,* Vol. 33, No. 13, Department of Health and Human Services Pub. No. (PHS) 85-1120. Hyattsville, Maryland: U.S. Public Health Service, September 26, 1985.

————. "Advance Report of Final Mortality Statistics, 1983." *Monthly Vital Statistics Report,* Vol. 34, No. 6, Supplement (2), Department of Health and Human Services Pub. No. (PHS) 85-1120. Hyattsville, Maryland: U.S. Public Health Service, September 26,1985.

————. "Advance Report of Final Natality Statistics, 1984." *Monthly Vital Statistics Report,* Vol. 35, No. 4, Supplement, Department of Health and Human Services Pub. No. (PHS) 86-1120. Hyattsville, Maryland: U.S. Public Health Service, July 18, 1986.

U.S. Bureau of the Census. Census of the Population, Vol. I, PC80-1-B1. *General Population Characteristics: United States Summary.* Washington, D.C.: U.S. Government Printing Office, May 1983.

————. Current Population Reports, Series P-20, No. 218. *Household and Family Characteristics: March 1970.* Washington, D.C.: U.S. Government Printing Office, 1971.

————. Current Population Reports, Series P-20, No. 399. *Marital Status and Living Arrangements: March 1984.* Washington, D.C.: U.S. Government Printing Office, July 1985.

————. Current Population Reports, Series P-20, No. 406. *Fertility of American Women: June 1985.* Washington, D.C.: U.S. Government Printing Office, June 1986.

————. Current Population Reports, Series P-25, No. 952. *Projections of the Population of the United States, by Age, Sex, and Race: 1983 to*

2080. Washington, D.C.: U.S. Government Printing Office, May 1984.

———. Current Population Reports, Series P-60, No. 127. *Money Income and Poverty Status of Families and Persons in the United States: 1980.* Washington, D.C.: U.S. Government Printing Office, August 1981.

———. Current Population Reports, Series P-60, No. 149. *Money Income and Poverty Status of Families and Persons in the United States: 1984.* Washington, D.C.: U.S. Government Printing Office, August 1985.

———. Current Population Reports, Series P-60, No. 151. *Money Income of Households, Families, and Persons in the United States: 1984.* Washington, D.C.: U.S. Government Printing Office, April 1986.

———. Current Population Reports, Series P-60, No. 154. *Money Income and Poverty Status of Families and Persons in the United States: 1985.* Washington, D.C.: U.S. Government Printing Office, August 1986.

———. Current Population Reports, Series P-70, No. 7. *Household Wealth and Assets Ownership: 1984.* Washington, D.C.: U.S. Government Printing Office, July 1986.

———. *1982 Economic Censuses. Women-owned Businesses.* Washington, D.C.: U.S. Government Printing Office, April 1986.

———. *Statistical Abstract of the United States 1986,* 106th edition. Washington, D.C.: U.S. Government Printing Office, 1986.

U.S. Department of Labor. "Labor Force Activity of Mothers of Young Children Continues at Record Pace." *News,* USDL 85-381, September 19, 1985.

———, Bureau of Labor Statistics. *Employment and Earnings.* Washington, D.C.: U.S. Government Printing Office, January 1976, January 1986, May 1986.

———. *Handbook of Labor Statistics.* Washington, D.C.: U.S. Government Printing Office, June 1985.

Notes on the Contributors

Nancy Barrett is Professor of Economics and Chair of the Economics Department at American University. She received her Ph.D. in economics from Harvard University. The author of numerous books and articles on economic policy, Dr. Barrett served on the senior staff of the Council of Economic Advisers, and as Deputy Assistant Secretary of Labor for Policy, Evaluation, and Research in the Carter administration.

Carolyn Becraft is Director of the Project on Women and the Military at the Women's Equity Action League (WEAL). Ms. Becraft, who served as an Army officer for more than five years, was on the Board of Directors of the National Military Family Association and was Chair of the Army Family Action Council. She is also a Fellow with the Inter-University Seminar on Armed Forces and Society.

Andrew Cherlin is Professor of Sociology at the Johns Hopkins University. Dr. Cherlin's studies have centered on trends in American family life. He is the author of *Marriage, Divorce, Remarriage* (1981) and coauthor of *The New American Grandparent: A Place in the Family, A Life Apart* (1986) with Frank Furstenberg, Jr.

Betty Parsons Dooley has been Director of the Women's Research and Education Institute since 1977. An early Texas feminist, she was active in state politics before moving to Washington. In 1964, she was a candidate for the U.S. House of Representatives from the 16th Congressional District of Texas. She served for seven years as Director of the Health Security Action Council, an advocacy organization that worked for comprehensive national health insurance.

Margaret C. Dunkle is Director of the Equity Center, a nonprofit organization concerned with human and civil rights. Ms. Dunkle became the first Chair of the National Coalition for Women and Girls in Education, and served as Special Assistant for Education Legislation in the U.S. Department of Health, Education, and Welfare.

Sara M. Evans is Associate Professor of History and Women's Studies at the University of Minnesota. A former Kellogg National Fellow (1983–86), Dr. Evans is the author of *Personal Politics: The Roots of Women's Liberation in the Civil Rights Movement and the New Left* (1979) and coauthor, with Harry C. Boyte, of *Free Spaces: The Sources of Democratic Change in America* (1986).

Rachel Benson Gold is Associate for Policy Analysis with the Washington office of the Alan Guttmacher Institute. She has written extensively on reproductive health care and public policy in the United States.

Algea O. Harrison is Associate Professor of Psychology at Oakland University. Her work is primarily on the psychological impact of the black experience in America. Dr. Harrison's articles have appeared in such publications as *Child Development, Journal of Social and Behavioral Sciences, Journal of Marriage and the Family, Teaching Psychology,* and *The Psychology of Women Quarterly.*

Marion F. Houstoun is Immigration Staff Specialist in the Bureau of International Labor Affairs of the U.S. Department of Labor. She has served as the Secretary of Labor's expert staff-level representative to the Select Commission on Immigration and Refugee Policy (1979–80) and President Reagan's Immigration and Refugee Policy Task Force. Ms. Houstoun's publications include the landmark 1976 study, *The Characteristics and Role of Illegal Aliens in the U.S. Labor Market: An Exploratory Study,* which she coauthored with David S. North.

Roger G. Kramer is a manpower analyst with the Immigration Policy Group, International Affairs Bureau, U.S. Department of Labor. Before joining the Labor Department, Mr. Kramer was the Senior Immigration Statistician at the Immigration and Naturalization Service. During the 1970s, he analyzed demographic trends in developing countries at the International Demographic Data Center of the U.S. Bureau of the Census.

The Honorable **Juanita Kreps** served as U.S. Secretary of Commerce from January 1977 to December 1979. The first economist to hold this position, she had been the James B. Duke Professor of Economics and Vice-President of Duke University. Dr. Kreps, who has returned to Duke University, serves on numerous corporate boards and has been an officer of many professional associations. She is the author and editor of several books and numerous articles in economic journals.

Wendy Lawrence is head squash professional at the Capitol Hill Squash Club. In 1984 she was ranked number 12 in the U.S. in women's squash. A Vassar graduate, she is a former Chairman of the United States Squash Racquets Association's Ranking Committee and winner of the 1984 Wedgewood Trophy for outstanding sportsmanship in squash in the United States.

Anne Nelson is Director of the Institute for Women and Work of the New York State School of Industrial and Labor Relations, Cornell University. She is the coauthor, with Barbara Wertheimer, of *Trade Union Women: A Study of Their Participation in New York City Locals* (1975). Among Ms. Nelson's most recent publications is "A Union Woman's Influence" (*Labor Studies Journal*, Winter 1986).

Marian Lief Palley is Professor of Political Science at the University of Delaware. She is author or coauthor of numerous articles and books, including, with Joyce Gelb, *Women and Public Policies* (1982, 1987). Dr. Palley is former Secretary of the American Political Science Association (APSA) and former President of APSA's Women's Caucus.

Cory L. Richards is Public Policy Director and Director of the Washington office of the Alan Guttmacher Institute. He serves as editorial director of the Institute's bi-weekly newsletter, *Washington Memo*.

Bernice R. Sandler has been Director of the Project on the Status and Education of Women (PSEW) at the Association of American Colleges since the project's inception in 1971. PSEW is the oldest national education project concerned with achieving educational equity for women. Ms. Sandler's work has centered on Title IX of the Education Amendments of 1972.

Representative **Patricia Schroeder** (Democrat-Colorado) is dean of the women in Congress. She succeeded Elizabeth Holtzman as Democratic Co-chair of the Congressional Caucus for Women's Issues in 1980. Rep. Schroeder is a member of the House Armed Services, Judiciary, and Post Office and Civil Service Committees and of the Select Committee on Children, Youth, and Families.

Donna Shavlik is Director of the Office of Women in Higher Education of the American Council on Education. An expert on women's advancement in higher education, Ms. Shavlik is a founder of the Council's National Identification Program for the Advancement of Women in Higher Education.

Representative **Olympia Snowe** (Republican-Maine) succeeded Margaret Heckler as Republican Co-chair of the Congressional Caucus for Women's Issues in 1983. She is a member of the House Foreign Affairs Committee, the House Select Committee on Aging, and the Joint Economic Committee.

Sally Steenland is Deputy Director of the National Commission on Working Women, where she directs the organization's media projects. She has also worked for Ralph Nader and for the National Citizens Committee for Broadcasting.

Anne J. Stone has been a research associate at WREI since 1981, having previously served on the Washington staff of then-U.S. Representative Elizabeth Holtzman. Ms. Stone has authored and coauthored policy analyses on various subjects, including the federal budget, employment issues for women, and tax reform legislation.

Judith G. Touchton is Deputy Director of the Office of Women in Higher Education of the American Council on Education. Dr. Touchton is an authority on the status of women in colleges and universities. She is currently engaged in producing *The ACE Fact Book on Women in Higher Education*.

Joyce Van Dyke is an independent writer and consultant specializing in women's issues and the theatre. Formerly a professor of English at Wellesley College, Dr. Van Dyke has published articles and reports on a range of women's and social policy issues, as well as on drama and theatre.

Betty M. Vetter is Executive Director of the Commission on

Professionals in Science and Technology (formerly the Scientific Manpower Commission). She is editor of the monthly *Scientific, Engineering, Technical Manpower Comments,* and coauthor, with Eleanor L. Babco, of *Professional Women and Minorities—A Manpower Data Resource Service.*

Ruth E. Zambrana is Assistant Professor at the University of California at Los Angeles, School of Social Welfare. She is on the Research Advisory Board of the National Network of Hispanic Women and is editor of the final report of the board's study, *The Work and Family Experiences of Hispanic Women.* Dr. Zambrana has published a wide variety of articles on health, work, and education among the Latino population. She is the editor of *Latina Women in Transition: Work, Health and Family.*

About the Women's Research and Education Institute

BETTY PARSONS DOOLEY, *Executive Director*
SARA E. RIX, Ph.D., *Director of Research*
SUSAN P. SCANLAN, *Outreach Director*
ANNE J. STONE, *Research Associate*
CHINA JESSUP, *Fellowship Program Director*

THE Women's Research and Education Institute (WREI) was established in 1977 as the nonpartisan research arm of the bipartisan Congressional Caucus for Women's Issues. Located in the nation's capital, WREI forms a critical bridge between researchers and policymakers concerned with issues of particular importance to women.

Since its founding, WREI has worked to (1) stimulate researchers to consider the broader implications of their work, especially as it affects public policy; (2) encourage the exchange of ideas and expertise between researchers with technical knowledge and policymakers familiar with the realities of the legislative process and political constraints; (3) examine policies from the perspective of their effect on women; and (4) promote the formulation of policy options that recognize the needs of both women and men.

Index

ABOUT THE EDITOR

Sara E. Rix is Director of Research at the Women's Research and Education Institute (WREI), where she specializes in social, policy, and comparative research and analysis. Her primary research interests are employment policy, retirement policy, and the economics of aging. She holds a Ph.D. in sociology from the University of Virginia.

Dr. Rix is on the board of directors of the National Coalition on Older Women's Issues. She is, or has been, an adviser on or consultant to projects of the General Accounting Office, Working Women, the Office of Technology Assessment, the National Senior Citizens Education and Research Center, the National Council for Alternative Work Patterns, and the 1981 White House Conference on Aging.

Dr. Rix has studied, written on, and spoken about the work and retirement income needs of middle-aged and older men and women for over 10 years. She is the coauthor of *The Graying of Working America* (with Harold L. Sheppard) and of *Retirement-Age Policy: An International Perspective* (with Paul Fisher). Before her coming to WREI, she was a research scientist at the American Institutes for Research.